The Patient Centered Value System

Transforming Healthcare through Co-Design

T0299934

Pull quotes for *The Patient Centered Value System: Transforming Healthcare through Co-Design*, by Anthony M. DiGioia, M.D. and Eve Shapiro

"The spiraling costs of healthcare and diminishing value for organizations, patients, and families requires a new, transformative approach to healthcare delivery. The Patient Centered Value System is *the* answer to lowering costs, improving clinical outcomes, and increasing the patient and family care experience. The PCVS has resulted in tangible improvements on all levels at the Connecticut Joint Replacement Institute at Saint Francis Hospital."

—Steve F. Schutzer, M.D.,
Medical Director, Connecticut Joint Replacement Institute, President, Connecticut Joint Replacement Surgeons, LLC

"*The Patient Centered Value System: Transforming Care through Co-Design* offers a highly readable and practical approach for dramatically improving patient outcomes and experiences. As health care consumers, we would definitely want our providers to be following the Patient Centered Value System principles, delivering high-quality, empathetic, and lower-cost patient care."

—Robert S. Kaplan,
Marvin Bower Professor of Leadership Development, Emeritus at the Harvard Business School

"This book captures perfectly the challenge that faces quality improvers everywhere: that lasting change can only be achieved through a change in mindset which places patients and families at the centre of the improvement agenda. The Patient Centered Value System is one of the few approaches which does just this. This system works. What it also does is transform the working lives of the staff applying it, reconnecting them powerfully with their core mission to care. It has been a privilege to use this approach with teams from around the United Kingdom, and a joy to see the changes they make when they see care through patients' eyes."

—Bev Fitzsimons,
Head of Improvement, Point of Care Foundation, U.K.

"DiGioia and Shapiro have achieved the goal of every author: to make understandable that which is complex, and to make implementable complex principles. When the subject is patient (and family)-centered care, those goals are both formidable and critical to the nation's health."

—John R. Ball, M.D., J.D,
Executive Vice President, Emeritus, American College of Physicians

"This book will teach you how to see. Whether you are a hospital CEO, as I have been, or a care giver at the front lines of care, as I have been, this book will open your eyes to the journey of a patient and family throughout care. The care systems of the future will be designed with and for our patients and their families. This book is the best guide to give you the tools and methods to co-design care with them."

—Maureen Bisognano,
President Emerita and Senior Fellow, Institute for Healthcare Improvement

The Patient Centered Value System

Transforming Healthcare through Co-Design

By Anthony M. DiGioia, M.D. and Eve Shapiro

CRC Press
Taylor & Francis Group
Boca Raton London New York

CRC Press is an imprint of the
Taylor & Francis Group, an **informa** business

A PRODUCTIVITY PRESS BOOK

CRC Press
Taylor & Francis Group
6000 Broken Sound Parkway NW, Suite 300
Boca Raton, FL 33487-2742

First issued in paperback 2020

ISBN 13: 978-0-367-73583-8 (pbk)
ISBN 13: 978-1-138-05596-4 (hbk)

Library of Congress Cataloging-in-Publication Data

Names: DiGioia, Anthony M., author. | Shapiro, Eve., author.
Title: The patient centered value system : transforming healthcare through co-design / Anthony M. DiGioia and Eve Shapiro.
Description: Boca Raton : Taylor & Francis, 2018. | "A CRC title, part of the Taylor & Francis imprint, a member of the Taylor & Francis Group, the academic division of T&F Informa plc." | Includes bibliographical references and index.
Identifiers: LCCN 2017014903| ISBN 9781138055964 (hardback : alk. paper) | ISBN 9781315165615 (ebook)
Subjects: LCSH: Patient centered health care. | Managed care plans (Medical care) | Health services administration.
Classification: LCC R729.5.H43 D54 2018 | DDC 362.1/04258--dc23
LC record available at https://lccn.loc.gov/2017014903

For patients, families, and providers everywhere.

For Don Berwick, Maureen Bisognano, Gene Lindsey, and Bev Fitzsimons for their enthusiasm, encouragement, and support of patient and family centered care, for demonstrating how to drive transformational change, and for continuing to inspire and lead the way.

For the early adopters of the Patient Centered Value System and its components, who have helped this dynamic methodology to evolve and transform the care and experiences of patients, families, and providers.

For the giants on whose shoulders the Patient Centered Value System is built: John Kotter, Tim Brown, Paul Bate, Glenn Robert, Herbert Simon, B. Joseph Pine II, Clayton Christensen, Stephen Denning, Robert S. Kaplan, and Michael Porter.

And, in gratitude, to my wife, Cathy (A.M.D.), and my husband, Howard (E.S.). We couldn't have done this without you.

Contents

List of Figures

List of Tables

Foreword

Everything possible begins with civility.

Robert Waller M.D.

Excellence in healthcare depends on the quality of relationships with patients and families—really listening to what they want and need—and remembering the values that led healthcare professionals to their calling in the first place. Gone are the days when the simple view that "the doctor knows best" suffices. Now, if we listen carefully and with open minds to what patients and families tell us, we can find the best compass toward improving our delivery of care and their care experience. This is healthcare "co-design," and it is the wave of the future.

Developing relationships with patients and families, practicing civility, and embracing transparency come first, but the spiraling costs of healthcare also need to be understood and brought under control for the benefit of patients, families, communities, providers, and organizations. Do the bills that patients and families receive from hospitals reflect the true cost of their care? Neither patients, nor families, nor providers can answer this question because the *true* costs of care—as opposed to charges or reimbursements—remain unknown. Providers and organizations need to know what it *really* costs to deliver care if they are to reduce costs while at the same time improving quality and experiences and providing real value.

In *The Patient Centered Value System: Transforming Healthcare through Co-Design*, Anthony M. DiGioia M.D. and Eve Shapiro present an approach both to co-designing care delivery with patients and families and to calculating the true costs of care for medical or surgical conditions over the full cycle of care. Section I of the book is written as the story of healthcare providers who are inspired to practice co-design by seeing the care experience through the eyes of patients and families using the powerful tool of "Shadowing" and the Patient and Family Centered Care Methodology. Section II of the book begins with a focus on Time-Driven Activity-Based Costing, first developed by Kaplan and Anderson (2007), which in the Patient Centered Value System uses Shadowing to calculate all of the costs—including the hidden costs—of delivering healthcare. Section III of the book explains the theoretical underpinnings of the Patient Centered Value System, and how this approach can be combined with process improvement approaches, such as Lean Thinking, that an organization may already be using. It describes organizations that have used the Patient Centered Value System, along with the results they have achieved.

I highly recommend this book to healthcare professionals of all types and at all levels, including chief executive officers, chief financial officers, and those responsible for quality, safety, and patient care. The Patient Centered Value System as the new operating system for healthcare delivery points the way to personal and professional satisfaction and the experience of joy in work while helping patients and families become true partners in care through co-design.

Donald M. Berwick, M.D.
President Emeritus and Senior Fellow,
Institute for Healthcare Improvement.

Reference

Kaplan, RS, Anderson, SR. 2007. *Time-Driven Activity-Based Costing: A Simpler and More Powerful Path to Higher Profits.* Boston, MA: Harvard Business School Publishing.

Preface

The existing deficiencies in health care cannot be corrected simply by supplying more personnel, more facilities and more money. These problems can only be solved by organizing the personnel, facilities and financing into a conceptual framework and operating system that will provide optimally for the health needs of the population.

Robert Ebert,
Dean, Harvard Medical School, 1965

In the more than 50 years between that statement and this moment, we have been on a frustrating journey, searching for an operating system and finance mechanism that could "provide optimally for the health needs of the nation." In 2007, the Institute for Healthcare Improvement crystallized Ebert's vision as the "Triple Aim":

- Improving the patient experience of care (including quality and satisfaction)
- Improving the health of populations
- Reducing the per capita cost of healthcare

More recently, that terse description has been given greater meaning by being restated as, "Care better than we've seen, health better than we've ever known, cost we can afford … for every person, every time" (Institute for Healthcare Improvement 2015–2016).

Since recasting Ebert's description of the "deficiencies in healthcare" into a pursuable objective that we can all accept and understand, we have diligently searched for easily spreadable methodologies in pursuit of the Triple Aim. Many of us have tried hard to adopt and spread Lean as this operating system and some have succeeded, but there has always been significant resistance as clinicians struggle to see how methodologies developed in manufacturing can be applied to the care of people.

Healthcare professionals have often been unable to connect the industrial methodologies of process improvement to their work without a sense that they are losing the essence of why they became clinicians in the first place. The "adaptive work" of continuous improvement, which seems to require them to give up what they value most, has often felt like a poor fit. Many a Lean transformation has stalled because of the perceived tension between clinical values and continuous process improvement toward the Triple Aim.

Since 2006, Anthony M. DiGioia, M.D. and colleagues at Magee-Womens Hospital, University of Pittsburgh Medical Center (UPMC), have been working to bring clinicians and medical institutions a continuous *performance* improvement methodology that has its roots in the values of good clinical practice. This book presents the outcome of this work, called the Patient Centered Value System. The Patient Centered Value System is a comprehensive approach to healthcare delivery that comprises three essential tools—Shadowing, the Patient and Family Centered Care Methodology, and Time-Driven Activity-Based Costing—while complementing and fully embracing current process improvement efforts such as Lean and the Toyota Production System as described later. The Patient Centered Value System integrates the scientific methods, clinical values, and objectives of continuous improvement. Reading about the Patient Centered Value System should feel familiar to anyone interested in quality, safety, efficiency, and the traditions of professionalism. The Patient Centered Value System feels as though it has evolved organically from a desire to improve the experience of care by seeing the entire care experience through the eyes of patients and families.

Section I of *The Patient Centered Value System: Transforming Healthcare through Co-Design* uses the technique of storytelling to quickly connect with readers facing new and challenging learning curves of their own. Over the course of a long career, I have played many of the roles depicted in the story: the enthusiastic Chief Executive Officer (CEO), the physician leader, and the reluctant and skeptical clinician. The roles that I have not played I have observed in others in numerous efforts to improve care and advance the mission of our organization against significant internal resistance and harsh externalities. I can testify that the characterizations in the story are effective presentations of the many ways that real people react to the challenges of change. The story demonstrates that adaptive change is both an interactive process and a challenging learning curve that must be climbed for both individuals and groups.

The book begins with a story that demonstrates the principles and objectives of Shadowing in action. As a former leader who has struggled with introducing the need for change, the dialog and the actions described in the story feel realistic. It is easy to recognize the leadership challenges and the need to build a guiding coalition of diverse stakeholders. What is most powerful about the story, for me, is how the CEO of Exemplar Memorial Hospital, Dr. Ben Highland, keeps bringing the reasons for change back to the best care of the patient, the hospital's mission, and the foundational principles of professionalism. As he introduces his colleagues to the what, why, and how of the Patient Centered Value System, the reader learns right along with them. The detail that Dr. Highland presents is so complete that readers should be encouraged to introduce the Patient Centered Value System in their own organizations simply by emulation.

Sections II and III of this book serve as the didactic resource written in the usual tradition of the medical literature that Dr. Ben Highland might have used in leading his colleagues to understand the power of the Patient Centered Value System. The story portion of the book and the technical portion cover the same issues in a highly complementary way. Repetition and review are the keys to learning.

The information in the Introduction is so useful to understanding the evolving state of healthcare and the theory and science of continuous change that it deserves special mention. If the book just began without some set-up to the story, many readers might miss some of the messages the story delivers. The Introduction should not be quickly glossed over. It has great merit as a stand-alone piece.

My favorite chapter is Chapter 8, "Time-Driven Activity-Based Costing in the Patient Centered Value System: A User's Manual," which demonstrates how to use Shadowing along with the costing approach developed by Robert S. Kaplan and Steven R. Anderson (2007) to determine the true cost of care delivery. Any organization that hopes to lower its costs to succeed in the era of value-based reimbursement needs to develop competency in combining Shadowing with Time-Driven Activity-Based Costing. This 'monograph' within a book makes the subject easy to understand and demonstrates nicely how it can be implemented.

Chapter 10, "Patient Centered Value System + Lean or Other Process Improvement Approaches = Rapid Improvement," is also of particular interest because it explains how to add the Patient Centered Value System to other process improvement approaches you may already be using to accelerate the pace of change. Lean is a management philosophy in continuous evolution. Just as the English language has continuously become richer and more effective by adopting new words and expressions from other cultures and languages, Lean too has always been in a process of continuous acquisition. Ever since a rainy Saturday morning when I first met Dr. DiGioia in downtown Boston to hear about the Patient Centered Value System, I have stressed how compatible his work is with our Lean efforts. How does "going to the gemba" really differ from Shadowing? The projects that are chosen as the focus for improvement in the Patient Centered Value System are quite similar to *kaizen,* or rapid improvement, events.

What *is* different about the Patient Centered Value System is the explicit focus on the patient and family as the core concern. In this book, the elimination of waste and the improvement of the care process are articulated more clearly as an extension of our professional accountability and values than often comes through to clinicians as they struggle with their prejudices against Lean as a form of "medical Taylorism." In Chapter 10, the authors embrace this compatibility between their methodology and other forms of continuous improvement, including Lean. This is huge!

Perhaps the two greatest barriers to success with any improvement methodology are "today's work" and the time and effort that individuals must devote to learning how to use any new methodology. Competent and committed leadership that extends deep into the enterprise can lower those barriers, yet patients and families who are given the opportunity to co-design the healthcare experience are the true catalysts for change.

Two additional barriers to change in many organizations are the costs of consultant help in managing the change process and revenue lost when frontline staff are required to learn the methodology. If one considers the broad spectrum of healthcare organizations across the nation, it is easy to realize that many just do not have the resources to invest in consulting and their staff doesn't have time to read and digest the message of a long technical treatise describing a new approach to practice. The authors of *The Patient Centered Value System: Transforming Healthcare through Co-Design* definitely considered these realities as they wrote this book. An interested reader can easily consume several chapters in one sitting and it is quite possible to cover the whole book over one weekend. It is easy to imagine a group of concerned clinicians or a senior management team going through this book in preparation for a strategic retreat that is scheduled when collectively they realize that business as usual is in its eleventh hour.

Read it as a story. Read it as a resource. Read it as a training manual. Just read it. This is a *must read* for anyone who cares about the future of healthcare.

Gene Lindsey, M.D.
CEO Emeritus, Atrius Health

References

Institute for Healthcare Improvement. September 2015–August 2016. *Leadership Alliance, Year 2.* Boston, MA.

Kaplan, RS, Anderson, SR. 2007. *Time-Driven Activity-Based Costing: A Simpler and More Powerful Path to Higher Profits.* Boston, MA: Harvard Business School Publishing.

Acknowledgments

The authors would like to thank Pamela K. Greenhouse for her substantive contributions to this book; the staff of the Innovation Center of UPMC, whose work over the last 10 years is reflected in its content; and the Trauma Care Experience Working Group of UPMC, whose real-life dedication to transforming care for patients and families is depicted in our story.

A special thanks to Charles Kenney for opening the unexpected door of opportunity.

Thanks to the leadership and providers at UPMC, who supported the efforts described in this book and allowed the UPMC Health System to be the early adopter and the pilot test site for the Patient Centered Value System and all of its components.

The authors would also like to thank Maureen Bisognano, Bev Fitzsimons, Helen Haskell, Gene Lindsey M.D., Dale Ann Micalizzi, and Steve Schutzer, M.D. for reviewing the draft manuscript.

And thanks to Traci L. McGowan, Administrative Assistant, the Bone and Joint Center, Magee-Womens Hospital of UPMC, for her help with manuscript preparation and Adam Petras, Designer, Creative Services, Innovation Center of UPMC, for his work on cover design.

About the Authors

**Anthony M. DiGioia** is creator of the Patient Centered Value System, a practicing orthopedic surgeon, and Medical Director of both the Bone and Joint Center and Innovation Center at the University of Pittsburgh Medical Center (UPMC). Tony graduated from Carnegie Mellon University in Civil Engineering, obtained a graduate degree in Civil and Biomedical Engineering, and then attended Harvard Medical School, completed his orthopedic residency in Pittsburgh, and undertook a Fellowship at Massachusetts General Hospital. Wanting to help bridge the gap between engineering and medicine, Tony was a world leader in the initial development of medical robotics and computer-assisted surgery. His work has always focused on bringing together diverse teams from multiple disciplines in order to listen to and meet the needs of patients and families. This broad focus led Tony to develop the Patient Centered Value System, which combines process and performance improvement with supportive technologies to improve clinical outcomes and patient and family care experiences while reducing costs.

 **Eve Shapiro**, principal, Eve Shapiro Medical Writing, Inc., has written on topics related to patient safety, patient centered care, systems improvement, transitions in care, physician–patient communication, medi- cal errors, and other subjects for audiences ranging from researchers and clinicians to patients and families. She has written books, articles, and other works for organizations such as the Agency for Healthcare Research and Quality, the Institute for Healthcare Improvement, the Joint Commission, the Robert Wood Johnson Foundation, the University of Pittsburgh Medical Center, and Consumers Advancing Patient Safety. Eve believes storytelling is the most powerful way to teach, gener- ate insight, promote understanding, and communicate essential truths.

Introduction

> Relationships will be the foundation of health care's
> new age ...
> **Donald M. Berwick, M.D.**

Relationships are at the heart of the healthcare experience. Or they should be, as Dr. Donald Berwick reminds us. Relationships between patients, families, and providers. Non-hierarchical relationships among an integrated network of providers who come from multiple disciplines to see care through the eyes of, and meet the myriad needs of, patients and families. Providers working in teams rather than asserting professional prerogative and working in silos. Really listening to patients and families and getting to know them as whole people. These are among the basic practices Don Berwick (2016) proposes in what he calls the new "moral era" in healthcare.

Now there is a relationship-based approach to transforming healthcare delivery called the Patient Centered Value System, which moves healthcare toward this moral era, enabling us to achieve the Triple Aim while responding to the many challenges and opportunities posed by an evolving and complex healthcare financing and delivery environment: that is, to improve the patient's experience of care (including quality and satisfaction), improve the health of populations, and reduce the per capita costs of healthcare.

Often, the most effective solutions to complex problems are simple ones. The Patient Centered Value System is a simple, replicable, and sustainable approach to viewing all care through the eyes of patients and families, identifying opportunities to improve value, and building implementation teams to drive change.

Central to the Patient Centered Value System is the concept of co-design, in which healthcare providers observe and listen to what patients and families have to say about their care experiences and then set about improving them (Bate and Robert 2006). The immediacy of the patient's and family's involvement as they go through their healthcare journey—telling us then and there what they want and need (Brown 2008, 2009)—is where co-design begins. In the context of the Patient Centered Value System, co-design of the healthcare experience means that healthcare providers design the ideal state of healthcare delivery *in collaboration* with patients and families after listening to their wants and needs. Providers then test and implement projects to close the gaps between the current state and the ideal as patients and families define it.

The Patient Centered Value System is a comprehensive approach to healthcare delivery comprising three equally important tools: Shadowing, the Patient and Family Centered Care Methodology, and Time-Driven Activity-Based Costing (Kaplan and Anderson 2007). Anthony M. DiGioia, M.D., and colleagues at the Innovation Center, Magee-Womens Hospital, University of Pittsburgh Medical Center (Meyer 2011; Bisognano and Kenney 2012) have developed this systematic approach to delivering patient and family centered care in any organization, whatever its size or setting.

Shadowing

Shadowing is the essential tool used in the Patient and Family Centered Care Methodology to enable healthcare professionals to see the current state of any care experience from the patient's and family's point of view through direct, real-time observation of their experience as they move through it, whether in doctors' offices, hospitals, clinics, imaging centers, long-term care facilities, rehabilitation centers, skilled nursing facilities, or other settings (DiGioia and Greenhouse 2011). Through first-hand observation, Shadowing enables providers to identify and stratify patients' needs and to engage them as active partners in their care. Shadowing is also used in Time-Driven Activity-Based Costing to determine the actual cost of care.

The Patient and Family Centered Care Methodology

The Patient and Family Centered Care Methodology is a six-step, grassroots, "bottom-up" meets "top-down" process improvement *and* performance improvement approach to delivering ideal care that focuses on the patient and family to guide improvement efforts. In the Patient and Family Centered Care Methodology, ideal care is defined by patients and families (rather than by healthcare providers) through the full cycle of care, including pre- and post-hospital services, outpatient, and inpatient care (Millenson et al. 2013; Bisognano and Kenney 2012; DiGioia and Greenhouse 2011; Meyer 2011; DiGioia et al. 2007).

One of the hallmarks of the Patient and Family Centered Care Methodology is the breaking down of the silos so prevalent in healthcare through the formation of teams, called Patient and Family Centered Care Working Groups and Project Teams, comprising staff from different parts of the organization—and, in some cases, from different organizations—so that healthcare, regardless of where it is delivered, meets the needs of patients and families both within and outside of hospital walls (Millenson et al. 2013; Bisognano and Kenney 2012; DiGioia and Greenhouse 2011; Meyer 2011; DiGioia et al. 2007, 2010).

The key principles of the Patient and Family Centered Care Methodology are viewing all care as experiences through the eyes of patients and families; engaging patients and families as full partners in co-designing* each step of care delivery; giving caregivers (i.e., anyone in the health-care setting who impacts the experiences of patients and families, whether directly or behind the scenes) implementation tools to close the gaps between their current state and the ideal based on what matters to patients and families; and creating and sustaining a sense of urgency to drive change.

The six steps of the Patient and Family Centered Care Methodology are as follows:

Step 1. Select a care experience
Step 2. Establish a Care Experience Guiding Council
Step 3. Shadow patients and families to co-design the care experience
Step 4. Expand the Guiding Council into the Working Group
Step 5. Create the shared vision of the ideal story
Step 6. Form Project Teams to close the gaps between current and ideal

The Patient and Family Centered Care Methodology has been used in healthcare settings in the United States and around the world since its inception in 2006.

Time-Driven Activity-Based Costing

While the Patient and Family Centered Care Methodology uses Shadowing to help caregivers see any care experience through the eyes of patients and families, Time-Driven Activity-Based

---

* The concept of co-design has its origins in customer co-creation (Prahalad and Ramaswamy 2004).

Costing uses Shadowing to identify actual costs and cost drivers (as opposed to charges, reimbursements, or costs at a more global level in each segment of care and over the full cycle of care) by identifying the actual care pathways and the four buckets of resources needed to calculate the true cost of delivering care for any medical or surgical condition—that is, personnel, space, equipment, and consumables. This provides organizations with the unique ability to reduce costs thoughtfully by making strategic cuts rather than across-the-board cuts, which is the more typical approach. In addition, Time-Driven Activity-Based Costing provides the structure and mechanism for driving down costs while protecting and/or improving patient and family experiences and clinical outcomes.

Taken as a whole, the Patient Centered Value System directly reflects Berwick's (2016) vision of the nine steps that will lead us to the new moral era in healthcare and, in fact, the parallels are striking (Table 1).

About This Book

The Patient Centered Value System: Transforming Healthcare through Co-Design is intended for a broad audience of those involved in healthcare delivery, redesign, and financing, including but not limited to organizational Chief Executive Officers, Chief Finance Officers, Medical and Nursing Directors, those involved in patient safety and quality improvement, doctors, nurses, and other frontline healthcare providers at all levels.

The book is divided into three sections. Since stories are an essential component of Shadowing and the Patient and Family Centered Care Methodology, Section I: The Patient Centered Value System in Action: A Story (a prologue entitled "The Epiphany" and Chapters 1 through 6), uses a fictional hospital and fictional characters to show how this approach works.

Table 1 Comparing Berwick's New Moral Era in Healthcare to the Patient Centered Value System

Step	Berwick's (2016) Nine Steps to the New Moral Era	How the Patient Centered Value System Relates to Berwick's Nine Steps
1	Stop excessive measurement and measure only what matters.	Measures only what matters—metrics related to the experience of patients and families; value as defined by end users (i.e., patients and families).
2	Abandon complex incentive programs for healthcare workers...simplify.	Replaces complex incentive programs with a simple approach to caring for and partnering with patients and families, driving change toward the ideal and resulting in renewed joy in work.
3	Decrease focus on finance.	Tightly couples clinical, experiential, and financial performance to improve quality and value for every stakeholder—patients, families, care teams, insurers, and organizations.
4	Avoid professional prerogative when it is in the way.	Redesigns care delivery processes so that the needs and desires of patients and families take precedence over all others' needs. Builds unique care teams that cross silos.
5	Recommit to improvement science.	An improvement science based on the design sciences, psychology, and experience-based design. Brings together the performance of people *and* processes.

(Continued)

Table 1 (Continued)   Comparing Berwick's New Moral Era in Healthcare to the Patient Centered Value System

Step	Berwick's (2016) Nine Steps to the New Moral Era	How the Patient Centered Value System Relates to Berwick's Nine Steps
6	Be transparent to patients, families, and communities.	Achieves transparency by viewing all care through the eyes of patients and families and welcoming their partnership to co-design improvements in care.
7	Be civil, show courtesy and respect— regardless of your role.	Breaks down silos and encourages teamwork to focus on the needs of patients, families, and communities.
8	Listen and empower those who are being served, especially the disadvantaged.	Engages patients and families as full partners in redesigning the system of care while reaching into underprivileged communities with programs designed to improve population health.
9	Reject greed from payers and providers.	Provides the tool to understanding what matters most to patients and families, which requires us to shift from volume-based to value-based care delivery.

With Chapters 1 through 6 each corresponding to a different step of the Patient and Family Centered Care Methodology, anyone interested in introducing this six-step methodology in their organization can use this story as a "how-to" guide. Although fictionalized, the problems presented in this story are real, are common in all healthcare settings, and are experienced by patients and families, along with caregivers, every day. The projects described to solve these problems are also real, have been implemented by Working Groups at UPMC, and can be implemented in any organization to move from the current state to the ideal. Chapter 7, "The Patient Centered Value System: Fact not Fiction", explains the connection between the first and second sections of this book.

In Section II: Determine and Drive Down the True Cost of Care Delivery and Achieve the Triple Aim, Chapter 8 explains how to understand and use the third component of the Patient Centered Value System—Time-Driven Activity-Based Costing combined with Shadowing—to help you determine the actual costs of care and how to drive down these costs without compromising quality, safety, or outcomes.

Section III: The Patient Centered Value System: Theory and Practice, presents the origins of the Patient Centered Value System (Chapter 9); how combining the Patient Centered Value System with Lean or other process improvement approaches can speed the pace of improvement in any size or type of healthcare organization (Chapter 10); and organizations that have used this approach, with their results (Chapter 11).

The Patient Centered Value System, a relationship-based approach to healthcare and performance improvement, is poised to usher in a much-needed, new age in healthcare.

References

Bate, P, Robert, G. 2006. Experience-based design: From redesigning the system around the patient to co-designing services with the patient. *Qual Saf Health Care* 15(5):307–310.

Berwick, D. 2016. Era 3 for medicine and health care. *JAMA* 315(13):1329–1330.

Bisognano, M, Kenney, C. 2012. *Pursuing the Triple Aim: Seven Innovators Show the Way to Better Care, Better Health, and Lower Costs*. San Francisco: Jossey-Bass.

Brown, T. 2008. Design thinking. *Harv Bus Rev* 85–92. (http://hbr.org/2008/06/design-thinking/)

Brown, T. 2009. *Change by Design: How Design Thinking Transforms Organizations and Inspires Innovation*. New York: HarperCollins Publishers.

Carman, KL, Dardess, P, Maurer, M, Sofaer, S, Adams, K, Bechtel, C, Sweeney, J. 2013. Patient and family engagement: A framework for understanding the elements and developing interventions and policies. *Health Aff* 32(2):223–231.

DiGioia, AM, Greenhouse, PK. 2011. Patient and family shadowing: Creating urgency for change. *J Nurs Adm* 41(1):23–28.

DiGioia, AM, Greenhouse, PK, Levison, TJ. 2007. Patient and family centered collaborative care: An orthopaedic model. *Clin Orthop Relat Res* 463:13–19.

DiGioia, AM, Lorenz, H, Greenhouse, PK, Bertoty, DA, Rocks, SD. 2010. A patient-centered model to improve metrics without cost increase. *J Nurs Adm* 40(12):540–546.

Hibbard, JH, Greene, J. 2013. What the evidence shows about patient activation: Better health outcomes and care experiences; fewer data on costs. *Health Aff* 32(2):207–214.

Institute for Healthcare Improvement. 2012. *Innovation Series 2012: A Guide to Measuring the Triple Aim: Population Health, Experience of Care, and Per Capita Cost.* Cambridge, MA: Institute for Healthcare Improvement.

Kaplan, RS, Anderson, SR. 2007. *Time-Driven Activity-Based Costing: A Simpler and More Powerful Path to Higher Profits.* Boston, MA: Harvard Business School Publishing.

Meyer, H. 2011. Innovation profile: At UPMC, improving care processes to serve patients better and cut costs. *Health Aff* 30(3):400–403.

Millenson, ML, DiGioia, AM, Greenhouse, PK, Swieskowski, D. 2013. Turning patient-centeredness from ideal to real: Lessons from 2 success stories. *J Ambul Care Manage* 36(4):319–334.

Prahalad, CK, Ramaswamy, V. 2004. *The Future of Competition: Co-Creating Unique Value with Customers.* Boston, MA: Harvard Business School Publishing.

THE PATIENT CENTERED VALUE SYSTEM IN ACTION: A STORY

1

Prologue: The Epiphany

> The greater danger for most of us is not that our aim
> is too high and we miss it, but that it is too low and
> we reach it.
>
> ### Michelangelo (1475–1564)

"I'm going to tell you a story," said Dr. Ben Highland, CEO of
Exemplar Memorial Hospital, looking out at his audience at
the hospital's annual staff meeting. "It's about what happened
when my wife, Jane, was a patient here three months ago. But
it's not only about what happened to her. It's also about what
happened to me. You see, I experienced her care, up close
and personal. No longer was I simply a doctor and a hospital CEO. Suddenly, more than anything, I was a very worried
husband. This is a story about my eye-opening experiences in
a place, and in a profession, I thought I knew well. I'd like to
share these experiences with you, and what they've taught me.

"Let me start by saying Jane's care itself was excellent most
of the time," Dr. Highland continued. "Because her doctors
and nurses are technically skilled, Jane's health improved and
after three weeks she was ready to come home. It was clear
that everyone caring for her—from receptionists to nurses,
nurses' aides, therapists, anesthesiologists, surgeons, pharmacists, and others—sincerely wanted to give her the best

possible care. And yet the care *experience*, for Jane and for me, was often a nightmare."

Seeing astonished looks on some of the faces in the audience, Dr. Highland asked, "Does this surprise you? It wouldn't if you suddenly became a patient yourself, or the family member of a patient," he said softly.

"You must be wondering why Jane was here, and why she was here for so long," Dr. Highland went on. "Since she has given me permission to speak about it," he said, "I can tell you that Jane was driving to the supermarket one drizzly Saturday morning. A truck ran through a stop sign. The wet road made it impossible for the driver to stop when he slammed on the brakes. He plowed right into Jane's car.

"Everything changed in an instant," Dr. Highland said as he cleared his throat and continued. "Jane left the house that morning a healthy woman. Next thing I knew," he went on, "a hospital social worker called my cell phone, saying, 'You didn't answer your home phone, Dr. Highland. I've been trying to track you down for the past half hour. Your wife has been in a car accident. She arrived in the Exemplar Memorial Emergency Department as a trauma patient. I don't know any of the details about the accident or her condition, but please get here as soon as you can.'

"I was playing basketball when the call came. How badly hurt was she, I wondered, suddenly beside myself with fear and panic. I felt myself break into a cold sweat. I must have sped all the way to the hospital, but to be honest I don't really remember *how* I got there.

"I *do* remember that when I got to the Emergency Department I couldn't find my wife. I was terrified, of course, fearing the worst."

Seeing heads nod, Dr. Highland continued, "There I was, searching everywhere for Jane, but no one seemed to know where she was. Finally, a nurse named Betsy—more like an angel, really—put her hand on my shoulder and said, kindly, 'You look worried sick. Who are you looking for?'

"When I told her, she replied, 'I'll find out whatever I can and I'll let you know. Just wait here.'

"True to her word, Betsy came back a few minutes later to tell me Jane was in the operating room. To say I was anxious would be an understatement, but at least now I knew where she was. I paced the floor for the four hours she was in surgery—it felt like an eternity to me—wanting nothing more than to see and talk to her, and to her doctor.

"During those four hours, not one person came to tell me how Jane was doing. Or how her surgery was going. Or how much longer the surgery was likely to take. There was not one hint of acknowledgement or compassion for what I, the husband of a seriously injured woman, was going through. The agony of this experience—essentially, being ignored precisely when I needed communication the most—was just the beginning of a very long and often difficult journey for both of us.

"Nothing about the experience was easy or straightforward, either for Jane or for me. Her experience in the hospital involved surgery, stays in the intensive care and medical-surgical units, and inpatient rehabilitation. After discharge, there was home healthcare, outpatient rehabilitation, and follow-ups with specialists and her primary care doctor to deal with. Breakdowns in communication, both inside and outside the hospital (when communication took place at all), were common. Why, I asked myself, did our care experience have to be this way?

"Jane's road to recovery was anything but smooth, and she often had to go back and forth between departments or units while in the hospital. And it was obvious that members of her hospital care team didn't always talk to each other—and that this lack of communication could have serious negative consequences. Let me give you a couple of examples. First, an intern said Jane was scheduled for a test the next day and shouldn't eat anything after midnight. Yet, the doctor who conducted early morning rounds seemed unaware of the time of the test or that Jane had been told not to eat. And then breakfast was delivered to her room. What, she asked, was she to make of that? Should she eat or shouldn't she? And whom should she ask? Jane pinpoints that at that moment she began to lose confidence in her care team. Second, Jane received different treatment plans, including different medication orders, from different doctors during her hospital stay. Was she, the patient, supposed to catch and make sense of these discrepancies? Who really was responsible for her hospital care? The answer was never clear.

"Then, after Jane was discharged, her hospital care team seemed to forget we existed. Because Jane left the hospital with inadequate discharge instructions, she was unsure about what to do when she got home and worried that she'd end up right back in the hospital. And, finally, because the hospital made a mistake in her home care orders, her transition from hospital to home was far from seamless. The point is that we can, we *must,* do better.

"Who do you think coordinated her care when she came home? *I* did!" Dr. Highland said. "Is this the way care should be? What, I wondered, would have happened if I hadn't been there to coordinate her care? What happens to other patients whose family members are either too overwhelmed or unable to be so involved?" he asked.

Hearing the buzz of whispers, Dr. Highland paused, then said, "Our experience taught me that we need to be acutely aware of the full cycle of care for patients and families, both inside and outside of this hospital.

"Why did we go into the healthcare field in the first place?" Dr. Highland asked. "Every day, I know we come to work wanting to deliver the best care possible. But think about and answer this question: can we honestly say we are realizing our highest ideals when caring for patients and families at every step? How long do you think it will be before you, yourself, become a patient or the family member of a patient? And when you inevitably find yourself in this position, what kind of care experience do *you* want?

"I've given you a lot to think about this morning," Dr. Highland said. "When we reconvene after lunch," he concluded, "I'd like to tell you about a healthcare delivery system we can adopt, right now, to improve the care experiences of patients and families, improve clinical outcomes, and reduce waste and costs. This system also enables care providers and those in administration to work together in a true partnership with patients and families. I hope you'll think about and discuss what I've said over lunch. Thank you."

Polite applause accompanied Dr. Highland as he walked offstage.

***

"When I spoke to you this morning," Dr. Highland told his audience after the lunch break, "I was speaking as a husband. Now, I am also speaking to you as Exemplar Memorial's CEO. I know that every member of the care team wants to deliver ideal care. Our staff, technology, and facilities are the best available. Why then," he asked, "do many of the care *experiences* of patients and families, like Jane's and mine, leave so much to be desired?

"Let's step back from the personal and consider our overall delivery of care for a moment. Why are patient satisfaction rates so low? Why do so many of our staff members tell us they spend time working around our broken systems to provide patient care? Why are patient stays often longer than they need to be? And why are readmission rates so high?"

Pausing for a moment, Dr. Highland continued. "Ask yourselves this question: Have you ever wondered where a patient and family member came from before they reached you? Have you ever wondered where they would go after they left your care? The patient's and family's care experience is not usually a straight line or a seamless journey. Instead, their journey is fragmented because they go from one silo to another—separate areas such as the Emergency Department; the operating room; the intensive care unit; the medical-surgical unit; inpatient rehab; outpatient rehab; and home healthcare—with little or no communication taking place between these areas as they travel from one to the next," Dr. Highland went on.

"In addition, a care experience such as our trauma care experience may take place over a long period of time, in multiple areas both inside and outside the hospital, with many different care providers. And while healthcare professionals come and go over the course of this journey," he said, "family members are right there, accompanying the patient every step of the way, from silo to silo. Family members are, for this reason, powerful, vital allies in providing safe care. It is *all* of our responsibility as caregivers—and this includes providers, those in administration, and support staff—to engage patients and family members as partners in their care. It is also up to us to break down the silos that separate us and compromise both patient care and the patient and family care experience. Jane's and my journey through the trauma care experience reminds us how important it is to involve patients and families in their own care. And how important it is to put patients and families at the center of care.

"Before continuing, I have a few more questions for you," Dr. Highland said, preparing to quiz his audience. "How many of you have been a patient, or the family member of a patient, in the last year? Raise your hands if this applies to you. Okay, about 90 to 95 percent. How many of you," he went on, "would say that care experience was an ideal care experience? Looks like only a small handful. How many who didn't have the ideal care experience came away with ideas for improvement? Great, back up to about 90 percent. Now, how many of you actually made changes when you went back to work? Only a few, I see—and we are the 'experts,' the 'insiders!' It isn't up to patients and families to make changes. Rather," Dr. Highland said, "it is up to *us*, working *together* with patients and families, to drive true change.

"To those of you who may be skeptical about our ability to deliver ideal care, I am here to tell you that transformational change is not only possible, it is within our grasp. There is a system called the Patient Centered Value System, developed by orthopedic surgeon Anthony M. DiGioia, III, M.D. Dr. DiGioia, whose original interest was in civil engineering and whose focus was on the science of robotics and the use of computer-assisted surgical tools in hip and knee replacement surgery, came to believe that it wasn't just the surgery that determined patient outcomes—it was everything else! He realized that patients would fare better if, rather than practicing in traditional silos, caregivers would consider the patient's and family's *entire* care experience through the full cycle of care, including preparedness for surgery; anesthesia; pain management; rehabilitation; and the need for home care. As his thinking evolved, Dr. DiGioia also came to believe that the way to ensure the best outcomes (for patients, families, and, ultimately, for organizations) would be to see the entire care experience from the point of view of patients and families—and to partner with them to co-design ideal care experiences.

"The Patient Centered Value System," Dr. Highland continued, "is an approach to transforming healthcare delivery that improves the patient's and family's experience of care, improves clinical outcomes, and reduces waste and costs. It is a simple, replicable, and sustainable approach to viewing all care through the eyes of patients and families, identifying opportunities to improve value, and building implementation teams to drive change. The Patient Centered Value System is a comprehensive approach to healthcare delivery comprising three tools: Shadowing, the Patient and Family Centered Care (PFCC) Methodology, and Time-Driven Activity-Based Costing.

"Shadowing is the essential tool that enables healthcare professionals to see the current state of any care experience from the patient's and family's point of view through direct, real-time observation of their experience as they move through it, in any healthcare setting—including doctors' offices, hospitals, clinics, imaging centers, long-term care facilities, rehabilitation centers, skilled nursing facilities, and others. Through firsthand observation, Shadowing enables providers to identify and stratify patients' needs and to engage them as active partners in their care," Dr. Highland said.

"Shadowing patients and families through their care experience also enables providers and organizations to determine their actual costs of care and the cost drivers—as opposed to charges, reimbursements, or costs at a more global level—in each segment of care and over the full cycle of care.

"The Patient and Family Centered Care Methodology is a six-step, easy to learn, customizable approach to delivering ideal care experiences every day, to every patient and family member, in any healthcare setting. Now, I realize it's a mouthful to say 'Patient and Family Centered Care Methodology' all the time," Dr. Highland continued, "so sometimes I'll refer to it as the PFCC Methodology."

Dr. Highland went on, "I *will* say that while the Patient Centered Value System is an easy approach to learn, it is, after all, a journey. And journeys, by their very nature, aren't always smooth. There will, inevitably, be hurdles to overcome, not the least of which may be our own understandable and perhaps inevitable fear of change. Nevertheless, our journey to transformational change is essential and we must start now. You know what they say," he smiled, "a journey of a thousand miles begins with one step. The time has come to take our first step.

"In the interest of full disclosure," Dr. Highland went on, "I will tell you that I was fortunate enough to work with Dr. DiGioia and experience the Patient Centered Value System firsthand in my previous position as a hospital Medical Director. I've also attended several PFCC VisionQuest workshops. In these interactive workshops, participants learn how to implement and sustain the Patient Centered Value System. The beauty of these workshops," Dr. Highland continued, "is that attendees can return to work the next day and start their own Care Experience Working Groups. To be honest," he confided, "I'd thought about introducing the Patient Centered Value System when I first came to Exemplar Memorial six months ago. But first I wanted to learn as much as I could about the current state. Now that I've seen the current state with my own two eyes, through the eyes of a husband as well as a CEO, I know the time has come to introduce the Patient Centered Value System here and now.

"Now, you may be wondering, how do the components of the Patient Centered Value System work?" Dr. Highland said. "Well, as an overview, this approach has three key elements. The first is seeing all care through the eyes of patients and families; the second is co-designing the care experience together with patients, families, and caregivers; and the third is moving from the current state to the ideal while overcoming the inevitable hurdles along the way.

"In the Patient Centered Value System, what some may consider 'soft' or 'little' things—like having clean rooms, keeping track of patients' dentures, eyeglasses, and even wedding rings, and serving nutritious food—are just as important as the big things, like ensuring improved clinical outcomes, quality, and patient safety while avoiding waste," Dr. Highland continued. "When it comes to healthcare, attention to detail in every aspect of care is essential. That means the big *and* little things. If we get the 'soft' or 'little' things right, patients and families will have confidence that we'll get the big things right, too. And vice versa. For example, what might patients and families think if a room is dirty? They might think cleanliness is not a priority and fear contracting a hospital-acquired infection.

"But there's also a real link, not just a perceived link, between our attention to the 'soft' details of care and all of care delivery," he continued. "For instance, disorganization may be a pattern at a particular nurses' station, or certain hallways may look cluttered. But these details, which some may think of as 'soft,' may reflect deeper systemic problems that could have adverse and costly consequences. The Patient Centered Value System will help us to see every detail of care and the system of care as a whole in ways we never have before, which will help us to go from the current state to the ideal. Seeing care through the eyes of patients and families is the only way we will really see and come to understand how any care experience, of whatever size or type, can be improved.

"Have you ever heard the story of the rock group Van Halen and the brown M&Ms?" Dr. Highland went on.

As audience members shook their heads, he said, "Van Halen was one of the first real rock band 'supergroups.' In the 1970s, they played in older arenas that had never held the enormous stages and heavy equipment they toured with. The group wondered, 'Are the floors of these arenas strong enough to support the immense weight of our stage, lighting, and sound equipment, or would the floors buckle under the weight? How can we be sure all of our set-up specifications have been followed precisely before we set foot on the stage? After all, the safety of the band, the crew, and the audience is at stake.'

"So this is what they did," he continued. "Buried deep within their contract was a clause stipulating that M&Ms would be provided for the group backstage—but that *every single brown M&M had to be removed.* If they found any brown M&Ms, they'd know that the contract hadn't been read carefully. If they couldn't get the little things, like M&Ms, right, chances were they wouldn't get the big things, like equipment set-up, right either. For Van Halen and for us, there really are no 'little' things. Everything is important, everything matters, and every aspect of care is inextricably linked.

"As I've said," Dr. Highland went on, "the segment of the Patient Centered Value System known as the PFCC Methodology is a standardized, replicable, six-step approach to transforming care delivery that supports each of the key elements I mentioned a few moments ago. *Together,* with your help and the help of patients and families, we will identify the first care experience needing improvement—this is Step 1. Next, in Step 2, we will invite several of you to serve as PFCC Champions on the Guiding Council. This is an exciting opportunity to help start and guide the entire process, so I hope those of you we invite will say yes! In Step 3," he continued, "the Guiding Council uses tools such as Shadowing patients and families to help determine our current state, to identify 'touchpoints'—that is, those places along the healthcare journey where any caregiver impacts the care experience of patients and families in any way—and to determine the true costs of care. I realize this may sound very new and different to you now," Dr. Highland paused, "but this methodology is very straightforward and easy to follow.

"In Step 4," he continued, "the Guiding Council *expands* to form a full Care Experience Working Group, whose members are determined by the patient's and family's flow through their full cycle of care. In other words, everyone who 'touches' or has an impact on the experience of the patient and family should be represented on the full Working Group. In Step 5, members of the Care Experience Working Group, along with patients and families, write the ideal care experience story as patients and families define it—in other words, how care *should* be delivered—to establish our ideal state. Comparing the current state with the ideal state will show us where the gaps are and will show us where we need to improve. Finally," he said, "in Step 6, based on the priorities of patients and families (and *not* our own), we will develop the first of many Project Teams that will start to close the gaps between the current state and the ideal, building high-performance care teams and changing our culture in the process."

Dr. Highland went on, "The components of the Patient Centered Value System comprise a performance improvement tool—and since it includes people *and* processes, this approach creates a culture to improve outcomes and safety, and to deliver great experiences while reducing costs.

"You've read and heard a lot over the last few years about the Triple Aim, first championed by the Institute for Healthcare Improvement and now adopted by healthcare systems worldwide—that is, achieving better care experiences, better health, and lower costs by improving the delivery of care. Because the Patient Centered Value System addresses both clinical care and processes, it is fundamental to our ability to achieve the Triple Aim," he said.

"The bottom line is this: we need to start now. Today is Friday. On Monday morning, we will launch the Patient Centered Value System at Exemplar Memorial Hospital. If we start right now, each of us will soon be able to say we made significant, transformational changes in the way we deliver care. The clock is ticking.

"Skeptical?" Dr. Highland asked with a smile. "One of the things you'll soon learn about the Patient Centered Value System is that this approach to care delivery will empower you to partner with patients and families in ways you may, until now, have only imagined—and to tap into the sometimes unused 'brain trust' in all of us who work in healthcare. Another thing you'll learn," he added, "is that once we begin to see the care experience through the eyes of patients and families, we will feel a sense of urgency to make needed changes right away—and we won't rest until we do!"

Dr. Highland smiled as he watched the audience rise and applaud.

Chapter 1

How to Introduce the Patient Centered Value System in Your Organization

A journey of a thousand miles begins with one step.

Lao Tsu

Dr. Ben Highland drove home, gratified by the audience's positive reaction to his presentation. A standing ovation, he thought with a smile. Now Ben eagerly anticipated Monday morning, when he would begin to use the momentum his talk generated to introduce the Patient Centered Value System at Exemplar Memorial Hospital.

Because he had followed the Patient Centered Value System at the University of Pittsburgh Medical Center, Ben knew that this approach leads to great care experiences for patients and families, improved clinical outcomes, and reduced waste and costs. And now, having experienced the current state of trauma care at Exemplar Memorial as a husband, transforming the trauma care experience took on a whole new level of urgency. We can't waste another day, another hour, another minute—he thought as he pulled into his driveway.

The first thing he did when he walked into his office Monday morning was call Dan Kahn, Exemplar Memorial's Chief Medical Officer, and Nancy Byrd, the hospital's Chief Nursing Officer, to see if they could come to a brief lunch meeting the next day. Ben was delighted when they both said yes. He wanted to introduce the Patient Centered Value System and the best way to do it, he thought, would be to start with Shadowing and the Patient and Family Centered Care (PFCC) Methodology. He would set up a whiteboard listing the six steps of the PFCC Methodology to guide their discussion.

Ben had three goals for this meeting. The first was to tell Dan and Nancy he intended to use the Patient Centered Value System to transform trauma care delivery at Exemplar Memorial and to elicit their support. Ben's second goal was to explain Shadowing and the six steps of the PFCC Methodology so Nancy and Dan would have a better understanding of what transforming any care experience entails. And because he wanted to start with trauma care, his third goal was to ask Nancy and Dan who should serve on the Trauma Care Experience Guiding Council. Ben wanted to waste no time in establishing this small but critical, core group of people who are essential for starting and sustaining the Patient Centered Value System for any care experience, in any healthcare setting.

Ben eagerly anticipated this meeting. As he knew from past experience, the Patient Centered Value System leads not only to improved care experiences for patients and families, but also to improved experiences for caregivers—meaning anyone in the healthcare setting who influences the experience of patients and families, whether directly or indirectly, including doctors and nurses, therapists and technicians, managers, schedulers, billers, and everyone in between. And, inevitably, the result of increased patient, family, and caregiver engagement is a change in the culture of the organization itself.

The next day, when the three colleagues were seated at the table in his office, Ben began: "Until Jane and I went through the trauma care experience at Exemplar Memorial, I assumed we deliver the ideal care experience for patients and families. And sometimes, and in some areas, we do. But," he continued, "we need to do *better* than that. We need to deliver the ideal care experience in every area of this hospital, to every patient and family member, every single time. When I followed the Patient Centered Value System at the University of Pittsburgh Medical Center, I learned firsthand that we can give patients and families great care experiences while improving clinical outcomes, reducing waste, and lowering costs. As you know, the University of Pittsburgh Medical Center is one of the largest healthcare systems in the country, with all the complexity one would expect to find in an organization of its size. I've seen firsthand what such a large organization can achieve with the Patient Centered Value System. But I also know that organizations and facilities of *any* size can use this approach to achieve remarkable results."

"To be honest, Ben, I'm skeptical that the Patient Centered Value System can really transform trauma care, but given the alternative—doing the same things and expecting different results—it might be worth a try," Dan said.

"After seeing what happened to Jane right here at Exemplar Memorial," Ben said, "I realized that doing the same things was no longer an option because the current state isn't working for patients and families. After Jane's accident," he went on, "we had a long and sometimes difficult journey not only through this hospital but beyond its walls. We saw with our own eyes how and where the care experience fell short and needs to be improved. While I was here with Jane, I also heard other patients and family members express frustration about their care experiences. Since then, the letters I've read from patients—and their husbands and wives, sons and daughters—saying *their* care experiences were also less than ideal have taken on new meaning. So, based on our own experiences and those of others, I propose we start the process of transforming care delivery at Exemplar Memorial with the trauma care experience. As you know," Ben continued, "Exemplar Memorial Hospital, as a designated Level I Trauma Center, is able to provide total care for every aspect of injury from prevention through rehabilitation. What do you think?" he asked, looking first at Nancy, then at Dan.

"Let's give the Patient Centered Value System a try and see what happens. It sounds like we have nothing to lose and maybe everything to gain," said Nancy. Dan reluctantly agreed.

Ben said, "We'll start by introducing the first two components of this approach, which are Shadowing and the Patient and Family Centered Care Methodology. The goal of Shadowing and the Patient and Family Centered Care Methodology is to take us from point A—what care delivery is now, or the current state—to point B, what care delivery can be, or the ideal state.

"When we Shadow, we ask patients and families how they feel about their care and their experience and capture the patient's and family's comments, questions, reactions, and concerns every step of the way. We also note the flow of care, the starting and ending times of each step in the care process, how long patients and families spend waiting, and other details we will use to construct flow and process maps. Shadowing therefore provides us with quantitative *and* qualitative information about how the current state looks and feels to patients and families. This makes Shadowing the perfect way to begin to engage patients and families as partners in co-designing the care experience. Since Shadowing is also part of Step 3 of the PFCC Methodology, I'll explain more about Shadowing soon.

"The first step of the PFCC Methodology is to decide where any care experience—in our case, the trauma care experience—begins and ends. Setting these parameters helps us to focus our efforts."

"Defining where the care experience begins and ends may seem obvious, but I assure you, it's not," Ben went on. "Ask any group of caregivers, 'Where does the trauma care experience begin and end?' and you're bound to get more than one answer. Some caregivers may say this care experience begins when the patient arrives in the Emergency Department. Others may say the trauma care experience begins when either the family or Emergency Medical Services calls to say they're on their way."

"Right," Dan said. "And some may say the trauma care experience ends when the patient is transferred to the intensive care unit (ICU) or from the ICU to a general inpatient unit. Others may say this care experience ends when the patient is discharged from the hospital."

"Well," Nancy said, "since most trauma care starts when the Emergency Medical Services (EMS) team gets a call telling them to go to the site of an accident, I think we should define the beginning of the trauma care experience as the time when the EMS team first gets the call. And as you've said, Ben, the patient's and family's care experience really does extend beyond our hospital's walls."

"That makes sense," Dan said, "but I have a question about how much flexibility we have in defining the beginning and the end of a care experience. What if we decide later that we want to broaden our definition of where any care experience begins and ends? I mean, what if eventually we want to understand the care experience of patients and families before or after our predetermined starting and ending points? Is it ever too late to make changes?" he asked.

"Great question," Ben said. "The PFCC Methodology is adaptable and allows us maximum flexibility. We can expand our definition of the beginning and end points at any time."

Dan replied, "In that case, for now I think we should define the trauma care experience as ending with the patient's

transition to home. This would encompass stays in inpatient
rehabilitation units or skilled nursing facilities *before* a patient
goes home. Ideally, the hospital would send all the right
information to these facilities and would coordinate the move
with the patient's family to enable a smooth transfer. But we
all know it's not a perfect world and it doesn't always happen
that way."

"Perfect may seem like a stretch," Ben said, "but we *are*
aiming for true care transformation."

"Ben," Dan said, "as I mentioned earlier, I'm trying to be
open but I do have some serious reservations. You've been
talking about Shadowing and the PFCC Methodology as a way
for us to see care as an experience through the eyes of the
patient and family. But I feel strongly that I serve my patients
best by seeing care through the eyes of a doctor. Why should
I change my point of view? What's in it for me?"

"Dan, of course your clinical and technical skills and judg-
ment as a doctor are essential and no one is asking you to
give those up. But, in addition, seeing the care experience
through the eyes of the patient and family gives us a new
perspective on the current state that we may have realized only subliminally, if at all. It makes us better and more
astute caregivers. This perspective, which is new and may
be uncomfortable for some of us in the beginning, will result
from partnering and communicating with patients and families
in a wholly new way. Believe it or not, this perspective will
evolve naturally as we move through Shadowing and the PFCC
Methodology as part of a high-performance care team rather
than on our own. This partnership will empower us to make
the changes in care delivery that we, and patients and families, know are needed."

"That certainly would be new," Dan replied. "Until now,
when I've seen changes I think should be made I haven't felt
able to move the needle in any meaningful or sustained way."

"The perspective of patients and families will show us
as a team, clearly and quickly, which aspects of the care

experience are not only less than ideal from their point of view, but which aspects of the care experience may compromise outcomes," Ben said.

"Seeing the care experience from the perspective of patients and families shows us that *every* detail of the care experience matters—this includes the cleanliness of the room, the courtesy and responsiveness of the caregivers, and the clarity of their communications," Ben continued. "If we can get what some may consider the 'little' things right, patients and families will be confident that we'll get the big things right, too. Whether right or wrong, confidence in 'little' things tends to breed confidence in, and be reflective of, bigger things (and vice versa)."

"That's true," said Dan. "When my wife was in the hospital they didn't empty the wastebaskets and sharps containers in her room often enough. Those overflowing cans made the room look dirty and disorganized, made the hospital staff look lax, and frankly concerned us both. We were afraid the nursing care could be lax, or that there could be an increased risk of contracting a hospital-acquired infection, too."

"That's exactly what I mean," Ben said. "But in addition to the importance of patients' and families' perceptions, we must also consider that problems in what some think of as 'soft' areas may be part of a pattern and indicate larger, systemic problems. This is why attention to every detail of care is essential. And details are what Shadowing and the Patient and Family Centered Care Methodology helps us to see and to address."

Then Nancy spoke up. "What I'm wondering," she said, "is how much of a difference Shadowing and the PFCC Methodology can really make in the way we deliver care. After all, our nurses believe they're already seeing the care experience from the patient's and family's point of view and delivering patient and family centered care."

"Nancy, there's no question our nurses do a great job," Ben replied. "But despite all that's been written about the importance of patient and family centered care, until now there has been no blueprint for delivering this kind of care consistently throughout an organization.

"By using Shadowing and the PFCC Methodology," Ben continued, "all caregivers will share the same understanding. All caregivers will be able to follow the same steps to transform care experiences for patients and families. And who do I mean by *all* caregivers? I mean doctors, technicians, aides, and housekeepers. I also mean anesthesiologists, pharmacists, dieticians, people in the billing department, those at reception desks, and valet parking attendants. It's not only nurses who need to deliver patient and family centered care to every patient and family member in every single circumstance, but it's every person in this *hospital* who comes into contact with patients and families. And even those who don't come into direct contact with them—like me—and so many others whom patients and families never see but who, nonetheless, affect their care experience."

"I've never thought about it that way before," Nancy said. "You know, Ben, I once read something in a medical magazine that has stayed with me: 'Starbucks takes an impersonal experience and makes it personal; healthcare takes a personal experience and makes it impersonal.' I think about that statement a lot," she said, "because, if anything, healthcare should be the most personal experience anyone ever has."

"Yes!" Ben exclaimed. "The question we need to ask is, how do we make healthcare the ideal experience it should be? And the answer? By Shadowing and following the six steps of the Patient and Family Centered Care Methodology. I realize these concepts are new. They are innovative. And they are, right now, unfamiliar. But once we start down the road to transforming care delivery beginning with the trauma care experience, these concepts will not only become familiar, they will become second nature—in fact, they will become part of the fabric of our organization."

"Care transformation can begin, and yield results, very quickly. And we don't need any new resources to implement this first phase of the Patient Centered Value System. Now, because I know our time is short," he continued, "I'd like to go over the six steps of the PFCC Methodology with you. I'd like to explain what the PFCC Methodology is all about before we begin implementation, and I'd like your recommendations about one of its key components. I've listed the six steps on this whiteboard to guide our discussion today."

Nancy and Dan looked up at the whiteboard and read the following six steps:

Step 1. Select a Care Experience
Step 2. Establish a Care Experience Guiding Council
Step 3. Shadow Patients and Families to Co-design the Care Experience
Step 4. Expand the Guiding Council into the Working Group
Step 5. Create the Shared Vision of the Ideal Story
Step 6. Form Project Teams to Close the Gaps between Current and Ideal

Underlining <u>Step 1</u>, Ben said, "By agreeing to transform the trauma care experience and by defining where this care experience begins and ends, we have just completed Step 1 of the PFCC Methodology.

"<u>Step 2, Establish a Care Experience Guiding Council</u> is what I'd like to discuss next," Ben continued. "The Trauma Care Experience Guiding Council will be an essential strategic group of committed, enthusiastic champions who will start and guide our use of the PFCC Methodology in Trauma services. The Guiding Council will start as a small, core group and will later expand to become the Trauma Care Experience Working Group. Don't worry," he said, "I'll explain what the Working Group is when we get to Step 4. For now, I'll just say that the Guiding Council is vital for ensuring high-level guidance and support.

"Establishing the Guiding Council is where I need your help," Ben went on. "I'd like to serve as the Administrative Champion for this first Guiding Council. My involvement as Administrative Champion will put the hospital's seal of approval on our use of the PFCC Methodology. Then, to round out the Guiding Council we'll need two Clinical Co-Champions who can inspire colleagues to make and sustain needed changes. And a PFCC Coordinator to schedule meeting rooms, send updates, ensure the prompt flow of information, and maintain lists of active, future, and completed projects. Now," he said, pausing for a moment, "who would you recommend for these roles?"

Dan spoke first. "Since we've decided to start with the trauma care experience, I think you should ask Scott Long, Medical Director for Trauma Services, to serve as one of the Guiding Council Clinical Co-Champions. I think doctors will be more receptive to the PFCC Methodology if they know a respected colleague is championing it."

"Good point," Nancy said. "And I think you should ask Kate Starr, Nursing Director for Trauma Care, to serve as the other Clinical Co-Champion. For the Trauma Care Project Coordinator," she added, "I'd ask Jackie Jordan, the hospital's Quality Improvement Project Coordinator. Having a PFCC Champion from outside of Trauma Services will help us to show that we're breaking down silos and working collaboratively across departments and functions."

"Great suggestions, thank you," Ben said. "I'll invite them to serve on the Guiding Council right after this meeting.

"Now, on to <u>Step 3, Shadow Patients and Families to Co-design the Care Experience</u>," he continued. "Step 3 provides the *tools* that enable us to see the care experience through the eyes of patients and families. Perhaps the most powerful of these tools," Ben went on, "and one of the three prongs of the Patient Centered Value System, is Shadowing. In the PFCC Methodology, as I've said, we Shadow patients and families through their care experience. Shadowing, combined with Care Experience Flow Mapping, enables us to see the current state clearly, both from our perspective as caregivers and from the perspective of patients and families. Shadowing will show us where patients and family members go during their trauma care experience, for how long, and the caregivers with whom they come into contact—and when we map the flow of care as we Shadow, we will see with new eyes the delays, waste, inefficient care processes, and 'hassles' patients and families deal with every day.

"Caregivers who Shadow and then create Care Experience Flow Maps suddenly have an 'Aha!' moment in which they say, 'I never *realized* this is how patients and families experience our care: it never occurred to me to think about where patients and families came from before they reached me; I never really *thought* about where they would go when they left my care; I never *knew* this bottleneck was a problem, or that an inefficient scheduling process could keep patients from accessing care in a timely way. I never really considered how many times staff come in and out of patients' rooms, which disrupts their rest and healing. Or how many 'silos' patients and families go through—not only in the hospital, but between the hospital and home—and how disconnected these silos can be, much to the detriment of patients and families.'"

"That's right," Nancy said. "We're used to working in our own distinct areas but we don't usually think of these as silos—you know, departments and units (like the Emergency Department, x-ray, inpatient units, the operating room, etc.), functions (such as nursing, medicine, physical therapy, dietary services, speech pathology, etc.), levels of care (e.g., front line staff, middle managers, and C-suite directors), and care settings (e.g., the ambulance, hospital, outpatient rehab, skilled nursing facility, and home care). But 'silos' is exactly what they are."

Ben nodded and continued, "Now let me explain how this process works. After Guiding Council members and others Shadow patients and families through the trauma care experience, they will map the flow of care exactly as patients and families went through it. The result, the Care Experience Flow Map, will (1) establish the current state of the trauma care experience, and (2) show us the touchpoints (which I'll explain in a minute) in this care experience.

"We'll also use Shadowing to help us determine the true cost of care at the level of the clinical condition through the full cycle of care as part of the Patient Centered Value System," he went on, "and we'll go into this later (see Chapter 8)—but for now, let's focus on using Shadowing to establish the current state and reveal touchpoints."

Ben continued, "The touchpoints on the Care Experience Flow Map are doctors, nurses, technicians, aides, valet parking attendants, housekeepers, receptionists, anesthesiologists, pharmacists, and others from areas both inside and outside the hospital. We'll use the touchpoints from the Care Experience Flow Map to help us decide who should serve on the Working Group. Which brings us to Step 4."

Ben underlined <u>Step 4. Expand the Guiding Council into the Working Group</u> on the whiteboard.

"Can you explain what the Working Group is?" Nancy asked.

"The Trauma Care Experience Working Group is the engine that will drive care transformation," Ben replied. "The Working Group will include at least one caregiver from each touchpoint shown on the Care Experience Flow Map.

"Based on my experience," Ben continued, "I think our Trauma Care Experience Flow Map will show that we'll need to invite—at a minimum—a caregiver from pre-hospital Emergency Medical Services, the Emergency Department, radiology, laboratory services, anesthesiology, surgery, the post-anesthesia care unit, the intensive care unit, the medical surgical unit, pharmacy, dietary services, housekeeping, and rehabilitation. I also think our Care Experience Flow Map will show we need to invite a valet parking attendant, someone from admissions, and someone from financial services. Finally,

I know that our Care Experience Flow Map will show that we'll want to invite caregivers from outside the walls of this hospital, such as representatives from off-site rehabilitation and skilled nursing facilities, and someone from home health—in short, anyone on whom the patient and family will rely after hospital discharge. Of course, only by Shadowing and Care Experience Flow Mapping will we be able to pinpoint the patient's and family's touchpoints in the trauma care experience. These touchpoints will determine the actual composition of this Working Group."

"I'm wondering," Dan said, "how people from all these different departments will work together to transform the care experience of patients and families."

"As Working Group members," Ben replied, "we transform the care experiences of patients and families by breaking down the silos that have traditionally separated us. Members of this Working Group will connect all the different aspects of the trauma care experience. Suddenly, people who never knew one another, let alone talked or worked together, will collaborate as a true care *team* to identify problems—and to fix them—quickly. And not only that," Ben went on, "but being part of the Trauma Care Experience Working Group will lead to a culture of ownership among all caregivers involved. The key to a culture of ownership is the power of caregivers—from all levels and all areas of the organization—to make decisions and co-design change in partnership with patients and families.

"You make it sound so easy, Ben," said Nancy. "But is it? Have you ever encountered resistance to what some may see as a 'different' approach?"

Ben replied. "The truth is, change—even positive change—can be stressful. It would be less than honest to pretend otherwise. But part of our challenge is to welcome the change we know is needed in healthcare. In order to get caregivers to accept and embrace the Patient Centered Value System, including the Patient and Family Centered Care Methodology, we must answer the unspoken but underlying question that is at the core of everyone's fear of change. And that is, 'What will happen to me?'"

"You read my mind," Dan said. "That's exactly what I was wondering. How *would* you answer that question?"

"The answer," Ben replied, "is that you will become an even better caregiver than you already are. By changing our perspective, we will grow professionally in ways we never expected. Seeing the care experience through new eyes will lead to a heightened sense of satisfaction as we contribute to making needed changes happen."

"So, what you're saying is, as challenging as making these changes may sound right now, introducing the Patient Centered Value System, including the PFCC Methodology, will be positive for patients and families as well as for the organization and for all of us," Dan said.

"That's right," Ben said. "Now, getting back to speaking of patients and families, it can be very helpful to include them as members of the Guiding Council and Working Group. Having the perspective of patients and families represented at Working Group meetings can serve as a consistent reminder of what's important to them."

Ben then went on to explain that while Step 3 enables the Working Group to understand the current state of the trauma care experience, Step 5 allows Working Group members to envision the ideal state.

Underlining <u>Step 5. Create the Shared Vision of the Ideal Story</u> on the whiteboard, Ben said, "The ideal state is the way patients and families want their care to be, all the time, in any situation or setting, with no constraints. In Step 5," he went on, "we use everything we've learned through Shadowing, surveys, and engaging patients and families and we write the ideal state of care from their point of view. Writing the ideal story as a team leads to a shared vision that will guide the Working Group as we move from the current state to the ideal. Then we begin to co-design the ideal care experience in partnership with patients and families.

"Let's say, in Step 5, I'm writing a story about the trauma care experience," Ben continued, "and I've already Shadowed patients and family members though their care experience. It doesn't matter what my role is—I could be a parking attendant, a surgeon, a dietician, a housekeeper, a receptionist, a therapist, a nurse, or serve in some other role. First, I'd write about what happened during the care experience from the patient's and family's point of view. Next, I'd write about what *could* have happened and what *should* have happened in an ideal world, also from their perspective. What happened represents the current state. What could and should have happened represents the ideal state as the patient and family define it.

"Now, what do you think we see when we compare these two stories—those that reflect the current state and those that reflect the ideal state of care?" Ben asked.

"We are bound to see differences," Nancy said.

"And gaps. Or even chasms," Dan added.

"Exactly—and, again, all from the patient's and family's point of view," Ben said. "And through discussion and the sharing of individual stories, 'your story' becomes 'our story'—the collective story and shared vision of the Trauma Care Experience Working Group. What the PFCC Methodology allows us to do," he continued, "is to transform the current state so it *becomes* the ideal state of care, which is ever changing. Actually, this is the perfect segue to Step 6, the nuts and bolts of care transformation itself."

Then Ben underlined <u>Step 6. Form Project Teams to Close the Gaps between the Current and Ideal</u> on the whiteboard.

"In Step 6," Ben said, "members of the Trauma Care Experience Working Group will break up into small Project Teams to:

1. Select projects
2. Establish Project Team co-leaders
3. Again, identify the current state through Shadowing

4. Recruit members from the Working Group for Project Teams
5. Create the shared vision of the ideal story
6. Close the gaps between current and ideal

"I see," said Nancy, "the six steps followed by Project Teams are the same as the six steps of the PFCC Methodology."

"If I understand this correctly," Dan said, "we can think about the work of the Project Team as a 'cycle within a cycle.'"

"Exactly," Ben said. "This construct is not only elegant, but it promotes learning by being self-reinforcing. And that's not all," he went on, "the PFCC Methodology is self-sustaining. Project Teams disband when their current projects are completed and re-form to take on new projects. New projects are identified by Working Group members and others who continue to Shadow the care experience periodically over time. Rather than a linear process that has a beginning and an end, the PFCC Methodology is a process of continuous improvement."

Then, glancing at his watch, Ben said, "I see our time is up and I don't want to keep you. You've been more than generous with your time. Thanks again for coming on such short notice, and thanks for your suggestions about who should serve on the Trauma Care Experience Guiding Council. And now," Ben went on, "based on your excellent suggestions, I'm going to find Kate, Scott, and Jackie to see if they'll agree to serve."

Then, even before they had risen from their seats, Dan and Nancy watched Ben grab his jacket and race down the hallway.

Chapter 2

Choose Your Champions: Establish the Care Experience Guiding Council

---

> The task of the leader is to get … people from where
> they are now to where they have not been.
>
> ### Henry A. Kissinger

Kate Starr, Nursing Director for Trauma Services at Exemplar Memorial Hospital, was so engrossed reading letters from former patients and family members that she didn't notice Ben Highland standing in her office doorway. "Knock knock," he said.

"Wow, Ben, great presentation last Friday," Kate said. "How's Jane doing?"

"Better every day, thanks. And now it feels great to be looking to the future. This is a brand new day at Exemplar Memorial Hospital," Ben said.

"I can't wait to hear what you have in mind. I've just been reading letters from patients and family members who were pretty unhappy with some of their experiences here," Kate said.

"You know," she continued, "I read letters like this every week, but only occasionally have I ever felt I could do anything to make the care experiences of patients and families any better. And when I have tried to make positive changes," she went on, "I didn't know how to sustain them. I felt I was tackling the same problems over and over again. Talk about frustration. To make matters worse, I felt alone in my efforts. Until now. I've been giving your talk a lot of thought, Ben, and I'm actually starting to believe we can make some positive changes here."

"I guarantee you, if we start now," Ben said, "you'll soon be reading letters from patients and families *raving* about their ideal care experiences in this hospital."

"So where do we start? And how can I help?" Kate asked.

"You must have read my mind. The reason I'm here is to invite you to serve on Exemplar Memorial's first Care Experience Guiding Council—the Guiding Council for Trauma Care."

"Ben, I'm honored to be asked. Can you tell me a little more about the Patient and Family Centered Care (PFCC) Methodology? And what is the Care Experience Guiding Council? What would I contribute?"

"In a nutshell, the PFCC Methodology, one part of the three-pronged Patient Centered Value System, is a six-step process for transforming any care experience, in any setting, by seeing all care through the eyes of patients and families. And by actively involving patients and families in co-designing the care experience."

"What do you mean by care experience co-design, Ben?"

"The principles of design science and experience-based design—to make things better for end users—are used frequently in business but not so often in healthcare. In healthcare, the end users are patients and families. And the 'things' we aim to make better are patients' and families' healthcare experiences and outcomes. According to experience-based design," Ben went on, "end users themselves are integral to co-designing any improvement process. The essential question for us is, how can we partner with patients and families to create ideal care processes and experiences?" (Interested readers can go to Chapter 9 for more information on design science and care experience co-design and re-design.)

"And the answer?" Kate asked.

"As patients and families move through their healthcare journey," Ben said, "we move through it with them to understand their experience from the 'inside out.' One of the ways we do this is by Shadowing patients and families through each step of their care experience. Shadowing, the first prong of the Patient Centered Value System, is used in both the PFCC Methodology (the second prong of the Patient Centered Value System) and Time-Driven Activity-Based Costing (the third prong) but for different purposes. In the PFCC Methodology, as we'll discuss in detail soon, Shadowing is used to engage patients and families as partners in co-designing the care process. (The use of Shadowing to determine the actual costs of care through the entire cycle of care in any care experience is the subject of Chapter 8.) For now, it's important to know that partnering with patients and families using Shadowing leads to improved care experiences and improved clinical outcomes. And using Shadowing to capture data for Time-Driven Activity-Based Costing leads to reduced waste and lower costs. Taken together, this is what we call the PFCC Trifecta. And that's not all—by engaging and empowering staff, the PFCC Methodology improves their experiences, too."

"Now, as to why I'm here," Ben said, "I'd like to tell you about the Care Experience Guiding Council. The Guiding Council is a strategic group of a few committed, enthusiastic

caregivers who will guide, sustain, and expand our use of
the PFCC Methodology in Trauma Services here at Exemplar
Memorial. I hope you'll agree to serve. If you can come to the
small conference room tomorrow from 12 p.m. to 1 p.m., I'll
explain the basics and let you decide."

"This sounds exciting, Ben. If the PFCC Methodology can
transform the care experiences of patients and families, and
help to engage staff, I definitely want to be part of it. You
know, we try hard to deliver ideal care to every patient and
family and we don't like falling short. It would be wonderful
to be able to deliver ideal care. And it would be wonderful to
do it in a way that the staff feel good about. Absolutely, I'll be
there," Kate said.

When Ben left Kate's office he almost collided with Scott
Long, the Medical Director for Trauma Services. "Just the man
I was looking for. Scott, do you have a minute?"

"Sure, Ben. What's up? Great meeting last Friday."

"Thanks, Scott. As I promised at that meeting, I'm
in the process of assembling Exemplar Memorial's first
Care Experience Guiding Council for the Trauma Care
Experience. And I'd really like you to serve as one of the
Champions."

"I'm flattered," Scott said. "But remind me—what is the
PFCC Methodology? And how would I be involved?"

"Are you free to come to the small conference room tomorrow from 12 p.m. to 1 p.m.? Kate Starr will be there, and I'm
on my way to invite Jackie Jordan. I'll give all three of you
an overview of the PFCC Methodology then. And I'll explain
the role of the Guiding Council and what your responsibilities
would be. Then you can decide."

"Sounds good, Ben. Sure, I'd be glad to come."

"Great…see you then," Ben called over his shoulder as he
headed toward the elevators.

When Ben Highland reached the Quality Improvement
Department on the fourth floor, he strode down the corridor
and stopped when he reached Jackie Jordan's office.

"Good morning, Jackie," he said as he walked in to find the Quality Improvement Project Coordinator focused on her computer screen.

"Good morning, Ben," she said, looking up. "I heard your presentation last Friday. *Very* inspiring. Everyone's talking about it."

"Thanks, Jackie. Now, as promised, our journey in using the Patient and Family Centered Care Methodology is about to begin at Exemplar Memorial. I'm here to ask you to serve on the first Care Experience Guiding Council for the Trauma Care Experience. What do you say?"

"Well..." Jackie started, but knowing what was coming, Ben held up his hand to stop her.

"I know. Of course you have questions. Like what is the PFCC Methodology, anyway? What is the purpose of the Guiding Council? And what would be your role?"

"You took the words right out of my mouth," Jackie said.

"Tell you what," Ben said, "if you come to the small conference room from 12 p.m. to 1 p.m. tomorrow, I'll explain everything. I hope you can you make it."

"Sure, Ben, I'll be there. Thanks for asking me," Jackie said.

***

When Kate, Scott, and Jackie filed into the small conference room the next day, they saw the following information written on a whiteboard:

Patient Centered Value System
Patient and Family Centered Care Methodology:

Step 1. Select a Care Experience
Step 2. Establish a Care Experience Guiding Council
Step 3. Shadow Patients and Families to Co-design the Care Experience
Step 4. Expand the Guiding Council into the Working Group
Step 5. Create the Shared Vision of the Ideal Story
Step 6. Form Project Teams to Close the Gaps between Current and Ideal

"Thanks for coming, everyone," Ben began as they took their seats. "I'd like to start by asking, why did you all go into healthcare? What was and is your mission? What matters most to you? What motivates you, what makes you want to come to work every day?"

Kate thought for a moment and replied, "Two things motivate me, Ben. The first is to provide care that enables patients and their families to be their healthiest, for the longest period of time. The second is to make ours the best care possible in every way."

Scott answered, "What matters most to me is that patients understand their medical procedures and treatment plans and are able to take care of themselves when they leave the hospital."

Jackie responded, "What matters most to me is to find out what patients and families want for themselves, and then provide healthcare that meets their needs."

"So, bottom line, the health and well-being of patients and families are what motivate and matter most to each of us. That being the case," Ben said, "how do patients and families answer when we ask what matters most to them? Then once they've told us, how can we show them we're listening? And the answer? Well, that is the purpose of this meeting.

"Last Friday I spoke publicly for the first time about what happened when Jane was a trauma care patient in this hospital—and when I was, quite simply, her husband. As I said then, our experiences changed my perspective on the way we deliver care to patients and families. When I arrived in the Emergency Department and couldn't find her—and when I was kept waiting for hours during her surgery without a word from anyone—I felt helpless. And powerless. And scared. When she was eventually transferred to an inpatient unit, she bounced around from one department to another, with caregivers communicating inadequately with each other and with us. Which made us feel anxious and uncertain. When it was time for her to go to an inpatient rehab facility, they didn't have all the information they needed after they admitted her. Which annoyed us and actually set Jane's recovery back. And when she was back home and no one called to see how she was doing or to answer our questions, we felt forgotten. And vulnerable. We had many other experiences, too, that were far from ideal.

"I knew then that what happened to us should never happen to anyone, anywhere," he continued. "But I have a feeling similar things do happen to patients and family members every day. That's why I've asked you here today. I'm determined to transform trauma care at Exemplar Memorial Hospital and I want you to be a vital part of this transformation as Champions. I hope you'll agree to help launch the PFCC Methodology, which is part of the Patient Centered Value System and our new operating system for healthcare delivery."

"What's the purpose of this Guiding Council, Ben, and what would our roles be?" Jackie asked.

"And why us?" Scott asked.

"I'll answer Jackie's question first," Ben said. "As I told Kate yesterday, the Trauma Care Experience Guiding Council will be a small, strategic group of enthusiastic, committed caregivers who will serve as Champions to start and guide our use of the PFCC Methodology, and who will then expand the Guiding Council into the full Working Group and Project Teams."

He continued, "The overarching purpose of the Trauma Care Experience Guiding Council is twofold: first, to establish the current state of trauma care at Exemplar Memorial, which we will do by Shadowing patients and families through their trauma care experience and creating a Trauma Care Experience Flow Map. This flow map will show us where patients and family members go during their trauma care experience and for how long, the caregivers with whom they come into contact, and the many 'hassles' patients and families face as they go through the care process. The Care Experience

Flow Map will enable us to see the opportunities for improving trauma care at a glance. Second, as I've already mentioned, the purpose of the Guiding Council is to set the stage for expanding into the Working Group and Project Teams.

"In addition," Ben continued, pointing to the whiteboard, "each of us will have individual roles and responsibilities on the Guiding Council, which are listed here" (Table 2.1).

Table 2.1   Roles and Responsibilities of PFCC Guiding Council Members

Member	Caregiver Name	Individual Responsibilities
Administrative Champion	Ben Highland	• Hospital's "seal of approval" • Help to overcome obstacles • Help to break down silos
Clinical Co-Champions	Kate Starr and Scott Long	• Establish current state • Coordinate Working Group's Shadowing and Care Experience Flow Mapping • Identify caregivers across the organization who represent touchpoints to create the Working Group
PFCC Project Coordinator	Jackie Jordan	• Maintain lists of active, completed, and future projects • Manage metrics tracking for active, completed, and future projects • With Clinical Co-Champions, coordinate Working Group's Shadowing and Care Experience Flow Mapping • Schedule meeting rooms • Send updates and ensure prompt flow of information

Expanding on these points, Ben said, "The Administrative Champion puts the hospital's seal of approval on our use of the PFCC Methodology and will guide our Working Group in using the six steps. The Administrative Champion also helps to break down silos and overcome obstacles and hurdles we'll face along the way.

"Kate and Scott," he continued, "as Clinical Co-Champions your roles will be to actively and enthusiastically promote the PFCC Methodology to your colleagues who work in trauma care, leading by example. Since your colleagues already know and respect you, having you in these roles makes perfect sense. You'll serve as role models and advisors for caregivers who need support throughout this journey. You'll guide your colleagues as they make needed changes and work to sustain them, and as they continue to evaluate and re-evaluate the current state of trauma care by Shadowing and re-Shadowing over time. And you'll identify caregivers across Exemplar Memorial who represent the touchpoints in this experience through Shadowing and Care Experience Flow Mapping. Once you've identified the touchpoints, you'll form the Trauma Care Experience Working Group. And you'll ensure that the soon-to-be established Working Group meets weekly, which is so important to sustaining the PFCC Methodology.

"Jackie, as PFCC Coordinator, you, too, will play a vital role," Ben went on. "You are a great communicator and organizer and are expert at juggling a multitude of details. You'll help determine and track active, completed, and future projects; and you'll maintain lists of all projects—whether they're current, completed, or planned for the future. You'll schedule meeting rooms, send updates, and ensure the prompt flow of information to all Working Group members. And you, along with Kate and Scott, will coordinate the Working Group's Shadowing and Care Experience Flow Mapping." Ben looked at the group and said, "I realize many of these terms and themes are foreign to you now. But don't worry. Before you know it, they will become familiar—and by following the PFCC Methodology they will soon become second nature.

"Now, as Scott asked," Ben continued, "why have I asked you to serve as Champions on the Trauma Care Experience Guiding Council? Because you are well-respected caregivers. Because you are trusted and well-liked by your colleagues. Because you have a reputation for getting things done. And because your skills will enable you to model the breaking down of silos—a fundamental principle of the PFCC Methodology—for the full Working Group.

"When we're talking about leading innovation and truly transformational change in our organization, which is what we're doing by introducing the PFCC Methodology at Exemplar Memorial," Ben went on, "we need as Champions caregivers who are empathetic and who communicate well with patients, families, and colleagues. Caregivers whom colleagues respect and see as role models and mentors. Caregivers who are good listeners. Who are so committed to care transformation that they will inspire others. And each of you, as Champions, embodies all these traits."

"Well, since you put it that way," Scott said, "this sounds like an exciting opportunity. I'm honored and I accept."

"Me too," Kate said.

"You can count me in," Jackie added.

"Excellent!" Ben exclaimed.

"As I've already said," he continued, "the PFCC Methodology is an easy to learn and easy to follow six-step process for delivering ideal care experiences to patients and families. As you can see, I've listed these six steps on the whiteboard. How do we achieve ideal care experiences? By seeing the full cycle of care—including pre- and post-hospital services—through the eyes of patients and families. And then by partnering with patients and families to co-design the care experience.

"As we've discussed," Ben went on, "we will improve the patient's and family's experience of care, reduce waste, and lower costs by using the PFCC Methodology. At the same time, breaking down silos by collaborating with other caregivers and working in partnership with patients and families will enable us to provide the best care possible, which will lead to improved outcomes and increased satisfaction for patients, families, and caregivers alike. Our goal in using the PFCC Methodology is to make sweeping *transformational* changes, rather than small or incremental changes, in the way we deliver care. Incremental changes will happen along the way, but these transformational changes will take us from the current state to the ideal state of care for patients and families."

"This does sound good, Ben, but some might say PFCC sounds a little 'soft,'" Kate said.

"That may be the perception of some," Ben responded, "but that is incorrect. First, when it comes to healthcare, attention to detail in every aspect of care is essential. Patients and families are acutely aware of their surroundings and are always concerned about the quality and safety of their care. If we get what some might call the 'soft' things right, patients and families will have confidence that we'll get the other things right, too. And vice versa. A dirty room could make patients and families think cleanliness is not a priority and fear getting a hospital-acquired infection; clutter might look to patients and families like a lack of organization, so their confidence in our ability to deliver coordinated care might be shaken; and a lack of courtesy might make patients and families think we don't care about their needs.

"And there is not only a perceived link by patients and families, important though this is, but a *real* link between our attention to such experiential details and the safe functioning of the system itself. Problems in these so-called 'soft' aspects of care may reflect larger, systemic problems. For example, cluttered hallways or a disorganized nurses' station might reflect a lack of attention to detail in aspects of care, which could have adverse consequences. Does a lack of courtesy to patients and families reflect an unwillingness to listen and take their concerns seriously? And does a lack of communication between care providers reflect a disconnect that could cause harm?"

As heads nodded, Ben continued. "Second, the PFCC Methodology is built on the shoulders of giants from many fields, including Nobel Laureate Herbert Simon, Clayton Christensen, John Kotter, B. Joseph Pine, James Gilmore, Tim Brown, Steven Denning, Regina Herzlinger, Don Berwick, and others. Their expertise in the fields of design science, organizational behavior and development, psychology, business, marketing, and change management serve as the theoretical underpinnings of the PFCC Methodology. In developing the PFCC Methodology, we integrated all of their approaches into a single tool designed specifically for healthcare.

"Third, a number of papers published in peer-reviewed journals have reported the benefits of using the PFCC Methodology in improving clinical outcomes and reducing waste and costs (DiGioia et al. 2007, 2010, 2012, 2015; DiGioia and Greenhouse 2011, 2012; Van Citters et al. 2013; Millenson et al. 2013). For example, the PFCC Methodology was used at Magee-Womens Hospital of UPMC to reduce readmissions within 30 days of weight loss surgery resulting from such complications as dehydration, wound infection, pain, vitamin deficiency, weight gain, and deep vein thrombosis/pulmonary embolism. The project reduced readmissions from an average of 9.5 to 1 in the initial 22-patient intervention group in the first 30 days, and these results have been maintained. In addition," he said, "the PFCC Methodology has been tested in the real world by dozens of other healthcare organizations and providers." (More information on projects and organizations using the PFCC Methodology appears in Chapter 11.)

"I can see the PFCC Methodology isn't 'soft' at all," Kate replied.

Scott said, "I agree. Moreover, the guiding principle of the PFCC Methodology makes perfect sense. *No* industry has survived without focusing on the needs and wants of its end users. And who are our end users? Patients and families. How can we survive as an organization, let alone thrive, if we don't focus on improving their care experiences and outcomes?"

"Absolutely! And how can we survive as an organization if, as so many businesses have found, we don't also find ways to eliminate waste and reduce costs? This is now more important than ever," Jackie said. (Chapter 8 explains how Shadowing combined with Time-Driven Activity-Based Costing as applied in the Patient Centered Value System can reduce waste and costs.)

Ben nodded and said, "Now, since we've decided to start first with transforming the trauma care experience, part of Step 1 has already been completed (to complete the rest of Step 1 we'll have to define the beginning and the end of trauma care, which we'll do very soon). And because you have just agreed to serve on the Trauma Care Experience Guiding Council, we have completed Step 2. We'll discuss each of the six steps in detail in the coming days as we put the PFCC Methodology into action." Then, glancing at his watch, Ben said, "Later this week I'll explain Shadowing, along with the other tools that comprise Step 3. How does tomorrow from 12 p.m. to 1 p.m. sound?" Ben asked. "In fact, if this day and time work for you, let's make this the standing time for our weekly Trauma Care Experience Guiding Council meetings."

"Sounds good, Ben. I have a feeling this is going to be a life-changing experience—not only for patients and families, but for us," Kate said.

"Exactly what I was thinking," Scott said.

"I'm looking forward to getting started," Jackie said.

After they'd gone and the room was quiet, Ben called his wife. "Jane," he said excitedly, "we've just completed Step 2 of the PFCC Methodology. Exemplar Memorial Hospital now has its first Guiding Council. I can't wait to introduce Step 3, when I'll explain the tools that make the PFCC Methodology so unique and effective. Jane, you of all people know how important this is. At last, we are on our way to transforming trauma care."

References

DiGioia, AM, Greenhouse, PK. 2011. Patient and family shadowing: Creating urgency for change. *J Nurs Adm* 41(1):23–28.

DiGioia, AM, Greenhouse, PK. 2012. Care experience-based methodologies: Performance improvement roadmap to value-driven health care. *Clin Orthop Relat Res* 470:1038–1045.

DiGioia, AM, Greenhouse, PK, Chermak, T, Hayden, MA. 2015. A case for integrating the Patient and Family Centered Care Methodology and Practice in Lean healthcare organizations. *Healthcare* 3(4):225–230.

DiGioia, AM, Greenhouse, PK, DiGioia, CS. 2012. Digital video recording in the inpatient setting: A tool for improving care experiences and efficiency while decreasing waste and cost. *Qual Manag Health Care* 21(4):269–277.

DiGioia, AM, Greenhouse, PK, Levison, TJ. 2007. Patient and family-centered collaborative care. *Clin Orthop Relat Res* 463:13–19.

DiGioia, AM, Lorenz, H, Greenhouse, PK. 2010. A patient-centered model to improve metrics without cost increase. *J Nurs Adm* 40(12):540–546.

Millenson, ML, DiGioia, AM, Greenhouse, PK, Swieskowski, D. 2013. Turning patient centeredness from ideal to real: Lessons from 2 success stories. *J Ambul Care Manage* 36(4):319–334.

Van Citters, AD, Fahlman, C, Golfmann, DA, et al. 2013. Developing a pathway for high-value, patient-centered total joint arthroplasty. *Clin Orthop Relat Res* 472(5):1619–1635.

Chapter 3

Shadow Patients and Families to Co-Design the Care Experience

> We watch what people do (and do not do) and listen
> to what they say (and do not say). The easiest thing
> about the search for insight—in contrast to the search
> for hard data—is that it's everywhere and it's free.
>
> **Tim Brown,**
> *Change by Design*

When Kate, Scott, and Jackie filed into Ben's office at noon
the next day, they saw him writing on the whiteboard,
Step 3. Shadow Patients and Families to Co-design the Care
Experience.

Ben turned to face the Trauma Care Experience Guiding
Council, thanked them for coming, and began: "The purpose of today's discussion is to explain one of the three
prongs of the Patient Centered Value System, which is also
part of Step 3 of the Patient and Family Centered Care (PFCC)
Methodology—Shadowing. Step 3 also includes tools that

enable any caregiver to see the care experience through the eyes of the patient and family—including the stories patients and families tell us, the letters they send, and the surveys they answer—but today we'll focus our discussion on the most powerful and enlightening of these tools, Shadowing, combined with Care Experience Flow Mapping."

"Shadowing is the direct, repeated, real-time observation of patients and families as they move through each step of a care experience. In our case, this is the trauma care experience. The Shadower is the person who conducts the Shadowing. The Shadower is charged with seeing the care experience through the eyes of the patient and family, recording every step of the care experience, and constructing the Care Experience Flow Map. The Care Experience Flow Map is either a graphic illustration or a list that details the touchpoints in a patient's and family's care experience, showing where patients and families go during the care process and for how long, as well as the caregivers with whom they come into contact.

"Of course," Ben went on, "since as Shadowers we can note only what we observe, caregivers who operate behind the scenes—such as those responsible for billing, chart review, and equipment sterilization—won't appear on the Care Experience Flow Map. Instead, these caregivers are identified in other ways—for example, through discussions among the Guiding Council and with staff, as well as through Shadowing as part of Time-Driven Activity-Based Costing, which we'll discuss another day. (Time-Driven Activity-Based Costing is the focus of Chapter 8.)

"The Care Experience Flow Map shows where the patient and family go, in what order, and at precisely what times, during their care experience. A Shadowing report provides a comprehensive 'snapshot' of the patient's and family's true trauma care experience, including what they see, what they say, and how they react as they move through each phase of their care experience. In other words," Ben said, "the Care Experience Flow Map should *show* the patient's and family's care experience; the Shadowing report should *tell* the story of the patient's and family's care experience from their point of view. Shadowing reports should identify opportunities for improvement expressed by the patient, the family, and caregivers—and include the Shadower's own ideas for improvement."

"When we Shadow," he continued, "we'll record our observations using the GoShadow™ app available at GoShadow.org. We'll note the touchpoints along with the objective and subjective details of the care experience. Specifically, when we Shadow, we'll document how long each step along the care pathway takes and capture the comments, questions, reactions, and concerns expressed by the patient and family at each touchpoint. The touchpoints and details we record in our notes will be the raw data we'll use to construct the Care Experience Flow Map and Shadowing report. The GoShadow app will help us to accomplish these tasks quickly and easily.

"Let me explain," Ben went on. "GoShadow enables you to automatically generate Shadowing reports that include Care Experience Flow Maps highlighting touchpoints and caregivers; time studies; and suggestions captured from patients, families, and providers during Shadowing. These reports will prepare you to determine the actual, or true, costs of delivering care and not just what we charge or costs for which insurers reimburse us. Shadowing and GoShadow are real-time co-design tools that allow you to engage patients and families in their own care and to work in partnership with them and other caregivers to design the ideal care delivery system.

"After creating our Care Experience Flow Maps and Shadowing reports, we'll present these to Guiding Council and Working Group members so that we can share what Shadowing revealed to us. Using slides to present Shadowing reports is an effective way to show the qualitative and quantitative information resulting from Shadowing, and to highlight the aspects of the care experience we'd like our audience to see," Ben continued.

"Now, who has questions?" Ben asked.

"Is there a particular format we should use to create our Shadowing report?" Jackie asked.

Ben replied, "The GoShadow app lets you generate Shadowing reports automatically in a consistent format and includes objective and subjective information that is well organized and structured, and has never been captured or presented before. Shadowing reports present the background and reasons for Shadowing a particular care experience, move on to present the quantitative and qualitative details of the patient's and family's care experience, and conclude with our recommendations for improvement as a result of Shadowing. This is where ideas for improvement projects come from. For example, the Shadowing report may reveal that different care providers give patients and families conflicting information. Or that patient education would be more effective if provided in a different format or at a different time. We all know we can do better. Shadowing reports will help us to pinpoint where and how."

"Who will be the audience for our Shadowing report, Ben?" Scott asked.

"We'll report our Shadowing findings first to the Guiding Council and then to the full Working Group at the Working Group kick-off meeting," Ben answered. "Later, when selected members of the Working Group Shadow the trauma care experience, they'll report their own findings to the entire Working Group and Project Teams. (I know we haven't discussed Working Groups or Project Teams yet, and we'll get to that soon.)"

"Can we back up a minute, Ben? Why is identifying touchpoints so important?" Kate asked.

"Great question," Ben replied. "As we'll see when we Shadow," he answered, "what we *think* is the flow of care and what the flow of care really is for a patient and family are not always the same. We'll also see that there is more to identifying the current state than just flow; understanding the *experience* at every step of the journey is just as important, as we will soon discover. "To explain what I mean," Ben continued, "first let's ask ourselves what we think is the current flow of the trauma care experience. We may think a patient who is rushed to a Level I Trauma Center would go to the Trauma bay, to imaging services, the operating room (OR), recovery, the intensive care unit (ICU), the medical-surgical unit, inpatient rehabilitation, outpatient rehabilitation, and home. But when we Shadow, we may find that the patient and family do not move from one touchpoint to another in such a smooth, straight line. Instead, Shadowing may show us that the patient has to go directly from the Trauma bay to the OR. Or that when the family arrives in the parking lot they can't find the entrance or parking near the Emergency Department (ED). Shadowing may show us that the patient has to stay in the recovery area all night because no beds are available in the ICU. Or that once the patient is out of recovery and in the ICU, she has to go back to the OR for another surgery. And Shadowing will show us when, and under what circumstances, the patient and family are reunited, both with each other and with the patient's care team.

"Before the year is out," Ben went on, "dozens of caregivers will be applying the PFCC Methodology to transform many care experiences throughout the hospital. That's how this innovative way of delivering care will soon become thoroughly embedded into the culture of Exemplar Memorial Hospital and become our new healthcare operating system."

Ben went on, "Shadowing enables us to see, hear, and understand every aspect of the patient's and family's care experience from their point of view *as they go through it,* over the full cycle of care. We see the care experience through their eyes, here and now. Where do patients and families go, and when? Shadowing will show us. How does the care experience look and feel to them? Shadowing will tell us. With Shadowing, we no longer have to rely on the memories of patients and families days, weeks, or months after a particular care experience.

"When we Shadow patients and families through their care experience," Ben continued, "we accompany them every step of the way. We see what they see, hear what they hear, wait while they wait, and talk with them about their care experience—all while taking careful notes. This gives us the opportunity to co-design ideal care delivery with patients, families, and caregivers as full partners.

"Have you ever noticed the way our memories can play tricks on us?" Ben asked. "If we don't take notes," he went on, "we tend to forget when something actually happened. Or who was there at the time. Or what we felt while it was happening. Writing down what takes place, and when, and noting the caregivers with whom the patient and family come into contact, provides us with hard data as opposed to fuzzy memories. As we Shadow, we note any questions, comments, concerns, or suggestions the patient and family express at the time. We also note our own—and other caregivers'—observations, reactions, and suggestions for improvement. The result of Shadowing is information we will use to transform the care experience for patients and families.

"While the outcome of Shadowing is data," Ben continued, "the heart of Shadowing is an emotional connection that develops when we put ourselves in the shoes of patients and families. Yes, when Shadowing we are observers—but we also become, if only briefly, part of the family unit. If something is less than optimal from the patient's or family's perspective, we want to do something about it, and quickly. This is what we mean when we say that Shadowing creates the sense of urgency to drive change. As you'll see, this sense of urgency is a powerful incentive to transform the current state into the ideal state of care for *all* patients and families.

"While I was at UPMC," Ben went on, "caregivers sometimes said that before they followed any of the other steps of the PFCC Methodology, they first Shadowed patients through a defined care experience. Why Shadow first? Because as you'll see when *you* Shadow, Shadowing provides an instant infusion of insight, understanding, and empathy for patients and families. Simply put, Shadowing is unique in enabling us to see the care experience through their eyes. Shadowing changes everything."

"How do we get started?" Scott asked.

Then Jackie asked, "What do we need to know before we start?"

"Preparation is key to effective Shadowing," Ben replied, "so I'm glad you asked. The process of Shadowing consists of three steps," he said, as he proceeded to write these steps on the whiteboard:

- Get ready
- Go Shadow
- Report

"Now," Ben said. "Let's talk about what each of these steps entails.

"First, when we get ready to Shadow, we need to define the care experience to be Shadowed. For trauma care," Ben said, "let's start with the call that comes in from the ambulance to tell us they're on their way. And let's end when the patient returns home after the hospital stay or inpatient rehabilitation. Although Shadowing may end when a patient is discharged, our involvement with patients and families continues once they're home. If a patient needs follow-up care with their primary care physician, specialists, or a home healthcare agency, this is all part of their care experience.

"Second, getting ready to Shadow involves selecting Shadower(s). Who do you think makes a good Shadower?" Ben asked.

"Just the question I was going to ask," Scott replied.

"The truth is," Ben said, "anyone can Shadow—any caregivers, including new hires, those on light duty, and those in the Quality and Safety department and Finance; members of a Guiding Council (like us) and Working Group; and volunteers, patient advocates, summer interns, and students in the health professions. The less familiar that Shadowers are with the care experience being Shadowed, the fewer preconceptions they will have. Which is exactly what we want. Shadowers should, ideally, be keen observers, be empathetic and open-minded, and be a 'fly on the wall' as they Shadow patients and families.

"Since it's essential for all members of the Guiding Council to understand the current state of the trauma care experience," Ben continued, "we'll divide our Shadowing of the full care experience into smaller, separate segments. We'll each Shadow a patient, then the family, and then we'll combine all of our observations on each segment to create our full Shadowing report. Because there are many touchpoints—and often different touchpoints—for patients and their families, breaking Shadowing up into small segments makes this an easy task. When we divide the full care experience into smaller segments and have different caregivers Shadow discrete aspects, each of us may Shadow a patient and family for only an hour or two at a time. When we're done we'll combine our notes on the segments so we can see the whole care experience over the full cycle of care, as well as its parts. Soon, when we've established the Trauma Care Experience Working Group, new Shadowers will similarly Shadow patients and families through this care experience. Then it will be *their* turn to combine the findings into a Shadowing report to present to the entire Working Group.

"Third," Ben said, "getting ready to Shadow involves gathering information about the trauma care experience before we Shadow. For example, when is the best time to start Shadowing? Should we Shadow during the day or at night, on weekdays or weekends? A nurse in the Emergency Department recently mentioned it's probably best to Shadow on a Friday or Saturday night, since that's the busiest time in the Trauma bay.

As part of this step," Ben continued, "we need to let caregivers know in advance that we're planning to Shadow. We could do this by e-mail, through announcements at staff meetings, by posting notices on bulletin boards, or all of the above. It's important to be open about our plans to Shadow so no caregiver feels put on the defensive. When we announce our plans to Shadow, we should let all caregivers know that Shadowing is not a 'secret shopper' program—that the purpose of Shadowing is to help us see all aspects of the trauma care experience through the eyes of the patient and family, not to observe and report on caregivers' performance. We should also let them know they will have the opportunity to add their insights about how to improve the care experience of patients and families. This is what we mean by including patients, families, *and* caregivers in care experience co-design. As I've learned, caregivers know that healthcare processes are 'broken' and they welcome Shadowing and the opportunity to be part of the solution.

"When we get ready to Shadow," Ben went on, "we also need to get permission from patients and families to Shadow their trauma care experience. We want to partner with and engage them throughout the course of Shadowing. Of course, the nature of trauma care is that patients and families don't choose to come to the hospital in advance, so we can't get their permission to Shadow ahead of time. (For other care experiences, such as those in which patients schedule their hospital admissions or clinic and procedure visits, Shadowers have ample opportunity to ask patients and families for permission to Shadow.) What we must do in trauma situations is ask the family's permission when they arrive in the Emergency Department and ask the patient's permission as soon as he or she is able to understand and respond to our request. So, for example, if the patient enters the Trauma bay and is taken immediately for imaging tests or to the OR, we should find the family when they arrive and ask their permission to Shadow *their* care experience, approaching the patient later.

"When approaching the patient and family, we should explain that our role as Shadower is to observe, record, and evaluate their care experience so we can improve the delivery of care for all patients and families, now and in the future. The vast majority of patients and families agree to Shadowing because they genuinely want to help us improve care, and they know how much we value their input."

Jackie was the first to speak up. "How should we record our Shadowing observations, Ben?"

"As I mentioned earlier, you can record your Shadowing observations by signing up for the GoShadow app at GoShadow.org to note your observations and construct your Care Experience Flow Maps and reports electronically."

"How can we ensure compliance with the Health Insurance Portability and Accountability Act (HIPAA) to protect patient privacy when we Shadow?" Kate asked.

"Good point. It's essential to ensure that the identities of all patients and family members remain anonymous when we Shadow and when we write our Shadowing reports. We can do this by assigning numbers or find other ways of identifying patients and family members."

"Do we need to get written consent from patients and family members as well as verbal consent before we Shadow?" Jackie asked.

"No," Ben replied, "the verbal consent of patients and family members is enough. But you can certainly get written consent if you'd like to."

"Do we Shadow segments in the trauma care experience just once, or is this something we should do more often?" Scott asked.

"Great question, Scott. Shadowing should be repeated periodically over time," Ben answered, "but how many times, and how often to re-Shadow, is up to individual caregivers. Since the current state is always changing, re-Shadowing enables us to evaluate the new current state and make changes to establish the new ideal as patients and families define it. We need to think of Shadowing as a cycle of evaluation, re-evaluation, and continuous improvement. Shadowing each segment of a care experience two or three times is ideal. But Shadowing even once will provide useful information and reveal opportunities for improvement.

"Well, what do you say?" Ben asked. "We've done a lot of talking. The time has come to Shadow. But one important thing before we start," Ben cautioned. "We need to let caregivers in the Emergency Department know we're going to Shadow, and when. And we need to explain what Shadowing is. Our work has to be completely open and above board so no one feels they're being scrutinized. Kate, would you let the ED charge nurse know we're planning to Shadow Friday night? Be sure to say that Shadowing is simply a way for us to observe the care experience from the patient's and family's point of view and help us to improve their care experience, now and in the future. And that the observations and input of the caregivers themselves is of great value to us, as well. I don't imagine you'll get any pushback but let me know if you do.

"But back to what I was saying," Ben continued, "let's Shadow a patient and family through their trauma care experience in segments and note each of the touchpoints, along with our objective and subjective impressions. When we're done, we'll put our findings together to create a Care Experience Flow Map. Then we'll be ready to move on to Step 4 of the PFCC Methodology."

***

Friday, 10 p.m. Kate and Scott are in the Trauma bay waiting to Shadow a patient's and family's trauma care experience when the call comes in. With the GoShadow app open, they are ready to record events as they unfold.

"Exemplar Memorial Hospital, this is Ambulance 12. We are currently en route to your facility with a 59-year-old male unrestrained driver, ejected 20 feet from car. Patient is unconscious, 3–4 on the Glasgow Coma Scale, two-inch laceration above right brow, right leg compound fracture, labored respiration with nasal flaring. Current vital signs: BP (blood pressure): 90/40, RR (respiration rate): 30, HR (heart rate): 120. Patient has been placed in full spine immobilization including C-(cervical) collar in place, O2 (oxygen) via NRB (non-rebreather mask) at 12 LPM (liters per minute), 18 gauge IV placed in left antecubital. ETA 10 minutes."

10:13 p.m. Overhead announcement, "Trauma Team Activation Room 1." The 10 members of the Exemplar Memorial Trauma Team (TT) respond to the page by donning protective gear and placing florescent pink labels on gowns to identify their TT roles, and then head down the ED hallway toward Trauma bay room 1.

10:13–10:23 p.m. Male patient wheeled into Trauma bay by three EMS staff who provide a brief updated report to TT while the team transfers patient from EMS stretcher to TT stretcher. TT intubates patient; assesses breathing; takes x-rays; inserts a second IV into right arm; administers IVF (intravenous fluid) and medications; collects blood samples and sends to lab; conducts neurological assessment; and conducts complete physical exam.

10:23 p.m. "Patient to the OR *now*," TT Team Leader tells the surgical team and trauma surgeon standing outside the doorway.

10:23 p.m. Surgical team and trauma surgeon use express elevator to take patient to OR.

10:25 p.m. Charge nurse pages social worker to contact family.

While Scott follows the surgical team as they wheel the patient to the OR, Kate waits in the Emergency Department to Shadow the care experience of the family members when they arrive.

10:42 p.m. Social worker arrives in the ED; asks charge nurse for patient's identification so she can phone the family.

10:50 p.m. Charge nurse says he doesn't know where patient's identification and belongings are.

11:10 p.m. Social worker searches for and finally finds patient's wallet, looks up home phone number, and calls:

"Hello, Mrs. Jones? My name is Carol Jameson. I'm a social worker at Exemplar Memorial Hospital. Your husband has been in a car accident. He was wheeled into surgery a little while ago. I'm sorry, I can't tell you anything about his condition. Please come to the Exemplar Memorial Emergency Department as soon as you can. Do you know how to get here? Can someone come with you?"

Kate hears the social worker give Mrs. Jones driving directions before hanging up the phone and waits for the family to arrive. Forty minutes later, Kate notes the following:

11:50 p.m. A woman in her mid-50s arrives in the ED with her adult daughter. The woman breathlessly tells the security guard, "I'm Karen Jones. My husband Kevin was in a car accident. He's in surgery. How is he? Where is he? When can I see him?" she asks.

"I just need to check your ID and take a quick look inside your purse first," the guard says.

"What? I ran out of the house so fast I forgot my purse. I had just gotten into bed. I called my daughter as soon as I got off the phone with the social worker, and Stephanie came to pick me up. Oh no, I had Kevin's doctor's name and phone number in there. And our insurance card. Not to mention my cell phone, house keys, and a little money," Mrs. Jones says distractedly.

The guard looks annoyed. "Well, I'm not supposed to let you in without an ID. Wait here," he says as he walks away.

"What?" Mrs. Jones calls after him in vain, crying to her daughter, "We've just spent 30 minutes trying to find this place and I'm worried sick about your father. How can he just walk away like that?"

Five minutes later the guard returns. "Your daughter's ID will have to be enough for now. Wait over there and someone will come to talk to you."

Kate glances at the clock on the wall and notes the interaction with the guard in her goShadow® app.

12:00 a.m. Kate walks slowly toward the chairs where mother and daughter sit in the cream-toned waiting room. They look up as Kate approaches.

"Hello, my name is Kate Starr," she says, extending her hand to Mrs. Jones. "I'm the Nursing Director for trauma care here at Exemplar Memorial. I've heard your husband has been in an accident."

"Yes. I'm Karen Jones and this is my daughter, Stephanie. Do you know what's happening to my husband, Kevin? The social worker told me he was in a car accident and that he's in surgery but that's all we know. How badly hurt is he? How long will the surgery take? When can we see him? How can we find out something? We're worried sick."

"I'm afraid we don't know yet, Mrs. Jones, but someone should be able to give us some information soon," Kate replies.

Then taking a seat beside mother and daughter, Kate begins, "I can only imagine how difficult this must be for you and your daughter. I don't want to intrude. But the reason I'm here is to ask your permission to Shadow your care experience while your husband is a patient at Exemplar Memorial. Shadowing, which is completely voluntary and confidential, involves observing and noting everything that happens to your husband, you, and your daughter while you're here. The goal of Shadowing is to help us understand how we can improve the care experience not only for you, but for other patients and families, now and in the future. Of course, how much of your care experience we Shadow is completely up to you. You can request privacy at any time."

After a moment's thought and a brief consultation with her daughter, Mrs. Jones responds, "I think that would be fine."

"Thank you, Mrs. Jones," Kate says.

"When the call came I panicked," Mrs. Jones tells Kate. "I was so out of my mind with worry that I ran out of the house without my purse. And even though the social worker gave me directions on the phone, we couldn't follow them. So we got lost. Can you imagine?" she asks. "Then, when we finally got here, we couldn't find the right parking garage. So I pulled up right in front of the ED but was told I couldn't leave my car there. All I want is to see my husband and to know that he's going to be alright!" she cries.

12:45 a.m. A nurse walks toward Mrs. Jones and Stephanie and says, "Mrs. Jones, your husband was just wheeled into surgery. His left leg was shattered in the accident. I can't tell you what his current condition is and I don't know how long the surgery will take. I'll give you an update as soon as I hear something." Before Mrs. Jones has a chance to reply, the nurse is gone.

"What?" Mrs. Jones cries. "On the phone the social worker told me Kevin had already been taken into surgery. Now a nurse says he has just gone into surgery. Why are different people telling us different things? Was there a delay getting him into surgery? I don't know who to believe or what to think."

Stephanie puts her hand on top of her mother's as tears streak down Mrs. Jones' cheeks. "What does it mean that we're hearing different things from different people? And that no one is telling us anything about Kevin's condition?" Mrs. Jones asks Kate. "Does that nurse know what it feels like to have someone you love in the hospital?"

With a compassionate look, Kate places a hand on Mrs. Jones' arm and thinks nothing like this should happen to the family member of any patient.

2:45 a.m. A nurse walks into the ED waiting room and says, "Mrs. Jones? My name is Iris. I'm sorry you've had to wait so long to hear something. Your husband was badly injured tonight. He has some broken bones, has lost a lot of blood, and needed major surgery. He's out of surgery now and is on his way to the Trauma ICU. I'm sure you and your daughter would like to see him. He's resting comfortably but

I don't want you to be shocked when you see him. He looks pretty bad, but that's to be expected under the circumstances. I know it's very late and neither of you has slept tonight. Can I get you some coffee before I take you to him?"

"I'm sorry, but I'm confused," Mrs. Jones says. "Someone told us we'd be going to the recovery room first. Until now we've felt forgotten. Practically invisible. I'm so relieved you're here to escort us. Is my husband going to be alright?" Mrs. Jones asks.

"Well, we are hopeful. We're monitoring him very closely. His surgeon, Dr. Goode, will come to talk to you," Iris replies.

2:55 a.m. Exhausted but relieved, Mrs. Jones and Stephanie decline the coffee and follow Iris.

***

3:00 a.m. Scott is already in the Trauma ICU, having accompanied Mr. Jones from the OR. Iris introduces Scott to Mrs. Jones and Stephanie.

Pulling Kate aside, Scott whispers, "Shadowing on over-night shifts is unusual and certainly isn't expected. The way Ben explains it, the point is simply to Shadow as much of a care experience as possible. That being said, though, I don't mind staying a little while longer. Why don't you go home, get some sleep, and continue Shadowing in the morning?"

"Sounds good, Scott, thanks. Now I know what Ben means by Shadowing in segments. It certainly makes the process of Shadowing more manageable," Kate says.

As Kate quietly takes her leave, Scott watches the eagerly anticipated family reunion. He watches eagerness turn to shock as Mrs. Jones gasps at the sight of her husband lying in the hospital bed. She is unprepared for what she sees. There are cuts and bruises all over his swollen face. His right leg—not his left, as the nurse had said—is in a cast from toe to hip. His neck is encircled by a cervical collar. Tubes are attached from his body to several machines. Stephanie begins to cry for the first time. Then, while Mrs. Jones bends over to kiss her husband's forehead, Mr. Jones opens his eyes, smiles weakly, and tries to talk. The fear that has gripped her ever since the call came dissolves in that instant. Scott watches as tears of relief fall from Karen Jones' eyes.

A few minutes later, a man approaches them and says, "Mrs. Jones, I'm your husband's surgeon, Dr. Goode. I can't stay long," he says, glancing at his watch. "Actually, I'm in a bit of a hurry. Your husband is lucky to be alive. He was unconscious when he arrived but I see he has opened his eyes and is trying to speak. That's a good sign. Mr. Jones required a splenectomy, packing for a liver laceration, and a thoracotomy for his chest injuries. We'll have to take him back to the OR tomorrow when he's stable so we can reassess and definitively control the bleeding."

Using the GoShadow app, Scott notes Dr. Goode's explanation and the questions Mrs. Jones asks in response: "Will my husband be alright? What's a splenectomy? A liver laceration? What kind of chest injuries? You mean you don't know if you were able to control the bleeding? Does that mean he could bleed to death overnight? And you didn't mention surgery on his leg but I see he has a cast. Oh my God, I don't understand what all of this means," Mrs. Jones cries.

"What it means," Dr. Goode says curtly, "is that he's not out of the woods yet. What we need now is time. Go home and get some sleep. Someone will call you in the morning."

Not wanting to leave but not knowing what else to say or do, Mrs. Jones and Stephanie kiss their husband and father goodnight and, heads bent, walk slowly to the door.

As Scott escorts Mrs. Jones and Stephanie to the exit nearest the Trauma ICU, he explains he has taken over Shadowing from Kate for a little longer. "When Mr. Jones is fully awake and able to understand and respond," Scott says softly, "I'll ask his permission to Shadow his care experience. If that's alright with you, of course."

Mrs. Jones and Stephanie nod, and Mrs. Jones says, "Thank you, doctor. You've given me hope that he *will* be alright, even if he looks really bad right now. Everyone needs a little hope. If I didn't have hope, I don't know how I'd go on."

"Your husband is in good hands," Scott says. "We'll see you in the morning. Thank you for allowing us to observe your care experience."

"I certainly hope you're right," Stephanie says. "You know, between the gruffness of the security guard when we first got here, the nurse telling us my father's left leg was shattered instead of his right, and what felt like the surgeon's brush-off, I'm a little worried about the quality of his care. I hope you were taking notes about how the surgeon spoke to us. Glancing at his watch and saying he's in a hurry, especially at this hour of the night? When we've been worried sick, haven't slept, and haven't heard a word for hours? Speaking to us like we could understand what he was talking about, then refusing to explain? He should have taken his time and explained everything to us."

"I'm not saying he was disrespectful on purpose," Mrs. Jones says. "He probably didn't even realize how he was coming across. But he ought to know better. He should have answered our questions instead of trying to rush us out the door."

Not wanting to criticize a colleague but at the same time seeing Mrs. Jones' point of view, Scott simply nods in response.

"Do you remember where you parked?" Scott asks Mrs. Jones. "It might not have been in the lot closest to where we are now. Would you like me to walk you to your car? After all, it's 3 a.m."

"Yes, thank you," Mrs. Jones says with a tired smile, "that is very kind. I know I haven't minced words tonight, doctor, and I hope you understand why. But I'd also like to say thank you for the care that you and your colleagues have given him. I hope I'll see you tomorrow."

***

Over the next few weeks, Ben, Scott, Kate, and Jackie took turns Shadowing different segments of the trauma care experience of Mr. Jones and his family. They Shadowed them through Mr. Jones' second surgery; his stays in the ICU and the medical-surgical unit; and his time in inpatient rehabilitation and then outpatient rehabilitation.

Guiding Council members shared their notes, observations, and their own often emotional reactions to what they had seen during Shadowing in their narrative reports. "Until I Shadowed Mr. Jones' trauma care experience," Jackie said one day, "I never realized how loud hallway conversations between caregivers can be overheard by patients and family members, and can not only seem disrespectful but can disrupt a patient's rest. I kept thinking, everyone shouldn't be hearing these conversations and poor man, he's trying to sleep."

"It's not right." Kate said. "I was thinking the same thing while we were Shadowing. I never really thought about the kind of 'welcome' patients and families should receive when they are unexpectedly called to the hospital and what they actually experience instead. It seems that Shadowing will give us a way to raise awareness and make changes all over the hospital."

Scott said, "I never realized the extent to which the so-called 'soft' aspects of care—like courtesy—can affect the way patients and families think about the 'hard' things, like the way caregivers communicate medical information."

Listening to what his colleagues had to say and agreeing with them all, Ben stood up and began to pace the room. "Since Shadowing relies on multiple Shadowers to capture each segment of a long care experience such as trauma care (and, ideally, Shadowing different patients and families through the same care experiences to be sure we're seeing the true current state), I also took a turn Shadowing Mr. Jones and his family. Let me tell you what Shadowing showed me," he said after Jackie and Kate had finished. "One Tuesday evening at 8:00 p.m., a nurse came into Mr. Jones' room on the medical-surgical unit. She was about to administer a medication that a nurse on the earlier shift had given him only an hour before."

Hands clasped behind his back, Ben stopped pacing and continued, "Mrs. Jones, who had hardly left her husband's side since he was brought to Exemplar Memorial, caught this. She questioned the nurse and insisted that her husband, having just received this medication, not receive it now. At first the nurse insisted Mrs. Jones was mistaken but agreed to double check. A few minutes later she came back and thanked Mrs. Jones for catching what amounted to a near miss. By being there and speaking up, Mrs. Jones helped that nurse avoid a medication error. And we all know how common medication errors are, despite our best intentions. What would have happened if Mrs. Jones hadn't been there?"

Ben let the uncomfortable silence hang in the air for 30 seconds before asking, "And what would have happened if I hadn't been Shadowing at the time? For one thing," he continued, taking a seat, "I wouldn't have seen that we need to redouble our efforts to improve our processes around medication administration. I also wouldn't have seen that we need to improve our processes around handoffs at shift changes so things like this don't happen.

"Because we've Shadowed the trauma care experience," Ben went on, "we now have several potential projects to bring before the Trauma Care Experience Working Group. And Working Group members who Shadow this care experience will add many of their own.

"The culmination of our Shadowing the trauma care experience," Ben said as he unfurled a new poster, "is that we've created this Trauma Care Experience Flow Map, which shows the touchpoints in Mr. Jones' and his family's care experience (Figure 3.1). The Care Experience Flow Map will enable us to form the Trauma Care Experience Working Group because it gives us the information we need to invite a representative from every touchpoint to participate.

"Not only that," he continued, "the Care Experience Flow Map, along with our narrative Shadowing reports, will guide us in selecting our first trauma care experience improvement

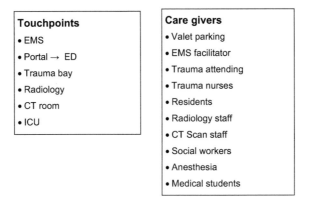

Shadowing results:
Emergency Department to ICU admission
Patient flow map

Touchpoints	Care givers
• EMS	• Valet parking
• Portal → ED	• EMS facilitator
• Trauma bay	• Trauma attending
• Radiology	• Trauma nurses
• CT room	• Residents
• ICU	• Radiology staff
	• CT Scan staff
	• Social workers
	• Anesthesia
	• Medical students

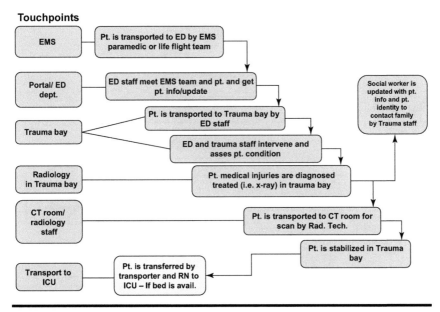

Figure 3.1   (a) The Patient Care Experience Flow Map.

projects. We'll share these with members of our about-to-be-formed Trauma Care Experience Working Group. Then, as required, Working Group members will Shadow and share their Shadowing reports and Care Experience Flow Maps with us. That's when we'll all be able to see the current state

Shadowing results:
emergency department to ICU admission
Family flow map

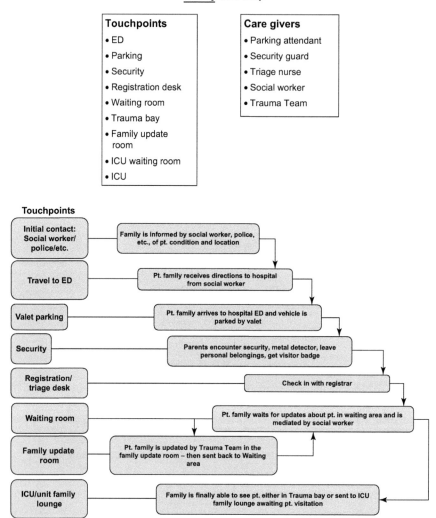

Touchpoints	Care givers
• ED	• Parking attendant
• Parking	• Security guard
• Security	• Triage nurse
• Registration desk	• Social worker
• Waiting room	• Trauma Team
• Trauma bay	
• Family update room	
• ICU waiting room	
• ICU	

Touchpoints

Initial contact: Social worker/ police/etc. — Family is informed by social worker, police, etc., of pt. condition and location

Travel to ED — Pt. family receives directions to hospital from social worker

Valet parking — Pt. family arrives to hospital ED and vehicle is parked by valet

Security — Parents encounter security, metal detector, leave personal belongings, get visitor badge

Registration/ triage desk — Check in with registrar

Waiting room — Pt. family waits for updates about pt. in waiting area and is mediated by social worker

Family update room — Pt. family is updated by Trauma Team in the family update room – then sent back to Waiting area

ICU/unit family lounge — Family is finally able to see pt. either in Trauma bay or sent to ICU family lounge awaiting pt. visitation

Figure 3.1   (Continued) (b) The Family Care Experience Flow Map.

from the patient's and family's point of view—including the 'hassles' they go through along their healthcare journey. When we see the gaps between the current state and the ideal as patients and families define it, we'll know where to target our improvement efforts."

Glancing at his watch now, Ben said, "We've done great work. I know it has taken us a couple of weeks to get to this point, but the time spent was well worth it. Now we're ready to move on to Step 4 of the PFCC Methodology. Why don't we talk about that tomorrow?"

Chapter 4

Develop Your Care Experience Working Group

Teamwork is the ability to work together toward a common vision. The ability to direct individual accomplishments toward organizational objectives. It is the fuel that allows common people to attain uncommon results.

Andrew Carnegie

The next day at noon, Kate, Scott, and Jackie were in the small conference room wondering where Ben was. On the whiteboard, he had written, <u>Step 4. Expand the Guiding Council into the Working Group.</u>

Suddenly, Ben bounded into the room. "Sorry to keep you waiting," he said, "I left something in my office that I wanted to share with you."

"What is it?" Kate asked as he handed her a letter, which she read aloud:

Dear Colleague,

It is with great pleasure that we invite you to become a member of the Trauma Care Experience Working Group. This is the team that will steer, shape, and own the innovative approach to improving the care experiences of patients and families known as the PFCC Methodology, which is part of the Patient Centered Value System. We hope you'll be willing and able to join us.

For those who are new to this approach, the Patient and Family Centered Care Methodology enables Care Givers like you to

- *See care through the eyes of patients and families*
- *Break down silos and develop unique high performance care teams*
- *Act on your sense of urgency to drive change*
- *Transform the delivery of care by co-designing experiences in partnership with patients and families*
- *Improve patient and family care experiences, including clinical outcomes*
- *Reduce waste and costs*

A Guiding Council has already been formed. The dynamic Champions who comprise this Guiding Council are ready to support you in making rapid patient and family centered improvements and are eager for you to share your expertise to ensure the Working Group's success.

Our journey begins with a kick-off meeting of the Trauma Care Experience Working Group this Tuesday morning. We look forward to your contributions. Together, in partnership with patients and families, we will transform care experiences and transform care delivery from the current state to the ideal. We hope to see you there.

Sincerely,
Ben Highland, your CEO

"Well, what do you think?" Ben asked.

"I think it sounds like an exciting opportunity," Scott replied.

"Who wouldn't feel honored to get this letter?" Jackie said.

"Let's look at the touchpoints we noted when we Shadowed Mr. Jones and his family," Ben said as he spread their Trauma Care Experience Flow Map on the table. "These touchpoints will tell us which areas of the experience need to be represented in the Working Group. We'll make an initial list of members to represent each of these areas, finalize the date and time for the kick-off meeting, and send this letter out to those on our list."

Kate, Scott, and Jackie examined the touchpoints on the Care Experience Flow Map. They immediately saw that Ben would need to invite caregivers from emergency transport, the Trauma Team, a social worker, a radiologist, an anesthesiologist, the director of emergency services, the ICU, the medical-surgery unit, and inpatient rehabilitation. He'd also need to invite a valet parking attendant, a security guard, someone from the Emergency Department (ED) information desk and ED admitting, a triage nurse, an ED nurse, an ED attending physician, an orthopedist, and someone from patient transport.

"Bringing together staff members—or rather caregivers—from all of these areas seems like a great way to break down silos and open lines of communication all over the hospital," Scott said.

Going over their initial list, Ben leaned back in his chair and said, "This is great but it's incomplete. Who's missing?"

Breaking the silence, he went on, "Some caregivers—like those from housekeeping, dietary services, and pharmaceutical services—don't appear as touchpoints on our Care Experience Flow Map. We'll need to invite them, too. These caregivers contribute behind the scenes for every patient and family at Exemplar Memorial. We'll also want to invite someone from Quality and Safety, and someone from Finance.

"How do we persuade those in Finance to participate? They might think patient and family centered care doesn't pertain to them," Kate said.

"As I've said all along," Ben replied, "the details of *every* aspect of care are important, including those related to finance. For example, we may reduce costs in one segment of care only to find that costs have increased in another. Or we may find that one change we make has a negative impact on quality. The only way to see the connection among these details is to follow the Patient Centered Value System, including the Patient and Family Centered Care (PFCC) Methodology *and* Time-Driven Activity-Based Costing (explained in Chapter 8). Before long, those in Quality, Safety, and Finance will see that what we're doing does, indeed, pertain to them. Plus," he went on, "once we've all experienced the Patient Centered Value System we'll understand that by focusing on the care experience of patients and families and implementing Time-Driven Activity-Based Costing, we'll be able to improve care experiences and clinical outcomes, reduce waste, and lower costs.

"But going back to who we'll invite to serve on the Working Group," Ben went on, "we'll want to invite a patient or family member. I know that having patients and families serve on a Working Group may not always be practical or feasible, but this is important to achieve if at all possible."

Ben continued, "The best way to engage and partner with patients and families is by having them sit on a Working Group. Now, aside from Shadowing and having patients and families serve on the Working Group," Ben continued, "there are other ways to engage and partner with patients and families. We can ask them to tell us their stories about their care experiences, either in writing or, even more powerfully, on audio or video recorders. Their stories can tell us why they feel the way they do about the care they received, how it can be improved, what went well and what didn't, what is most important to them, and so on.

"We can also ask patients to complete short, simple, focused surveys about every aspect of their care experience," Ben went on. "This can include the ease of parking, wayfinding, the amount of time spent waiting for care and information, the quality of nursing care, the communicativeness of all caregivers, including the surgeon and anesthesiologist, the cleanliness of the hospital, the noise level, and even the food. After all, as I've said, every detail matters. Their answers will help us to see every aspect of the care experience through their eyes.

"And gathering existing reports on patient satisfaction, such as Hospital Consumer Assessment of Healthcare Providers and Systems (HCAHPS) surveys, will tell us what patients think about their care experience as a whole, as well as what they think about specific aspects," Ben said. "The HCAHPS survey will tell us how patients rated such things as getting through to the office, the ease of making appointments and finding their way, waiting times, cleanliness, courtesy of all caregivers, teamwork of healthcare providers, explanations of procedures, and more."

Then getting back to the subject at hand, Ben said, "To establish our Trauma Care Experience Working Group we'll need to ask department managers whom they would recommend so we can finalize our list."

After Kate, Scott, and Jackie nodded in agreement, Ben said, "We're almost done. Now we just need to set a time for the Working Group kick-off meeting, which will be followed by one-hour weekly Working Group meetings on the same day, at the same time, each week. As the invitation letter says, I chose Tuesday because that allows us to set the Working Group's agenda early in the week. And I think we should start at 7:30 a.m. so this meeting won't conflict with our other work. Agreed?"

"Sounds good to us," Kate, Scott, and Jackie said.

"Well then, that does it for today. Very productive meeting. Thanks for coming. I'll get these invitation letters out this afternoon. Mark your calendars for 7:30 a.m. on Tuesdays as our standing time for Trauma Care Experience Working Group meetings. As the Guiding Council, we'll meet for a half-hour every Tuesday, either right before or right after the Working Group. We can decide that later," Ben concluded.

***

Ben stood at the head of the large conference room table at 7:30 a.m. the following Tuesday morning. Kate and Scott were at his side. To mark the kick-off of the Trauma Care Experience Working Group, an elaborate breakfast was spread out in the center of the polished table. The members of the Guiding Council wore black and white uniforms and served breakfast to the attendees, making them feel like VIPs. This was the Guiding Council's way of showing Working Group members how the PFCC Methodology should make patients and families feel during their care experience.

Jackie heard snatches of conversation as she walked around the table handing out information packets that included a flyer explaining GoShadow™ (available at GoShadow.org).

"… of course, I'm honored to be invited …."

"… how exciting … it sounds so innovative!"

"… what do you think is involved?"

"… who are all these people?"

"… how much of my time is this going to take?"

"… why did Dr. Highland ask *me*?"

"… I'm not sure what I have to offer …"

"… what's wrong with the care we deliver now?"

"Welcome, everyone," Ben began. "Thank you for coming to today's kick-off meeting of the Trauma Care Experience Working Group. We know how busy you all are, and we appreciate your taking the time to be here.

"Let's start by watching a segment from the old television medical drama, 'ER.' As you'll see," he continued, "the caregivers in this scene are working urgently to save a young mother's life. As you watch, put yourself in the shoes of the patient and her children."

Ben then nodded to Jackie, who walked over to the computer and started a scene from the television series. As the scene unfolded—that of a young mother being wheeled into the ER on a gurney after suffering a stroke—those around the table were unsurprised that very little was explained to the patient or to her children when they arrived. After all, they had witnessed and even participated in similar scenarios themselves.

When the clip concluded, Ben said, "You've just watched the current state of trauma care for one fictional patient and her family. But what's wrong with this picture? Putting yourselves in the shoes of the patient and her children, what would *you* have wanted the caregivers to do differently? What kind of care experience would *you* want?"

Suddenly, the care experience looked quite different to those around the table. "If I had been the patient or one of her children," said Rose, a hospital pharmacist, "I would have wanted to be approached with greater sensitivity. I may have just had a stroke and may have been in denial as this patient was, but I would have wanted the doctors and nurses to explain what was happening, to tell me what they were doing and why, and to let me know what would happen next. For goodness sake," she added, "don't be patronizing and don't keep me in the dark. Respect me enough to tell me what's really going on."

"I agree. But to tell the truth," said Patrick, a technician, "if I'd been in the caregivers' place I probably would have done the same thing. I think I would have felt such urgency to save the patient's life that I wouldn't have thought about how frightened she was or how anxious and confused her children were. It's obvious to me now, watching this clip, but if I'd been there at the time I doubt I would have noticed their distress. What should they have done? What should we do in similar circumstances?"

"We should use the Patient and Family Centered Care Methodology to see the current state through the eyes of patients and families and then to transform care to the ideal they need it to be," Ben answered. "At our recent annual meeting," he went on, "I mentioned that PFCC is *the* way to transform care by seeing every aspect of the care experience through the eyes of patients and families. Many of you may be wondering, 'What is PFCC? We already provide patient centered care. Why do we need it? How would I be involved? How much of my time is this going to take? How much is it going to cost? And how can I, as one person, really make a difference?'

"The purpose of today's meeting," he continued, "is to briefly explain what PFCC is and to discuss your roles in launching and sustaining it. Our goal? To transform the trauma care experience for patients and families by the time of Exemplar Memorial's next annual meeting."

Ben heard a buzz around the table.

"The reason we're here," he continued, "is that regardless of our area of expertise or position in this hospital, each of us is a caregiver because each of us, whether directly or indirectly, influences the care experiences of patients and families."

All eyes were on Ben as he said, "Your invitation letter mentioned that one of the goals of PFCC is to break down silos—and that means silos both within the hospital and between every segment of the continuum of care—including pre- and post-hospital services. Each of us works in a different area of the hospital and some of us, like Rick from EMS, work to an even greater extent outside it. Others, like Jim from Finance and Anne from Quality and Safety, work behind the scenes for patients and families. When we work *together* to deliver ideal patient and family care experiences using PFCC, we tear down traditional silos and can focus on the entire care experience of patients and families—not just on what happens in our own area. And using this approach we will co-design the ideal care experience in partnership with patients and families. As part of the Trauma Care Experience Working Group, we value the contributions each of us can make to this innovative approach.

"PFCC consists of six steps," Ben went on. Pointing to the easel behind him listing the six steps, he said, "Let's go through each of these steps briefly now, keeping in mind that the best way to learn is by doing.

"<u>Step 1</u> of PFCC is <u>Select a Care Experience</u>. In consultation with Dan Kahn, Exemplar Memorial's Chief Medical Officer and Nancy Byrd, our Chief Nursing Officer, we decided to introduce PFCC at Exemplar Memorial starting with trauma care. Since an essential part of Step 1 is to define where the care experience begins and ends, we've decided to define the beginning of trauma care as the time the Emergency Department gets a call from the field and the end as the day of the patient's follow-up appointment in the trauma surgeon's office after discharge."

"Interesting, that's not how I would have defined the beginning and the end of trauma care," whispered Dr. Stan Berman, an Emergency Department attending physician, to Rachel, a social worker. "I would have said trauma care starts when the patient is wheeled into the ED as a patient and ends when the patient is transferred to another area of the hospital. Dr. Highland's definition is much broader."

"I think that's how many of us might have defined the beginning and the end of trauma care, but his definition makes a lot of sense," Rachel whispered back.

"<u>Step 2</u>," Ben continued, "is <u>Establish a Care Experience Guiding Council</u>. The Guiding Council includes three to four members whose roles are to set the stage for PFCC by determining the current state and then expanding into the full Working Group. I will serve as the Administrative Champion. As such, my role is to put the hospital's seal of approval on our use of PFCC, help us overcome the inevitable obstacles, and help break down the silos that exist within our organization as they do in every healthcare organization.

"Kate Starr, Nursing Director for Trauma Care, and Scott Long, Medical Director for Trauma Care, will serve as the

Clinical Co-Champions. Kate's and Scott's role," Ben went on, "is to help establish the current state of the trauma care experience and coordinate Shadowing and Care Experience Flow Mapping, which we'll talk about in a minute.

"Jackie Jordan, our Quality Improvement Project Coordinator, will serve as the PFCC Project Coordinator," Ben continued. "Jackie will maintain PFCC project lists; help Kate and Scott to coordinate Shadowing and Care Experience and Flow Mapping; reserve meeting rooms; and send updates to ensure the prompt flow of information. Jackie will be responsible for ongoing and timely communication, which is essential to the success of PFCC.

"Now we're on to <u>Step 3, Shadow Patients and Families to Co-design the Care Experience,</u>" Ben continued. "This critical step helps us see the care experience through the eyes of patients and families," he said, looking at Alice, a former patient whom Ben had invited to serve on the Trauma Care Experience Working Group. "Before we can transform the care experience," he went on, "we first have to understand what patients and families experience now—that is, the current state. Then we have to learn what patients and families want and need—either instead of, or in addition to, what they are currently experiencing. This is what we mean by the ideal state," he said as Alice nodded.

"How can we understand the current state and learn how patients and families define the ideal state of care?" asked Donna, an Emergency Department anesthesiologist.

"There are a number of ways," Ben replied. "We can ask patients and families their opinions about the care they experienced after the fact. We can read their responses to surveys. We can read the letters they send us. But the most powerful way to see the care experience through the eyes of patients and families is to Shadow their care experience as they go through it. Shadowing shows us every aspect of their care experience in real time—what happens and when, the types and quality of interactions that take place, and how patients and families react all along the way. And that's not all. Shadowing shows us redundancies and problems with transitions we never knew existed. Outcomes that can be improved. Waste that can be eliminated. Costs that can be saved."

"Scott and I just finished Shadowing a patient and family through their trauma care experience," Kate said. "Shadowing profoundly affected our understanding of their experience from beginning to end and made us more determined than ever to do better. Let me read you our Shadowing report to illustrate what we mean."

Without mentioning the patient's or family members' names, Kate read the Guiding Council's Shadowing report of the trauma care experience of Mr. Jones and his family (Figure 4.1). (One segment of the Shadowing report can be found in Chapter 3.)

After reading their Shadowing report, Kate put the report into broader context. "While this man was a patient at Exemplar Memorial, his wife was here with him every single day. The patient, his wife, and their daughter found several aspects of their care experience disturbing. These ranged from the inconvenience of losing the patient's belongings to three things they said caused them great anxiety.

"First," Kate continued, "the patient's wife and daughter couldn't find the patient or learn anything about his condition for far too long after they'd arrived in the Emergency Department in a state of panic; second, there was a lack of communication among their many caregivers, which led to a feeling that no one was in charge as well as a medication error being narrowly averted; and third, the patient and his wife felt overwhelmed by a medication regimen prescribed at discharge with such inadequate instructions that they were unable to follow them correctly."

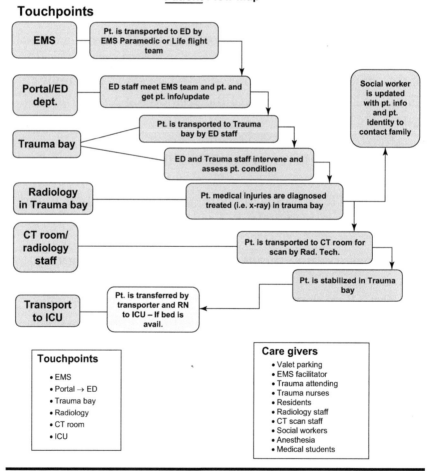

<u>The Level I Trauma Care Experience</u>
Shadowing Results
Segment: Emergency Department Through ICU
Admission or Transfer to a Trauma Unit

Request: To capture the patient and family experience from the time the patient and family enter the Emergency Department until the time they are transferred to the ICU

Shadowing Results: Emergency Department to the ICU
Admission
<u>Patient</u> **Flow Map**

Touchpoints

EMS	Pt. is transported to ED by EMS Paramedic or Life flight team
Portal/ED dept.	ED staff meet EMS team and pt. and get pt. info/update
Trauma bay	Pt. is transported to Trauma bay by ED staff
	ED and Trauma staff intervene and assess pt. condition
Radiology in Trauma bay	Pt. medical injuries are diagnosed treated (i.e. x-ray) in trauma bay
CT room/ radiology staff	Pt. is transported to CT room for scan by Rad. Tech.
	Pt. is stabilized in Trauma bay
Transport to ICU	Pt. is transferred by transporter and RN to ICU – If bed is avail.

Social worker is updated with pt. info and pt. identity to contact family

Touchpoints
- EMS
- Portal → ED
- Trauma bay
- Radiology
- CT room
- ICU

Care givers
- Valet parking
- EMS facilitator
- Trauma attending
- Trauma nurses
- Residents
- Radiology staff
- CT scan staff
- Social workers
- Anesthesia
- Medical students

Figure 4.1   Sample of a Level I Trauma care Shadowing report.

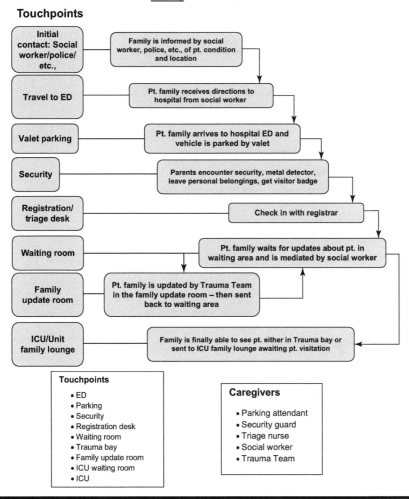

Shadowing Results: Emergency Department to the ICU Admission
<u>Family</u> **Flow Map**

Touchpoints

Touchpoints	
• ED	
• Parking	
• Security	
• Registration desk	
• Waiting room	
• Trauma bay	
• Family update room	
• ICU waiting room	
• ICU	

Caregivers

- Parking attendant
- Security guard
- Triage nurse
- Social worker
- Trauma Team

Figure 4.1 (Continued)   Sample of a Level I Trauma care Shadowing report.

Observations by Shadower and suggestions from patients and families

Arrival to ED

Patient experience

- Trauma team preps the bay–ready and waiting to act fast
- Patient is transported to ED by EMS or Life Flight Team
- EMS wheels patient in through an Emergency room entrance
- Someone in the front of the ED clarifies that it is "the trauma"

Family experience

- Valet parking – if they drove themselves here
- Enter building and check in with security
    - o Get bags checked, walk through metal detector, leave prohibited items with security holding, and receive a visitor tag
- Proceed to check in at the registration window
- Have a seat in the waiting room until further notice
    - o "This remodeling is clearly a planned event. So why didn't they PLAN any accommodations?"
    - o Outdated, dingy, HOT, crowded
        - The last place anyone would want to be when dealing with a traumatic family experience
    - o Accommodations
        - No bathroom (unless you ENTER the ED or LEAVE the ED)
        - No privacy
        - "Lousy phone reception"
        - No water!
        - No vending machines
        - "No options"
        - Nowhere to go unless you leave ED – which family members mostly will not do

Figure 4.1 (Continued)   Sample of a Level I Trauma care Shadowing report.

Trauma bay

- Patient enters trauma bay and is transferred from a stretcher to a bed
- Patient enters and Trauma Team immediately begins to assess condition, work together as a team
    - o If patient is awake they are questioned and communicated with –if not, the trauma team must work together and at times reference EMS
    - o Monitor hook up, vitals, IV placement, Allergies and Social History
- Organized chaos
- Personal introductions
- Ask then tell
- Belongings?
- Lacking "Big Picture" communication
    - o (Family update room, Trauma bay, not at all)
- Overall impression – Trauma Team excellent chemistry
- Once stabilized, the next step can happen, i.e., a patient is taken to get a CT scan (9 of 9 patients)

Radiology experience

- Enter scan room
- Radiology staff introduce themselves (sometimes)
- Quickly explain process to patient
- Orders vs. plan of care (stretcher)
- Pain meds are given if needed
- Staff communicates with patient via microphone or recorded voice as needed

Meanwhile, back to the family…

Family experience

- Family (if present) usually remain in the ED waiting room until patient is either stabilized or transferred out of the ED
    - o During this time a social worker is the family's only link to the patient – *vital for a positive family experience*
        - ▪ Social workers do an EXCELLENT job of communicating with *everyone* involved–including the Trauma Team

Figure 4.1 (Continued)   Sample of a Level I Trauma care Shadowing report.

- Once family is checked in a social worker is notified and promptly greets the family in waiting room
  - o Introductions
  - o Status updates (vague)
  - o Exchange contact information
  - o Lay out expectations
  - o Ease anxiety
- Once the patient has a definite destination outside of the ED the social worker transports them accordingly

ED to Inpatient Admission Experience

- Once stabilized, patient is transferred out of the ED and onto a predetermined Unit or ICU
  - o Often times this Touchpoint creates a bottleneck due to a shortage of beds on the trauma and ICU units
  - o Can be stuck in the ED for 10 minutes or several hours

ICU admission – Two different experiences:

Patient A:

Patients arrival to ICU

- Controlled chaos
- Respect Care Giver role in this process
- Warm welcome
- Coordination Care Giver and care
- Wanted to work here!

Families Arrival to ICU

- Family is updated within 30 minutes
- Communication: Where is the Chapel?
- Patient was receiving family updates
- If patient is not announced by social worker, how does the staff know they are in the family lounge?

Figure 4.1 (Continued)   Sample of a Level I Trauma care Shadowing report.

Reuniting patient and family

- Staff prepared patient for family visit
- Nurse escorted and provided explanation of condition
- Mother approached within 10 minutes about a research project

Inpatient stay

- Plan of care transparency
- Great verbal communication despite patient being sedated

Patient B:

Patients arrival to ICU

- I was with the family during patient's arrival

Families Arrival to ICU

- A surgeon speaks to family about expected surgery about 10 minutes after family arrives – "Will know in an hour or two if patient can have the surgery"
- No update for over 2 hours – brother calls for one
- Doctor arrives 11 minutes later with an update – looks like she was forced to be there
- Called back to see the patient 25 minutes later

Reuniting patient and family

- X-ray is in patient's room when family arrives
- Family is told to wait in the hallway outside of the room until they are done
  - Mom sees name spelled wrong on computer
- There are issues between nurses and patients going on all around and in front of the family within their first 10 minutes on the unit
- Nurse asks mom for her phone number but does not give mom any contact information

Inpatient Stay

- During the first 3 weeks of this inpatient stay, the patient has been heavily sedated and the family has been receiving little to no information from the staff
  - No orientation to the unit for the family – visiting hours, parking
  - Family is unaware that they can round with trauma team
  - The only information that the family receives is a research study business card and a unit brochure (entire time the patient was on the unit)
  - Never any certainty, always "I'll get back to you" or "*Someone* will be out to update your *shortly*"

Figure 4.1 (Continued)   Sample of a Level I Trauma care Shadowing report.

Resulting Improvement Projects

- Trauma packet/Family resource packet
- Trauma website
- Electronic trauma list
- Emergency Department environment of care
- Restructuring of the Trauma Team: Patients and families need to still know who their physician and caregivers are
- Traumatic brain injury patient education
    - Include transfers – not just for discharge patient

Figure 4.1 (Continued)   Sample of a Level I Trauma care Shadowing report.

"Putting ourselves in the shoes of patients and families by Shadowing is a powerful experience," Kate went on. "When we Shadowed, we saw how much precious time was wasted because a social worker couldn't find the patient's identification so she could call the family. We saw and felt the family's agitation as they arrived in the Emergency Department and waited anxiously for some word about their loved one. We felt their frustration as we observed their insensitive treatment by a security guard, their confusion when a surgeon explained the patient's condition in a way they couldn't understand. We saw, as if for the first time, how disruptive our hallway conversations can be to the patient's rest. And, most serious of all, we saw a medication error narrowly avoided only because the patient's wife intervened and a nurse took her concern seriously."

"Shadowing the current state of the trauma care experience made me feel the need to make the changes that are so obviously necessary, here and now," Scott said. "Without Shadowing, the current state wouldn't have been so obvious. In fact, we may never have realized what we can and should be doing better in very specific ways. Shadowing made us realize that we can't afford to wait another day. We know we can do better, we must do better for patients and families, and I'm convinced the PFCC Methodology is the way to close the gap between the current state and the ideal."

"And what is the ideal?" Ben asked. "The ideal is what patients and families say they want and need at any point during their care experience—that is, if they can put it into words. The ideal is also what Shadowers, in seeing the care experience through the eyes of patients and families, know it can and should be. The ideal is what we want and need when we are patients ourselves, or when we are the family members of patients.

"We come to understand the ideal when we Shadow and re-Shadow patients and families during their care experience," Ben continued. "We also come to understand the ideal through our own storytelling, which we'll get to when we discuss Step 5. Shadowing reports, along with Care Experience Flow Maps (the visual representation of touchpoints in the trauma care experience and the 'hassles' patients and families encounter as they move through their care experience) are critical tools that will guide our care transformation efforts.

"Step 4, Expand the Guiding Council into the Working Group, is where we are now," Ben said. "We have all been invited to serve on the Trauma Care Experience Working Group because each of us represents a touchpoint on the Trauma Care Experience Flow Map. And each of us has been invited to serve because we are dedicated to patient care, interested in collaborating with patients and our colleagues, and committed to excellence, all of which will enable us to go from the current state to the ideal state of care delivery for patients and families.

"You may have worked in this hospital for many years but you may not know the person sitting on either side of you," Ben went on. "That's because healthcare organizations tend to operate in silos. We come to work every day and work in the same department, with the same colleagues. So, we may not know the valet parking attendant, the Emergency Department receptionist, or the EMS transport technician; the anesthesiologist or the Trauma Team surgeon; the dietician or the pharmacist; or the OR nurse, the social worker, or the housekeeper. But at one time or another," he went on, "patients and families who enter this hospital come into contact with caregivers representing each of these touchpoints, either directly or indirectly. So, since we're going to be working closely together as members of this Working Group, let's introduce ourselves, stating our name, area of responsibility, and position at Exemplar Memorial," Ben said.

One by one, starting with the members of the Guiding Council, the members of the Trauma Care Experience Working Group went around the table introducing themselves. Ben was right. This was the first time many of them had met.

"Now," Ben asked. "Have you ever wondered where patients and families were before they came to you? Have you ever thought about where they will go after they leave your area? The most common answer to this question is 'no.' And that's a problem. Why? Because not knowing can lead to unnecessary redundancies in care; frustration and anxiety for patients and families; and confusion and missed opportunities for communication, increasing the potential for suboptimal transitions and even errors. As a result, the patient's and family's care experience suffers, clinical outcomes suffer, and unnecessary costs are incurred.

"That is the bad news. The *good* news," Ben said, "is that by working together using the PFCC Methodology we are aware of the wants and needs of patients and families from the beginning to the end of their care journey—from the moment we get the call from the field, to their arrival in the Trauma bay, until their follow-up appointment in the trauma surgeon's office after discharge. We will use the PFCC Methodology to disrupt the traditional silos and work together to improve patient experiences and clinical outcomes—and we'll apply Shadowing and the Time-Driven Activity-Based Costing components of the Patient Centered Value System (the subject of Chapter 8) to reduce waste and lower costs."

Leaning back in his chair, Dr. Paul Goode said, "Ben, you've talked about the benefits of the PFCC Methodology for patients, families, and the hospital itself. But I don't think patients and families know the first thing about their care. Why should I listen to them when all I want to do is deliver the care *I* know they need? After all, I'm the doctor and the expert, not them. What difference should their feelings make to the care I deliver? Why should I take the time to learn about and apply this methodology? What's in it for me?"

"Paul," Ben responded, "first, we need to think of and treat patients and families with the respect they deserve. After all, how would *you* want to be treated if you were the patient or a family member of a patient? Patients and families may not be clinical experts—you're right, that's our job. But they *can* sense when something isn't right with their care, when they're not being listened to, or when their concerns aren't being taken seriously and acted on. You of all people should know that such failures can have disastrous consequences. The literature is replete with examples of medical errors that have occurred as a result of not listening to and acting on the concerns of patients and families. Enlisting patients and families as partners in their care—in effect, in co-designing the care experience with them—is essential to patient safety. The PFCC Methodology enables us to co-design care with them in a systematic way."

Dr. Paul Goode said nothing. Ben could see it would take some time to convince him.

"If I'm being honest," said hospitalist Dr. Donna Murphy, "change makes me uncomfortable. And the PFCC Methodology sounds like such a big and disruptive change. I'm not sure this will be at all easy to implement and I want to know what will happen to *me* if we introduce it here."

Ben replied, "No question, Donna, the unknown usually feels threatening and fear of change is perfectly normal. But for the sake of patients and families as well as for our own, we need to dive in despite our fears. You'll soon see that your initial fears will be replaced by enthusiasm for care transformation. I've seen it happen time and again—physicians who most strongly resisted adopting the PFCC Methodology soon became its strongest supporters. I believe this will happen to you, too," he said, looking not only at her but at Paul Goode as he spoke.

Moving on, Ben said, "Let's talk briefly now about Step 5 and Step 6, since we'll devote our next couple of Working Group meetings to these Steps. <u>Step 5, Create the Shared Vision of the Ideal Story,</u> is both inspiring and revealing. Storytelling is at the heart of the PFCC Methodology and is used by everyone involved in transforming the patient's and family's care experience, including caregivers. Imagining and then writing about the ideal patient and family care experience from the patient's and family's point of view enables us to put ourselves in their shoes. When we Shadow (or listen to the Shadowing reports of other caregivers), we become partners with patients and families and empathize with them as never before. After Shadowing we ask them what we could have done to make their care experience ideal. Then we integrate our observations and their suggestions into our stories. Telling the story of the ideal patient and family care experience should be easy to do if we also remember that we are not only caregivers, but at some point, we have also been (or will be) a patient or the family member of a patient.

"Writing the story of the ideal trauma care experience will help us visualize its details," Ben went on. "It will set the stage for our Trauma Care Experience improvement projects, and will move us from storytelling to what author Ty Montague, in his book *True Story: How to Combine Story and Action to Transform Your Business,* calls "storydoing."

"When we compare our ideal story with what *currently* takes place," Ben continued, "we may see gaps, and even gaping holes, between what actually happens during the care experience and what *should* happen. The steps we decide to take to bring the current state into alignment with the ideal will determine our Trauma Care Experience improvement projects.

"Which is a perfect segue to <u>Step 6, Form Project Teams to Close the Gaps between Current and Ideal</u>," Ben said. "As you'll learn when we talk about this step in detail very soon, Step 6 is our guide to transforming the current state into the ideal state of care for patients and families. Project Teams, as you'll soon see, are the engines that will drive our care experience transformation efforts and take us from the real to the ideal.

"We have only two more things to talk about briefly before we wrap up today," Ben said. "The first is the PFCC Fund, which is a simple budget process used to support our Working Group projects. The second is the schedule of future meetings."

He went on, "Empowerment is a key concept of the PFCC Methodology, and this includes fiscal empowerment. The PFCC Fund is a budget, and a process, that will help us accelerate the work being done by Project Teams. As each Project Team is formed," he continued, "it has the authority to spend up to $1000 on care transformation *pilot projects,* which will allow us to start and complete these projects efficiently. While $1000 may not sound like a lot, you'll find that many, if not most, of the projects will require little to no funding—such as those involving revising processes or refining communication approaches. The PFCC Methodology enables us to achieve a lot without large expenditures and, in fact, tends to help us reduce costs. We'll learn about all the details of the PFCC Fund when we discuss Step 6 in depth. (Step 6 is the subject of Chapter 6.)

"I know we've shared a lot of information in a very short time and that you all need to get to work," Ben said. "The only thing we still need to address is dates for our weekly Trauma Care Experience Working Group meetings."

Surprised glances shot around the table.

"You mean we have to meet every *week?*" Dr. Goode asked from his seat in the back. "I'm sorry, Ben, I really don't have time for that."

"Paul," Ben replied, "I know you're busy. I'm busy. We're all busy. But transforming the trauma care experience for patients and families is a top priority at Exemplar Memorial. It's going to take an ongoing commitment from each of us."

"Dr. Goode, you may be surprised to learn that the PFCC Methodology doesn't take as much time as you might think.

We spend more than an hour a week now working around and trying to fix broken processes and systems," Jackie said.

Then Dr. Ron Knightley, director of Emergency Department services, spoke for the first time. "I'm excited about the chance to improve the trauma care experience for patients and families. The PFCC Methodology sounds like a unique opportunity to make a difference. I'm honored to be part of this Working Group and I'm enthusiastic about working to build high performance care teams to meet this challenge. Paul, you are a respected colleague and skilled surgeon. I hope you will give the PFCC Methodology a chance just as we're all willing to."

Many of those around the table nodded in agreement.

Ben continued, "The PFCC Methodology enables caregivers to deliver ideal care by engaging patients and families in an inherently personal way. Believe me, we'll see the positive results of our improvement projects quickly but we have to keep at it. One-hour weekly meetings create the momentum for making steady, sustained progress toward our goals. I have every faith you'll all be believers once we get started.

"The Trauma Care Experience Working Group will meet every Tuesday at 7:30 a.m., so please mark your calendars. We've scheduled meeting dates for the entire year. Jackie, as our PFCC Coordinator, will send out the list of dates.

"Thanks again for coming today," Ben concluded. "At next Tuesday's meeting, we'll focus on Step 5, writing the story of the ideal trauma care experience. Between now and then, ask yourselves two questions: First, if you were a trauma patient, what would you want your care to look and feel like? And second, if you were the family member of such a patient, what would be important at each step of your loved one's care? Alice's participation in this step will be especially helpful. At that meeting, we'll write a story that reflects our answers. The story will guide us in working toward a shared vision of the ideal state. I look forward to seeing each of you then," Ben concluded.

Chapter 5

Create a Shared Vision by Writing the Story of the Ideal Care Experience

When it comes to inspiring people to embrace some...new change in behavior, storytelling isn't just better than other tools. It's the only thing that works.

Stephen Denning

Ben had just finished writing Step 5 on the conference room whiteboard the following Tuesday—Step 5. Create the Shared Vision of the Ideal Story—as members of Exemplar Memorial's Trauma Care Experience Working Group took their seats.

"Good morning, everyone," Ben began. "The purpose of today's meeting is to follow Step 5 of the Patient and Family Centered Care (PFCC) Methodology. We're going to write the story of the ideal trauma care experience from the perspective of a patient and family."

Dr. Paul Goode, trauma surgeon, was the first Working Group member to speak. "Ben, this sounds like a waste of time. Why do we need to write a story about ideal care? And why from the perspective of a patient and family? This sounds 'pie-in-the-sky' and 'touchy-feely' to me."

"Not at all," Ben replied. "First, writing a story about the ideal care experience as if we were the patient and family helps us to build on what we observed, learned, and felt during Shadowing. There is nothing 'touchy-feely' about this. When we Shadow patients and families through their trauma care experience, we see, through their eyes, which aspects of the current state need improvement. We aren't usually aware of their concerns since we're so focused on our own roles, on doing our jobs as caregivers as well and as efficiently as possible. So it's easy for us to overlook other things that matter to patients and families. The beauty and utility of Shadowing and writing the ideal story is this: understanding ideal care as patients and families define it enables us to set goals for improvement and then work to achieve them."

Ben continued, "Let me make this perfectly clear, Paul. This is not 'pie-in-the-sky' thinking. What we're doing in Step 5 is '*blue-sky*' thinking. When we free ourselves from any constraints, real or imagined, as we write the ideal story, we're aiming for *transformation*, not simply incremental improvements, although those will come as well. You'd be surprised how much is possible when we set our sights high enough.

"There's no doubt that we come to work every day intending to do our best," Ben went on. "But when we understand what our patients and families experience in real time, what *we* think is our best often isn't good enough. The problem is, unless we see the care experience from their point of view, we may not even realize we're coming up short—or see what we could and should be doing better."

Ben saw Dr. Goode nod almost imperceptibly.

"Based on the Shadowing report we heard last week," Ben continued, "let's design the ideal trauma care experience in the form of a story that shows care as patients and families think it should be. When we compare our ideal story with the current state revealed in our Shadowing report, the gaps between the two will become apparent. The next step, which we'll get to soon in Step 6, is to take on projects to close those gaps."

Scott Long, Medical Director of Trauma Care and Guiding Council Co-Champion, spoke next. "Paul, one of the consequences of providing care in silos, as hospitals do, is that we don't usually think about where patients and families may have been before they came to us, where they're going next, or what interactions they may have had with other caregivers along the way. That's where Shadowing comes in. Shadowing enables us to follow the patient and family from one segment of care to another, from beginning to end—to see the entire care experience as a continuum, the way patients and families do. And to talk with them about their care experiences as they go through them. When we see the current state of an entire care experience through their eyes and then brainstorm ways to close the gap between the current state and the ideal, we need to aim high. Transformational change requires imagination, vision, and dedication to continuous improvement. As Ben says, it requires 'blue-sky thinking,' by which we raise the bar so we can exceed expectations, not just meet them."

"Let me see if I understand what you mean by 'blue-sky' thinking," said Nadine, the ER receptionist. "This may seem a little far-fetched … but if my daughter and I were both hospitalized after a car crash and were taken to different hospitals, I'd be able to see and talk to her and her doctors on a camera from wherever I am—you know, like Skype."

"That sounds 'blue-sky' to me," Ben said.

Then shifting gears, he said, "Let's take a step back for a moment. Before we draw on the Guiding Council's Shadowing report to brainstorm ideas about how we can redesign the ideal trauma care experience, let's take a moment to think about the last time we were patients, or the family members of patients, and how we felt about our care experiences. Who would like to share their experiences with us?"

Alice, a former trauma patient and now a Working Group member, spoke up. "I had an experience that made me anxious but that also turned out to be dangerous. I was getting out of the hospital after surgery. When I was discharged I was told I needed to take a bunch of different medications. How was I supposed to afford them all? No one even asked me if I *could* afford them. And then how was I supposed keep track of when to take them? No one asked me if I needed help or whether I understood. I ended up doing everything wrong and had to come back to the Emergency Department the next night. Is there some way patients can get their prescriptions filled before they leave the hospital? Why didn't they take more time to explain things before I left the hospital and make sure I understood what to do? And provide a contact person for me to call if I had questions when I got home, or check in with me so I wouldn't even have to call?"

Next, Jen, a radiologist, said, "Alice, I'm so sorry you had that experience. Hearing stories like this makes me angry. I want to improve the care experience for patients and families who have stories like yours. Now I actually have a positive story to tell involving trauma care. I think we'd all want our trauma care experience to be like the one my husband Jake and I had after his motorcycle accident last year."

Jen continued, "The social worker told me the trauma doctors and nurses were right there waiting for Jake when the ambulance pulled into the Trauma bay. They examined him thoroughly, took x-rays, and gave him the pain medication he needed, all in the space of 10 minutes. When the social worker called to tell me what had happened, I panicked. But she was so calm and kind that I was able to calm down a bit, too. She gave me detailed driving directions and told me a valet parking attendant would be waiting for me when I pulled up to the front door. She was true to her word. A young man wearing a windbreaker with the words 'Valet Parking' on the back was waiting for me. He greeted me with a smile and parked my car. There was a security guard at the entrance to the Emergency Department. His manner was gentle and he told me where to wait.

"I walked into the waiting room and the social worker was waiting for me with a packet of information," Jen went on. "She explained what was inside: a map of the hospital and complex, information for family and friends, a card to help me access pastoral care, and two cafeteria meal tickets. The social worker told me Jake needed surgery immediately and he was already in the operating room (OR), but that I would be reunited with him in the intensive care unit as soon as the surgery was over. A nurse gave me updates on Jake's surgery twice while he was in the OR. I always knew what was going on. I felt that all caregivers involved—from the social worker and Emergency Department receptionist to the surgeon, nurses, radiologists, and transport technicians—were functioning as a team, communicating with each other and with me. I felt included and respected, and I felt Jake was getting the best care possible. Under such terrible circumstances, it probably doesn't get much better than that."

Ben nodded and said, "Thanks, Jen, for sharing your story. Like Jake and Jen, when we are patients or family members we don't want to feel anxious or confused. We *do* want to feel included, informed, and confident that the care team is top notch and are all on the same page with each other and with us. The question is, 'Is what Jen and Jake experienced during trauma care always the case at Exemplar Memorial?' If it is, that would be outstanding. But if not, why not? And if not, what can we do to transform the current state into the ideal? Learning the answers to these questions is where Shadowing comes in. Since Shadowing is vital to writing the story of the ideal care experience, it's worth going over once more what Shadowing is and what it entails before moving on."

He continued, "When we Shadow patients and families through their trauma care experience—which, as you know, the Guiding Council has already done and which some of us will also do in Step 6—we observe what happens along the way and we listen to everything patients and families have to say about their care experience as it unfolds, both the good and the not-so-good.

"When we Shadow, we also note the suggestions of care-givers and our own observations about any aspect of the care experience that can be improved. And we ask patients and families to suggest three things that would have made their care experience ideal, in case they want to suggest something that didn't come up during Shadowing. Then," Ben went on, "based on all of this information, we write Shadowing reports and present our findings to the Working Group. The Working Group uses the Shadowing report to write the ideal story from the perspective of a patient and family. This is where we are now. Recalling the patient's and family's perspective in the trauma care Shadowing report we heard last week, let's start by tossing out some ideas so we can redesign the ideal care experience from the patient's and family's point of view."

"But what if what patients and families say they want is unrealistic?" asked Jim, from Finance. "What if it costs too much or simply isn't feasible?"

Ben responded, "Jim, we're not going to be constrained by costs or limitations of any kind, real or imagined, in writing the ideal story. As we've said, this is 'blue-sky' thinking, and the sky's the limit. Ideas that may sound impossible, even outlandish, now could soon become the current state. If we don't aim high, we're liable to make only small, incremental improvements when what we really need is sweeping, trans-formational change. And in my experience, most transforma-tional changes really don't end up costing much, if anything. I think you'll soon see why we should aim high. You'll be surprised at what we can achieve.

"We need to keep in mind one question," Ben said. "What was the perspective of the patient and family member we Shadowed through their trauma care experience? Patients and families don't know what's possible or impossible—they just know what they experienced and what they need. And it's *their* perspective, not ours, that should guide our ideal story.

"In writing our ideal story," he went on, "let's keep in mind that attention to every detail of care, including details some call 'soft,' is important. For example, when we're patients and family members, we're acutely aware of our surroundings. When we see that all our belongings are stored safely, our rooms are spotless, and our caregivers are courteous, we have confidence in the other aspects of our care, too. And when we see that our caregivers are communicating well with us, we have confidence that they are also communicating well with one another and that nothing will 'fall through the cracks.'"

Kate Starr, Nursing Director for Trauma Care and Guiding Council Co-Champion, interjected, "One thing to be aware of before we start is the flow of care for patients and families involved in trauma care. When the Guiding Council mapped the flow of care after Shadowing, we realized that, both initially and often later on, the flow is different for patients and their families. So we need to keep two distinct flows in mind as we write our ideal story."

"That's right," Ben said. "Where trauma care is concerned, patients usually arrive from the field either by ambulance or helicopter, and their family members are notified and arrive later. When family members arrive, they are confused, panicked, shocked, frightened, and coming into an unfamiliar environment that may feel intimidating just when they are feeling their most vulnerable. The same may be true when the patient is in surgery and the family is waiting to be reunited with the patient in the recovery room. That's why we must ask ourselves not only what patients say they need, but what family members say they need, when we write our ideal story."

Alice nodded in agreement.

Ben continued, "This is how Step 5 works. For the rest of this meeting, we'll brainstorm, throwing out ideas about the ideal trauma care experience, keeping in mind what we learned from Shadowing. Jackie, our Working Group coordinator, will write our ideas on a flip chart. Is there a creative writer among us who will volunteer to take the final pages and turn our ideas into a narrative, or story?"

Mia, a physical therapist, raised her hand. "I like to write," she said, "Why don't I give it a try?"

"Wonderful, Mia, thank you," Ben replied. "At next Tuesday's meeting," he continued, "we'll read what Mia has written and add to it, creating our story of the ideal trauma care experience together. Last week I did most of the talking. Today, it's your turn. Alright, let's go!"

Their ideas came flying. Jackie listed them in the order in which the trauma care experience tends to unfold. Caregivers who had until now been quiet and afraid to speak up began to express ideas enthusiastically. In the process of brainstorming ideas for the ideal care experience, this Working Group was becoming more than a roomful of individual caregivers. These housekeepers and surgeons, radiologists and social workers, dietitians and nurses, receptionists and pharmacists, parking attendants and physical therapists, and the others, were now in the process of becoming a team.

Alice spoke first. "As the wife of a trauma patient, knowing where my husband is and what kind of care he's receiving from the moment I walk into the Emergency Department until we're reunited is essential. And returning all of our belongings before discharge is important. Not only our wallets and cell phones, but our jewelry, eyeglasses, and dentures," Alice said.

"As a trauma patient, having the cervical collar removed as quickly as possible would make me a lot more comfortable," said Ed, the building engineer.

"Having one team assigned to care for me wherever I go in the hospital, instead of having different doctors and nurses come and go who I don't know, would put me at ease," said Ken, the neurosurgeon.

"Leaving the hospital with all the medications I need, and knowing how and when to take them, would make me feel more confident about going home," said Dottie, the OR nurse.

"All great ideas. Now where's the 'blue sky'?" Ben asked.

After a moment, Paul Goode said, "If all my doctors used social media, a secure version of something like Twitter, to communicate with each other and with me about my care in real time, decisions could be made more quickly and everyone would be on the same page."

"That's more like it! Let's keep the ideas coming," Ben said.

Before they knew it, the hour was up. As promised, Mia tore the pages off the flip chart and immediately began to turn them into a story of the ideal trauma care experience. The following Tuesday morning, she presented it to the Working Group.

In response to Kate's reminder that patients and families often take different paths through a healthcare setting, the next Tuesday the Working Group brainstormed a bit more and wrote two ideal stories—one focused on a patient we'll call Mrs. Romero, and another focused on her husband. Here are the stories the Working Group wrote:

Ideal Trauma Care Experience
of Mrs. and Mr. Romero

Mrs. and Mr. Romero had recently become grandparents. Mrs. Romero was on her way to babysit for their granddaughter when the car she was driving was hit from behind.

Mrs. Romero: I awake to the sound of sirens and someone telling me I'm going to be alright. I'm lying on a hard board and have a collar around my neck. Someone who says he's the Emergency Medical Technician tells me I've been in an accident. He tells me I'm strapped to a hard board and have a collar around my neck as a precaution. He says they are taking me to the Trauma Center, Exemplar Memorial Hospital. I hear him relaying information about me and the accident over the radio. He tells me when we get to the Trauma Center there will be a number of people to take care of me and I'll be in good hands.

When I arrive at the Trauma Center, someone begins talking to me immediately. She explains what the Trauma Team members are doing. She asks me about my pain frequently and soon gives me pain medicine. I'm wheeled into an x-ray room where x-rays are taken and then into another room where my blood is drawn.

A patient care technician takes my belongings and puts them in a bag large enough to hold everything, including my coat. He shows me the bag and puts a label on it with my name. The social worker comes in and asks me who in my family to contact. She calls my husband and lets me know she has done so, telling me she gave him clear directions and information about where to go when he arrives. I begin to relax knowing my husband is on his way.

A doctor is at my bedside in the Emergency Department shortly after I arrive and tells me about my injuries and the tests they're doing in a way that's easy to understand, even in the state I'm in. The test results and x-rays are read swiftly and I'm so relieved the doctor is able to remove my cervical collar fairly quickly. Based on the injuries shown in the x-rays, the doctor explains that an orthopedic surgeon will be coming to see me next.

Before I know it, the orthopedic surgeon is here and explains that I need surgery to place a rod in my thigh bone. She says she will ask an anesthesiologist to administer a nerve block to further relieve my pain before, during, and after surgery.

"What is a nerve block? How does it work? Is it risky?" I ask the surgeon apprehensively.

Just as I get the last question out, an anesthesiologist comes to see me in the Emergency Department and explains that having a nerve block means that patients need less narcotic medication for pain relief after surgery. I'm glad to hear this because the pain medicine the nurse has given me through my IV has made me a little nauseous. The anesthesiologist asks the nurse to take me to the pre-op holding area where he will administer my block. Thankfully, I am able to stay in the same bed for the transfer.

The anesthesiologist is waiting for me in the pre-op holding area and gets started right away. He explains that the block will last through and after surgery because a pump will continue to give me numbing medicine for a couple of days. I don't remember much after that until I wake up after surgery in the intensive care unit (ICU).

Mr. Romero: In the middle of the night the telephone rings at home. The caller identifies herself as a social worker at Exemplar Memorial Hospital. In the kindest way possible, she tells me that my wife has been in a car accident and has been transported to the Emergency Department. My immediate reaction is fear and panic.

The social worker tells me she understands that I'll want to be with my wife as quickly as possible. She asks if I know how to get to Exemplar Memorial. I tell her that I've never been to that part of town before. She asks if she can e-mail directions to me, which she does immediately. She also sends a text message with directions to my cellphone. She tells me she will be there to meet me when I arrive.

I have no trouble following the directions and arrive in the Exemplar Memorial driveway. A valet parking attendant wearing a jacket labeled "Valet Parking" opens the car door and helps me out. The social worker comes up to the car and says, "Hi, I'm Mary Smith, the social worker. We talked on the phone?"

I identify myself. Mary Smith says, "It's nice to meet you, Mr. Romero. The valet will take care of your car. You can come with me."

Mary Smith waits while I go through the security desk and the metal detector. She gives me the phone number for the Trauma Concierge, who is available for me to call 24 hours a day and who can answer my questions while my wife is being cared for.

She then escorts me to the Emergency Department family lounge, which I see is a private room with comfortable furnishings, a computer, a universal cell phone charging station, coffee, water, and a telephone. She asks if I would like a bottle of water and a snack and provides it right away. A sign on the wall informs me that it's okay to use my cell phone in that room and that the room has Wi-Fi access.

The Trauma Concierge meets me in the family lounge and gives me information about what to expect in terms of receiving updates on my wife's condition and when I can expect to see her. She gives me a care package complete with toothbrush, deodorant, and a bar of soap. She also gives me a brochure that provides unit-specific information as well as hospital maps and hotel phone numbers. She asks if I would like to have a visit from someone from Pastoral Care. I ask to see a chaplain. She pages him and before I know it he is there to comfort me. Later on, I learned that if I'd been in a state of extreme anxiety, the Trauma Concierge would have alerted the Trauma Stress Team to pay me a visit.

Within 10 minutes my wife's nurse, Maryanne, comes out and briefly explains that my wife is in the intensive care unit, awake, and asking for me. She tells me they are assessing my wife as well as controlling her pain, and that she is having specialized imaging done as part of her workup.

The surgeon comes to see me five minutes later and tells me that although I will see cuts and bruises on my wife's face and arms, the surgery to install the rod in her thigh bone went well and she is doing fine. Taking a deep breath, I ask the surgeon how much pain my wife will be in. She tells me my wife is receiving a nerve block now and has a patient-controlled analgesia pump available if needed, and that they will switch her to oral pain medication in a few days to continue to control her pain. The surgeon then escorts me to my wife's bedside. My wife is woozy but says her pain is under control. I am relieved to see her.

Mrs. Romero: I start to feel better as soon as my husband walks into the intensive care unit. Two nurses approach my bedside, one from the ICU and one from the Trauma unit, where I will go next. Nurse Maryanne and Nurse Alan share information about my condition and plan of care. They include my husband and me in their conversation and ask if we have any questions. Then Nurse Alan wheels me to a room in the Trauma unit that has monitoring capabilities and can also be turned into a regular room when I don't need as much specialized care. This means I won't have to move to a different unit as my condition improves. My room is available immediately and I am quickly settled in. The staff of this unit has advanced training in addressing the needs of trauma patients like me.

When I arrive on the Trauma unit, Nurse Alan is quick to ask me about my pain. He says to let him know if I begin to feel uncomfortable and explains that the goal is to prevent pain rather than try to catch up with it after it has returned. He reminds me that I will have the nerve block for three days following surgery, and reassures me that before the block is removed the care team will administer oral pain medications, wean me slowly off the nerve block, and reassess my pain level frequently. There is even a space on the whiteboard located at the foot of the bed for the nurse to write the last time I received a dose of pain medication. My anxiety lessens now that I know there is an effort by my care team to control my pain.

My personal belongings and valuables, placed in storage on my arrival, are delivered to my room ahead of me and I'm relieved to see them there in my closet when I arrive.

The Trauma doctor comes into my room and explains my injuries to my husband and me in greater detail than he was able to do earlier. He uses the computer at my bedside to show us the x-rays. We develop a plan of care that is agreeable to all of us. A large screen on the wall across from my bed lists my allergies, medications, vital signs, and progress notes from the various doctors caring for me. This screen is updated automatically every hour. I like being able to see what all of my caregivers are seeing so I can correct anything that's wrong. The last time I was in the hospital someone had forgotten to list one of my allergies on a chart—and since I couldn't see the chart from my bed, I didn't catch it. Luckily, my husband did.

Before he leaves, the Trauma doctor assures me he will be overseeing my care and communicating closely with any medical consultants that may need to be involved. He says everyone on my care team will communicate in real time using a secure version of Twitter. I appreciate knowing that up-to-date information is always available to my entire care team. He also gives us his cell phone number so we can call him with questions at any time.

There is no such thing as "visiting hours" in this hospital. Visiting hours are 24 hours a day, 7 days a week. Although quiet times are enforced so I can rest without interruption, my husband sleeps in my room at night and my children visit when they can. At night, the lights on the unit are dimmed, soft music plays in the background, and carts move noiselessly from room to room. My room is spacious, with a flat screen TV, DVD player, and computer, which puts patient education websites at my fingertips and enables me to send e-mails or text messages to members of my care team. I use either my bedside computer or the telephone to let the Exemplar Memorial kitchen know what I would like to eat whenever I'm ready for a meal. Their menu includes a range of healthful and tasty dishes.

Each morning at the same time, the healthcare team—consisting of my doctor, nurse, nurse practitioner, consulting doctors, case manager, pharmacist, physical therapist/occupational therapist, and nutrition specialist—speak with my husband and me about the plan of care for that day. An insurance expert comes to the first and last meeting. All team members introduce themselves and explain their roles. If a particular time is inconvenient for me, we can arrange another time to meet. These visits are efficient and helpful; the team works well together.

The unit social worker spends a good amount of time meeting with my husband and me to discuss what we'll need before I go home. My husband is then able to arrange for the necessary equipment to be installed, like bathroom handrails.

When it's time for me to go to physical therapy, my therapist (whom I will see throughout my hospital stay) enters my room with a wheelchair and transports me to the gym at the end of the hall. I work one-on-one with my physical therapist twice a day. Other patients are also having physical therapy in the gym. We support and encourage each other as we work hard to regain our functioning. Seeing my new friends actually makes me look forward to physical therapy. At this time every day, my room is cleaned by the same housekeeper, who I know by name.

On the day of my discharge, the doctor who cares for me throughout my hospital stay comes to see me, giving my husband and me verbal discharge instructions and phone numbers to call with questions and in case of emergency. I look at my calendar and make my follow-up appointments with my doctor then and there.

A few minutes later, Nurse Amy comes in with printed discharge instructions. She reinforces the information my doctor gave me and allows ample time for my husband and me to ask questions. Then she asks me to repeat the instructions in my own words to be sure I understand.

George, a patient care technician, packs up my personal belongings. I get dressed and feel confident. I am ready to go home.

Just before I am discharged, Gwen, the pharmacist on the Trauma service, hands me my medications, explains each prescription, gives me printed information about each one, and stresses that it is safe to continue taking the prescription pain pills when I need them during the next two weeks until my first outpatient appointment. She says I will need them less and less as my healing progresses and explains how to wean myself off of the pain medicine when I feel ready. Constipation can be a side effect of the pain medicine so she gives me tips on how to prevent it. Because I had hardly any pain during my hospital stay, I am confident I will be fine at home. Gwen explains how I can reach her if I need to; I really appreciate that because I know how hard it is to get in touch with a doctor when you have questions.

My husband gives Gwen his valet ticket and she calls the parking garage to have our car brought to the hospital's main entrance. The escort arrives in our room and takes us down in an express elevator to an exit where our car is waiting. It is not congested, so I am able to take my time getting into the car. The valet makes sure my seatbelt is secured and that we have all of our belongings. Saying goodbye, he wishes us well.

***

The air in the conference room vibrated with Working Group members' enthusiasm for achieving the ideal as they wrote their story. While brainstorming, some voiced ways to achieve the ideal on the spot. "What if we do this...?" one began, or "What if we do that?" Smiling, Ben reminded them that the purpose of Step 5 is not to solve the problems but simply to envision the ideal.

"We will work to transform the current state into the ideal when we get to Step 6 next Tuesday morning," he said. "In the meantime, keep that energy and those ideas flowing."

Chapter 6

Close the Gaps between the Current State and the Ideal

> The real voyage of discovery consists not in seeking
> new landscapes but in having new eyes.
>
> **Marcel Proust**

Ben walked into the conference room the following Tuesday
morning and saw members of the Trauma Care Experience
Working Group seated around the table and talking anima-
tedly. He wrote on the whiteboard, <u>Step 6. Form Project Teams
to Close the Gaps between Current and Ideal.</u>

"Today is the day we've all been waiting for—because
today we start Step 6 of the Patient and Family Centered Care
(PFCC) Methodology, the 'nuts and bolts' of transforming the
current state into the ideal as patients and families define it.
For the benefit of our new Working Group members, let's
recap the Shadowing report that reflects the current state and
the ideal story we wrote at our last meeting. Scott, would you
reread both to the Working Group?" Ben asked.

Scott Long, Medical Director of Trauma Care and Guiding Council Co-Champion, read both aloud. (The Shadowing Report and the ideal story are presented in Chapters 4 and 5, respectively.)

When Scott finished, Ben asked, "When we compare the ideal story to the current state, what gaps do we see? What problems rose to the top for patients and families during Shadowing? The gaps between the current state and the ideal from the patient's and family's perspective should be the focus of our improvement efforts.

"This is how Step 6 works," Ben went on. "First we'll discuss the gaps we see from the patient's and family's point of view. Then we'll decide which gaps we'll close as our first improvement projects. A new Working Group like ours usually starts with three to five projects, depending on their complexity. The projects we select should start with 'low-hanging fruit'—meaning those we think will be easiest to implement in the shortest amount of time—and move progressively to those that are more complex. The advantage of starting with 'low-hanging fruit' is that we'll see results quickly and feel a sense of accomplishment early on. This sense of accomplishment will generate enthusiasm for the PFCC Methodology and will propel us forward."

Ben nodded to Jackie Jordan, the PFCC Project Coordinator, who stood ready to write all of their ideas on the whiteboard.

Arthur White, a charge nurse in the Emergency Department, raised his hand and said, "I was on duty the night Kate Starr Shadowed the trauma care experience of Mr. Jones and his family. I couldn't find his belongings. I broke into a sweat because the social worker needed his ID so she could call his wife. He looked so bad I knew every minute counted. That delay meant his wife didn't find out he was here until 25 minutes later. That is the current state. In our ideal story, Mrs. Romero's belongings are immediately put into a large bag as soon as she arrives and an Emergency Medical Technician gives it to the Emergency Department charge nurse right away. The bag is labeled with her patient identifier and a tracking number. When the social worker arrives in the Emergency Department to call the family, the charge nurse hands her the patient's ID without delay."

"This is a perfect example of gaps that represent 'low-hanging' fruit. Now, what other gaps do we see between the current state and the ideal?" Ben asked.

Dr. Paul Goode, Trauma surgeon, responded. "I've never seen this so clearly before, but the Shadowing report shows a big gap between the real and the ideal where the organization and coordination of the medical team itself is concerned. In the current state, many doctors and medical interns see Mr. Jones in the Emergency Department; others see him and his family in the intensive care unit; and a whole new team of doctors sees them when they move to other parts of the hospital.

"The organization of the care team matters for many reasons," he went on. "The fragmented nature of care as reflected in the current state can lead to important information 'falling through the cracks,' both among caregivers themselves and between caregivers and the patient and family. For example, tests are sometimes missed or repeated unnecessarily; diagnosis and treatment decisions by different caregivers may be contradictory; medication orders may differ from one doctor to another; and there is no one doctor who patients and families can look to as their 'quarterback' to cut through the confusion."

Dr. Goode continued, "Fragmented care leads to patients and families being anxious and uncertain (which I'm starting to see can really affect their outcomes), delays that can negatively impact the flow of care, and patients whose safety is—let's be honest—at risk. In our ideal story, one team of doctors takes care of Mrs. Romero in the Emergency Department and then stays with her from then on, no matter where she goes while she's here. This is the same team that maintains communication with her husband. Having a single care team is a good way to ensure ongoing communication, patient safety, and continuity of care."

Ben smiled at what sounded like Dr. Goode's 'conversion' to the PFCC Methodology but said nothing.

Jeanne Marshall, Nursing Director on the orthopedic unit, spoke next. "So many patients and families tell us they feel most vulnerable when nurses change shifts. They're afraid nurses going off duty will forget to tell nurses coming on duty important details about their care, and with good reason. We know that nurses are constantly interrupted, including during shift changes. And since so much information about each patient must be conveyed in such a short amount of time, details sometimes 'fall through the cracks,' as Dr. Goode said. I realize no one omits information purposely, but we need a better process to ensure accurate and complete reports during these busy times."

"I hate to interrupt," Dr. Goode said, "but would everyone in this Working Group just call me Paul?"

Jeanne nodded and went on, "In the current state, nurses on the medical-surgical unit who are going off duty neglect to tell the nurses coming on duty that the doctor has just ordered one of Mr. Jones' medications to be discontinued. It's important that Mr. Jones not receive even one more dose. Mr. and Mrs. Jones are aware of this change, since the doctor has just been in to see them. But because the change of shift report occurs at the nurses' station, the patient and his wife are unaware that this detail has not been communicated. As it turns out, the doctor reports this change to the nurses himself so the patient's safety is not compromised. But what if he hadn't done this?"

After a moment's pause she went on, "In our ideal story nurses conduct their change of shift report at Mrs. Romero's bedside by including her and Mr. Romero, asking them to add or correct information as needed. Including the patient and family in the nursing change of shift report not only puts the patient and family at ease—this practice enhances patient safety."

Debbie, an informatics specialist, said, "I see a big gap between the verbal-only driving directions the social worker gives Mrs. Jones, the patient's wife, in the current state and the verbal, e-mailed, and texted directions the social worker gives to Mr. Romero in our ideal story."

Rick, the Emergency Medical Technician, said, "The Shadowing report notes that Mr. Jones' cervical collar—which is extremely uncomfortable—stays on for quite some time. In our ideal story, the collar comes off as soon as it can be removed safely."

Susan, from admitting, said, "The Shadowing report shows that in the current state, the security guard is curt and offers Mrs. Jones and her daughter no information, kindness, or sensitivity. In our ideal story the security guard is courteous and helpful."

John, from transportation services, spoke next. "What about leaving Mrs. Jones and her daughter to fend for themselves when it comes to parking their car, which is the current state? In our ideal story, a valet parking attendant is waiting for Mr. Romero to arrive in the ED and parks his car for him."

"The gap that seems more like a gaping hole to me," said Anne, from Quality and Safety, "relates to the patient and family reunion. In the current state, it takes far too long for Karen Jones and her daughter to be reunited with their husband and father; it takes too much time for them to learn what's going on; and Mrs. Jones and her daughter feel unnecessary anxiety and fear during that long period of uncertainty. In our ideal story, the social worker meets Mr. Romero as soon as he arrives in the Emergency Department. He is given information and is updated on his wife's condition regularly and often until they are reunited in the recovery room."

Peter, a physician assistant, said, "I'm really struck by the gap where discharge is concerned. The Shadowing report shows that in the current state, caregivers rush through discharge instructions and don't use the 'teach-back' method to be sure Mr. Jones and his family understand what they need to do when they get home. And a nurse hands them prescriptions we *assume* they'll fill in a timely way and take correctly. What if, instead, we were to handle patient discharge the way we do in our ideal story? Have a doctor give clear verbal discharge instructions and then have a nurse follow up with written and verbal instructions using 'teach-back' to be sure the patient and family understand what they need to do at home? And then again, right before discharge, have the pharmacist come in and hand patients their medications, not just prescriptions; explain clearly how and when to take them, also using the 'teach-back' method; and allow plenty of time for the patient and family to ask questions and voice concerns. If we could close the gaps between the real and the ideal, patients and families would be better able to take care of themselves at home. As things stand, too many patients land right back in the Emergency Department soon after discharge."

The Trauma Care Experience Working Group spent a few more minutes comparing the current state to the ideal state and identified other gaps, including collecting and storing patients' belongings; procedures to secure the trauma bay; the timing of radiological procedures; pain prevention; the tailoring of meals to meet each patient's needs; the condition of family lounges; wayfinding; and others.

"There are so many gaps that need to be closed," said Rachel, a social worker. "How do we decide where to start, and where do we begin?"

"All good questions," Ben replied, "Let's start by looking at the list of gaps we've just identified," he said, pointing to the whiteboard on which Jackie had written Future Projects.

"Which five areas do patients and families say are in greatest need of transformation right now?" Ben asked. "Those are the ones we'll tackle first."

After much discussion and some heated debate, it was clear that the Trauma Care Experience Working Group thought all of the ideas on the list were important.

When their discussion wound down, Kate Starr, Nursing Director for Trauma Care and Guiding Council Co-Champion, said, "Alright, let's take on five projects to start with. We'll keep all of our other ideas on the <u>Future Projects</u> list. We'll tackle each of these one at a time. When Project Teams complete one project, they'll reform to start another. The way we *prioritize* our projects is to listen to what patients and families have said is most important to them. We'll want to start with the 'low-hanging fruit' because, as Ben said, such projects are easy to implement, yield results quickly, and generate enthusiasm among members of the Project Team. So ... what is the consensus of the Working Group as to which projects are most urgent from the perspective of patients and families?"

Arthur White, the Emergency Department charge nurse, said, "We'd like to focus on collecting and storing patient belongings. This 'low-hanging fruit' sounds like such a simple thing, but it's so important. Having the needed materials and a good process in place prevents delays—and keeps patients from being upset and inconvenienced, both on admission and at discharge. Losing items such as eyeglasses and dentures can be costly and can delay a patient's recovery, and losing items like patients' wedding rings can be especially painful for them and their spouses."

Paul Goode said, "We'll focus on restructuring the Trauma Team."

Jeanne Marshall replied, "We suggest focusing on including the patient and family in the nursing change of shift report."

Joan Gardner, Nursing Director of the post-anesthesia care unit, said, "We'll focus on the patient and family reunion."

Rose Brooks, a hospital pharmacist, said, "We'd like to focus on discharge prescriptions and medication education."

"Excellent choices," Ben said, while on the whiteboard, Jackie wrote the heading <u>Current Projects</u> and listed the five projects the Working Group had just chosen:

1. Collecting and Storing Patient Belongings
2. Restructuring the Trauma Team
3. Including the Patient and Family in the Nursing Change of Shift Report
4. Redesigning the Patient and Family Reunion
5. Revising Discharge Prescriptions and Medication Education

"Now that we've identified our first projects," Ben said, "we'll follow the six steps of the PFCC Methodology as Project Teams—which is why we consider Step 6 a 'cycle within a cycle.' You won't have to learn any new steps, since these are the same six steps we've been following all along as a Guiding Council and Working Group. Now we're simply going to follow these steps as we work on the projects we've chosen."

Turning to the whiteboard, Ben listed the six steps within Step 6. "Here's what I mean," he said:

Step 1. Select a project
Step 2. Assign Project Team co-leaders
Step 3. Shadow patients and families to co-design the care experience
Step 4. Recruit members of the Project Team
Step 5. Create a shared vision of the ideal story
Step 6. Close the gaps between current and ideal

"These steps should sound familiar," Ben said, "because we've just taken these steps to select our overall project (improving the trauma care experience), form our Guiding Council and select our Guiding Council Co-Champions, evaluate the current state through Shadowing, expand the Guiding Council into the Working Group, and create a shared vision of the ideal story. Now, in Step 6, we're ready to close the gaps between the current state and the ideal for each of our projects by following these six steps."

Ben continued, "By selecting projects based on the perspective of patients and families, we've just completed **Step 1** of this 'cycle within a cycle.' Now, on to **Step 2.** Who will volunteer to be the co-leaders of each project?"

Arthur White, the Emergency Department charge nurse, and Michael Glass, from patient transport, volunteered to co-lead the project to improve the collecting and storing of patient belongings.

Trauma surgeon Paul Goode and hospitalist Donna Murphy volunteered to co-lead the project to restructure the Trauma Team.

Jeanne Marshall, Nursing Director of the orthopedic unit, and Linda Goodman, a nurse manager of one of the step-down units, offered to co-lead the project to include the patient and family in the nursing change of shift report.

Dr. Ron Knightley, Clinical Director of Emergency Department Services, and Joan Gardner, Nursing Director on the post-anesthesia care unit, offered to lead the project to redesign the patient and family reunion.

Maria Gonzalez, Medical-Surgical Nursing Director, and Phil Hart, Pharmacy Director, agreed to serve as co-leaders of the project to revise discharge prescriptions and medication education.

"Thank you all," Ben said. "The first thing you'll need to do is to define where your projects' care experiences begin and end; evaluate the current state through Shadowing; and create a Care Experience Flow Map to illustrate the touchpoints and 'hassles' patients and families encounter as they move through their care experience (**Step 3**); then, you'll need to recruit members to serve on your Project Teams based on these touchpoints (**Step 4**); create a shared vision of the ideal story for your project as if you were the patient and family member (**Step 5**); and close the gaps between the current and the ideal state (**Step 6**).

"When you've formed Project Teams," Ben went on, "plan to meet once a week for 1 hour—although eventually you may be able to accomplish the needed work in shorter meetings. The weekly Project Team meeting is the engine that drives our care transformation efforts. Then at weekly Working Group meetings you'll report on your team's progress."

"Just one question, Ben," Paul Goode said. "In talking about our proposed projects, we haven't mentioned the possibility of failure. How real is this possibility, and what can we do if a project fails?"

"That's a great question, Paul. Failure is always a possibility and is often our best teacher—as long as we're willing to learn its lessons. Let me give you an example. Several years ago, I was part of a Surgical Care Experience Working Group. The Project Team I was on developed electronic boards that showed families where their loved ones were—such as in the pre-operative area, in surgery, or in the recovery room. Think of the arrival and departure boards you see at airports, and you'll get the idea. We thought we'd done a great job, that the information on the boards was clear. But Shadowing showed us that families didn't understand the boards because they were written in 'hospitalese.' So what did we do? We rewrote the information on these boards in collaboration with patients and families, re-Shadowed, and continued this process until families told us these boards were helpful rather than confusing. Today, these boards are visible in family lounges, the cafeteria, and the gift shop—using tracking numbers rather than names, of course, to protect patients' privacy."

Then Dr. Ron Knightley spoke up. "It seems what you're saying, Ben, is that failure isn't a sign that we should stop what we're doing—it's a sign that we need to figure out why something isn't working and try a different approach."

"Exactly," Ben replied. "Sometimes even Working Groups fail. Working Groups that are initially active and productive may slip into inactivity. This can happen for any number of reasons: a lack of executive leadership support, Working Group restructuring, a Champion leaving the organization, or a lack of Champion engagement. The important thing is to recognize the signs of inactivity, such as neglecting to meet weekly; determine the underlying causes; and take steps to re-energize a Working Group that seems to be flagging.

"When this happened to a Working Group I was once part of," Ben continued, "we enlisted the help of a new clinical Champion, held a new kick-off meeting, restructured our Project Teams, redefined the care experiences we sought to transform, and, of course, re-Shadowed. Bottom line: failure is a signal that something needs to change. It's up to us to figure out what that something is until the Working Group has been re-ignited."

With that, Ben looked around the room and said, "Thanks for coming, everyone. Now, if there are no other questions, that's a wrap."

***

The next day, each pair of Project Team co-leaders met briefly to define the beginning and end of their segments of the trauma care experience.

Arthur White and Michael Glass defined collecting and storing patient belongings as beginning when the patient's clothes and other belongings are removed on arrival in the Emergency Department and ending when these items are returned before hospital discharge.

Donna Murphy and Paul Goode defined the beginning of their project to restructure the Trauma Team as the moment the patient arrives in the Emergency Department and the ending as the time of hospital discharge.

Jeanne Marshall and Linda Goodman defined the beginning of their project to include patients and families in the nursing change of shift report as the start of each report and the ending as the conclusion of that report, anywhere in the hospital where shift change reports are conducted.

Joan Gardner and Ron Knightley defined the patient and family reunion as beginning when the Exemplar Memorial social worker calls the family to let them know they need to come to the Emergency Department and ending when the patient and family are reunited.

Maria Gonzalez and Phil Hart defined the patient discharge process as beginning with the first conversation about discharge between caregivers and patients and families—usually several days before discharge—and ending when patients and families drive away from the hospital, bound either for home or a rehabilitation facility.

Having decided where their projects begin and end, Project Team co-leaders were ready to Shadow. They downloaded the GoShadow app (available at GoShadow.org) to record their Shadowing observations.

Over the course of the week, each pair of Project Team co-leaders Shadowed the segments of the trauma care experience that defined their projects. Project Team co-leaders divided their Shadowing responsibilities, each Shadowing a different segment of their defined care experience. While Shadowing, they noted everything that happened during the patient's and family's care experience, and when; each area of the hospital patients and families visited; all caregivers with whom patients and families came into contact, along with their interactions; all comments, questions, and suggestions made by patients, families, and caregivers; and their own observations. When their Shadowing was complete, they combined their notes into five separate Shadowing reports.

At the end of each Shadowing session, they asked patients and families, "If you could name three things that would have improved your care experience and made it ideal, what would they be?" and noted the answers, along with their own observations about which aspects of the care experience were in need of transformation, in their Shadowing reports.

The co-leaders of each Project Team then used their Shadowing reports to create five Care Experience Flow Maps: one showing the touchpoints in the collection and storage of patient belongings; the second mapping the touchpoints in the organization of medical teams; the third showing the touchpoints in the nursing change of shift report; the fourth illustrating the touchpoints in the patient and family reunion; and the fifth showing the touchpoints in the discharge prescriptions and medication education process.

Project Team co-leaders brought their Shadowing reports and Care Experience Flow Maps to the next Working Group meeting. At that meeting, they passed out copies of these maps and read their detailed Shadowing reports aloud. After reading their Shadowing reports, one co-leader from each Project Team summarized the current state for the Working Group this way:

Collecting and Storing Patient Belongings: Current State

"We Shadowed a patient who arrived by ambulance after a motorcycle accident," Arthur White began. "Caregivers on the Trauma Team immediately removed his helmet, cut off his clothes, pulled off his shoes, and removed his watch. The charge nurse had to search for a bag to put the patient's clothes and other belongings in since none was handy. When he found a bag, it wasn't large enough to hold the patient's helmet. So, he put the helmet in a corner on the floor. It took him another few minutes to find a label that would stick to the bag so he could write down the patient's name but the label started to peel off as soon as he affixed it to the bag. We knew the helmet would be lost—and if the label were to peel off the bag completely, his clothes and the rest of his belongings would be lost, too.

"When we Shadowed a different patient during discharge, what do you think we saw? It took 30 minutes for the nurse to find the patient's belongings. And when she finally handed the patient his bag, he said several items, including his eyeglasses, were missing. If we could streamline the process of collecting and storing patients' belongings," Arthur White concluded, "patients would leave the hospital with everything they had when they came in. And giving patients back their belongings at discharge is cheaper than paying to replace those we've lost. Furthermore, patients' recovery would not be impeded because we lost essential items such as eyeglasses or dentures."

Restructuring the Trauma Team: Current State

"When the patient came to the Emergency Department she was met by a number of different attending physicians, residents, and other doctors who evaluated her injuries," Paul Goode said. "She was first taken to the Trauma intensive care unit—Unit F—and then to the step-down Trauma Unit G. Each time the patient was moved, even to different places within the Trauma Unit, a different team of doctors came to see her. The patient did not know who her doctor was. When she was moved to the medical-surgical unit, what happened? A completely different set of doctors told her they were managing her care, but there was no person she could identify as 'her doctor.'

"When she was on the medical-surgical unit, the doctors who said they were managing her care came to see her at different times of the day. Often, they would ask her the same questions and give her what sounded like different diagnoses or conflicting treatment recommendations, which confused her and made her feel anxious and, at times, fearful.

"And sometimes different doctors came in to see her, not because of unit or room changes but because of the many levels and types of doctors involved in trauma care and in academic settings—residents, fellows, attending physicians, hospitalists, and so on. This patient asked us, 'How can I find out who my main doctor is? With so many doctors coming in and out of my room, I don't know who's in charge of my care. It feels like nobody is listening to me. Why do some doctors tell me one thing and other doctors tell me another—don't they talk to each other? I wish I had a doctor who would be my "quarterback" to help me understand and makes sense of it all. In a hospital, of all places, I feel like no one is taking care of me.'

"To see the fragmentation of care through the eyes of the patient and family was truly eye-opening. We realized that having a consistent care team who communicates effectively with patients, families, and with each other can lead to more confident patients and families, earlier discharge times, fewer unnecessary readmissions, and resulting cost savings. Now, more than ever, it's clear that the current state needs to change—and it needs to change now."

The Nursing Change of Shift Report: Current State

"We Shadowed the Exemplar Memorial nursing change of shift report process in the medical-surgical unit one evening," Jeanne Marshall said. "An 80-year-old man had come in with signs of trauma a week earlier and now had blood in his stool. At the nurses' station, the nurses going off duty did not tell the nurses coming on duty that the patient was scheduled for a colonoscopy.

"The patient, who had been fasting all day, told the nurses who had come on duty that he was hungry. The patient's daughter had just stepped out to make a few phone calls and was unaware that a dinner tray had been delivered to her father's room. By the time she returned, her father had begun to eat.

"Thirty minutes later a patient transport technician came to take the patient for his test. The nurses, realizing they had not been fully informed, told the technician the patient had just eaten. They rescheduled the patient's colonoscopy for the following evening. Of course, this meant the patient would have to fast all over again and there would be further delay in finding the source of his bleeding.

"It's clear from this example that the current state of the nursing change of shift report can compromise clinical care and patient safety while negatively affecting the patient's care experience. We can and must do better."

Patient and Family Reunion: Current State

"When we Shadowed the patient and family reunion," Dr. Ron Knightley began, "we found the current state similar to what Kate and Scott found when they Shadowed this segment for the Guiding Council in Step 3 (described in Chapter 3). But the situation for the patient and family we Shadowed was a little more complicated.

"The patient was flown to the Exemplar Memorial Emergency Department by helicopter from a hospital 30 miles away," he continued. "The social worker from that hospital called the family to come to the Emergency Department, but by the time they got there the patient was already en route here. The family was frustrated and upset but told the social worker they'd drive to Exemplar Memorial. They'd never been to this area before and asked the social worker for directions. The social worker gave the family verbal directions but they got lost on the way.

"When the family finally arrived, they didn't know where to park so they left their car in front of the Emergency Department and it got towed," Ron went on. "The security guard was gruff and did not tell the family where to go for information about the patient. When the family found the Emergency Department receptionist, she had to page the social worker. It took 15 minutes for her to meet the family. It took 45 minutes for the family to learn something about the patient's condition and whereabouts. The family was frightened, angry, and exhausted. They asked for a chaplain but somehow that message didn't reach the on-call chaplain. They wanted coffee and something to eat but the cafeteria was closed. They said they felt completely alone. The family was finally reunited with the patient three hours after they'd arrived and remained in a state of confusion and anxiety the entire time.

"Shadowing this segment of the trauma care experience enabled us to see it for the first time from the family's point of view. It seemed like everything that could have gone wrong did go wrong. Mercifully, their loved one's surgery was successful. But in ways large and small we failed this family. We will not rest until we institute measures to ensure nothing like this happens again. And when we do," Ron Knightley concluded, "we'll have loyal patients and families who will recommend us to their family and friends. There's no advertisement more powerful than word of mouth. And although this isn't our focus by any means, an undeniable by-product of delivering ideal care experiences to patients and families is increased market share. We can't wait to get started."

Discharge Prescriptions and Medication Education: Current State

Maria Gonzalez began, "A trauma patient was being discharged from the medical-surgical unit three weeks after arriving in the Emergency Department. The doctor came in to give the patient and family verbal discharge instructions, and a nurse came in next to reinforce the doctor's instructions and give the patient and family printed discharge information. After asking whether they had any questions, to which they answered 'no,' the nurse gave them two printed prescriptions and said someone from patient transport would take them to their car shortly.

"When the nurse left, the patient said, 'I didn't want to tell the nurse, but I won't be able to get these prescriptions filled today. I have no way of getting to a pharmacy and my drugstore doesn't deliver. I guess I'll just wait till tomorrow afternoon when my daughter should be able to help me. That'll be alright, won't it?'" she asked.

"Then, biting her lip, the patient said, 'Once I get my medications I hope I remember when I'm supposed to take them. I think the nurse said to take one pill 30 minutes before meals three times a day, and the other an hour after meals twice a day. What if they look alike? The nurse didn't ask me, but I'm already taking three other medications at home, all at different times of the day. It's so confusing. What if I make a mistake?'

"I said nothing to the patient in response but was so concerned I immediately reported this conversation to the unit nursing supervisor," Maria said. "This situation is a medication error and hospital readmission waiting to happen. That poor woman—she was leaving the hospital but didn't know whether she'd be able to take care of herself at home. Seeing what patients and families have to grapple with firsthand makes me want to fix this problem immediately. And consider the readmission costs that could be avoided by changing our protocols and practices," Maria Gonzalez concluded, "Ethically and fiscally, we must make these changes now. We simply cannot wait."

After Maria's summary, Kate Starr said, "Congratulations. You've just completed **Step 3** of the PFCC 'cycle within a cycle' (Shadow Patients and Families to Co-design the Care Experience). Because your Shadowing reports and Care Experience Flow Maps are so precise, we can see how the current state of these care experience segments look and feel to patients and families; how they look to caregivers and to you; and how the powerful tool of Shadowing helps to generate enthusiasm for changing the current state to the ideal.

"Now it's on to **Step 4**," Kate went on. "Since Shadowing has clarified all of the touchpoints in these segments of the trauma care experience, it's time to recruit members from these touchpoints to serve on our five Project Teams."

Scott Long added, "We recommend a 50/50 split when forming these teams: ideally, half the members of your Project Teams should come from inside this Working Group and half from outside it."

"How should we decide whom to invite from either inside or outside the Working Group?" asked Phil Hart.

"A good question," Scott replied. "For the project focusing on improving discharge prescriptions and medication education, you and Maria would want to include a pharmacist, a nurse, and a social worker, who are represented on this Working Group. And since education involves creating print and Web-based material for patients and families, you may want to invite caregivers from our Office of Education and perhaps the Communications Department, even though they're not members of this Working Group. Our advice is to keep the Project Teams small but to involve caregivers whose areas of expertise can help to advance a particular project and achieve our goal of care transformation," he said as the meeting adjourned.

***

At 7:30 a.m. Wednesday morning, each pair of Project Team co-leaders met to decide whom to invite to serve on their Project Teams. Arthur White and Michael Glass, co-leaders of the project to improve the collection and storage of patient belongings, invited a Trauma Concierge, an Emergency Department nurse, an Emergency Medical Technician, a medical-surgical nurse, a housekeeper, and someone from information technology who was not a Working Group member.

For their project to restructure the Trauma Team, co-leaders Paul Goode and Donna Murphy invited the Trauma intensive care unit Medical Director, an Emergency Department attending physician, an orthopedic surgeon, and a neurosurgeon. They also invited a medical intern and someone from e-records who were not members of the Working Group.

Jeanne Marshall and Linda Goodman, co-leaders of the Project Team to include patients and families in the nursing change of shift report, invited a patient care technician, a physician assistant, a medical-surgical nurse, and someone from the office of patient safety. They also invited a patient advocate and someone from public relations who were not members of the Working Group.

Dr. Ron Knightley and Joan Gardner, co-leaders of the project to transform the patient and family reunion, invited Alice, a former trauma patient, someone from patient transportation services, parking operations, Emergency Department admissions, and a social worker, all of whom were members of the Trauma Care Experience Working Group. They also invited a security guard and a dietician who were not Working Group members.

Maria Gonzalez and Phil Hart, co-leaders of the project to transform discharge prescriptions and medication education, invited a hospital pharmacist, a Trauma Unit doctor, someone from case management, a trauma nurse practitioner, and someone from home healthcare services. Taking Scott's advice, they also invited people from the Office of Communications and the Education Department who were not Working Group members.

Project Team co-leaders were delighted that everyone they invited agreed to serve. They gave Project Team members who were not members of the Working Group information on the GoShadow app.

"All five Project Teams have chosen to meet separately on Wednesday mornings at 7:30 a.m.," Ron Knightley told the Working Group the following Tuesday. "We start tomorrow. Our first task will be to review the ideal story we wrote as a Working Group, but this time focusing on the segments of the trauma care experience we Shadowed. Then we'll be ready to write our Project Teams' ideal stories from the perspective of patients and families."

"In other words," Ben said, "you're about to start **Step 5** of the 'cycle within a cycle.' The Working Group looks forward to hearing your ideal stories next week."

***

At 7:30 a.m. the next morning, each Project Team co-leader gave Project Team members a copy of the Working Group's ideal story focusing on the entire trauma care experience. They also handed out copies of their own Shadowing reports and Care Experience Flow Maps focusing on their specific projects: collecting and storing patient belongings, restructuring the Trauma Team, the nursing change of shift report, the patient and family reunion, and discharge prescriptions and medication education.

Project Team members reread the Working Group's ideal story, revisited co-leaders' Shadowing reports and Care Experience Flow Maps showing the current state, and wrote the following ideal stories for their projects as if they were the patients and families:

Collecting and Storing Patient Belongings: Ideal Story

When I was wheeled into the Emergency Department after my motorcycle accident, a team of doctors raced to my side, cut off my clothes, and removed my watch. I remember thinking my wallet's in my pants pocket so I hope they don't lose it. A young man, who I later learned was one of my nurses, put my helmet (which had been removed in the ambulance), along with my clothes, shoes, eyeglasses, and watch, into a very large blue nylon drawstring bag. I saw him write my name on a label and place it in the center of the bag. I didn't think about this again until I was discharged. When my discharge nurse delivered the bag to my room with all my belongings, I was relieved to find everything there, including my helmet, eyeglasses, and wallet. I was glad not to have to file a claim to get reimbursed for the cost of all my things. Being without them for any length of time would have been inconvenient, to say the least.

Restructuring the Trauma Team: Ideal Story

I was comforted when I came into the hospital and a team of doctors met me in the Trauma bay saying they would be my doctors all through my stay, wherever I went in the hospital. I felt even more at ease when the Trauma surgeon told me, "We are your doctors now and will be your doctors until you are discharged. We will communicate closely with each other and with you and your family. We will all know what's going on with your care as long as you are here. We will work closely together so nothing about your care will 'fall through the cracks.'"

That is exactly what happened. The doctors who took care of me in the Emergency Department saw me during and after surgery, and in the post-anesthesia care unit, the intensive care unit, and the medical-surgical unit. They met every morning by my bedside at 7 a.m. to conduct rounds and they included the nurses, my husband, and me every time.

They gave me a sheet of paper that listed each of their phone numbers and the best times to reach them if I had any questions before I saw them the next morning, and even after I'd been discharged.

I knew each doctor by name. I really liked the way they spoke to one another, in a very respectful, collegial way. They spoke to my husband and to me the same way. I felt completely at ease and confident that I was getting the best care possible.

My doctors agreed on the time I'd be discharged the next day. Because I was able to tell my husband the time they planned to discharge me, he was there by the time the discharge nurse came in. As soon as we were done he drove me home. I knew another patient was waiting for a bed, so I was glad she didn't have to wait long.

Nursing Change of Shift Report: Ideal Story

I was approaching the end of a five-week hospital stay that began with my being airlifted to the Exemplar Memorial Emergency Department. I'd spent time in the operating room, the post-anesthesia care unit, the intensive care unit, the medical-surgical unit and, finally, inpatient rehabilitation. Wherever I went in the hospital, nursing shift changes were the times I felt most secure. The nurses conducted their change of shift reports at my bedside. At each shift change, my nurses, my husband, and I shared information so we were all on the "same page" about my care. The nurses going off duty asked us to listen to their reports and add or correct anything they may have omitted or gotten wrong. If we had questions, they answered them clearly and completely. The nurses took their time. We never felt rushed. They made us feel like partners in my care. We were impressed by the fact that even though these nurses worked on different shifts, they acted like a team. We felt they all cared about getting the information right and genuinely cared about us.

Patient and Family Reunion: Ideal Story

A social worker at our local community hospital called to tell me that my husband had been brought to the Emergency Department by ambulance after having been hit by a car. When I arrived, she told me he had just been taken by helicopter to Exemplar Memorial Hospital, but she would help me if I wanted to drive there. She handed me a packet of information and a pass that would identify me to everyone who worked at Exemplar Memorial as the loved one of a patient. The information packet included detailed driving directions and maps and even links I could download to my cell phone for directions.

I put the pass on the driver's side windshield as I prepared to drive to Exemplar Memorial. The maps and directions were so detailed that I didn't get lost. When I got there 30 minutes later and the parking lot guard saw the pass, he directed me to the Emergency Department. When I showed the pass to the concierge in the Emergency Department, she quickly handed me a bag of amenities, told me where my husband was and what condition he was in, and asked a nurse to take me to him. It was a relief to be reunited with him so quickly. That pass really seemed to "part the waters" for me. Now I tell all my friends and relatives to go to Exemplar Memorial if they need a hospital. And many of them have, telling similarly great stories. No doubt about it, we are Exemplar Memorial's biggest fans.

Discharge Prescriptions and Medication Education: Ideal Story

By the time I was discharged from the hospital, I had everything I needed and felt confident about going home. A few days before I was discharged, a social worker met with me and my wife to discuss what we'd need to arrange before I could go home, like having a bathroom rail installed and finding a home health aide, which my wife took care of with recommendations from the social worker.

The morning of my discharge, a doctor came in to explain everything I'd need to do and took his time explaining how and when to take my medications. He asked me if I had any questions—and when I did, he answered them clearly. He even asked me to repeat what he had said in my own words so he could be sure I understood. When there was something I was a little unsure of, he wrote down the directions for me. Before he left, he gave me his cell phone number and told me to call him if I had any concerns, any time. I would never abuse this privilege, but it made me feel more secure to know I could call him if I needed to.

When he left, a nurse came in and carefully went over everything the doctor had said. She gave me printed instructions that I could review at home. She told me a pharmacist would be coming in with my medications in a few minutes, and then I'd be ready to go home.

Sure enough, as if on cue, Rose, the pharmacist, came in with my two prescriptions—not printed prescriptions, mind you, but the actual bottles of pills. What a relief to be able to go home and take the medicines right on time! No having to wait to see if someone could drive to the pharmacy, or worry that the pharmacy might not be open. Having those medicines and really understanding how and when to take them gave me peace of mind during a stressful time. For the first time, I didn't worry that I'd land right back in the hospital. This time, I knew I'd be able to take care of myself at home.

***

At the next Working Group meeting, the Project Team co-leaders read each of their team's ideal stories aloud. Occasionally, Project Team members would slip into talking about the ideal care experience from their point of view as caregivers. Kate and Scott, as Guiding Council Co-Champions, gently reminded them that they needed to be seeing, thinking about, and describing the ideal care experience as if they were a patient and family member. "It's not about us," they would say, "it's really all about how *patients and families* define the ideal care experience." These reminders helped to keep Project Teams on track.

"Great work," Ben said after the Project Team co-leaders finished reading their ideal stories. "Now you're ready to start **Step 6** of the PFCC 'cycle within a cycle': close the gaps between the current state and the ideal. If you'd like to put your projects on a 'fast track' to 30-day implementation, the PFCC Methodology includes a fast-track option, too," he added as he handed out PFCC Project fast-track cards. (See Figure 6.1) "The full Working Group looks forward to your

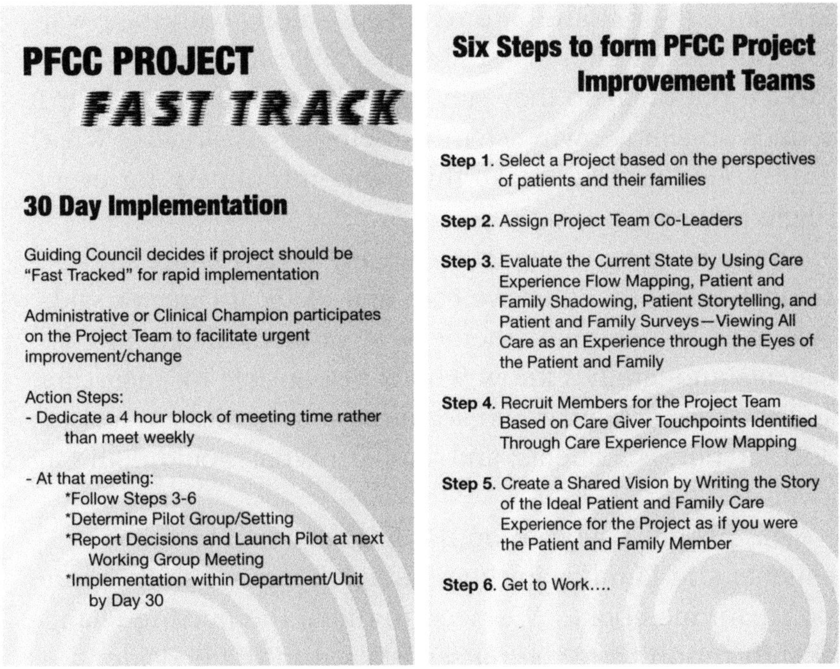

PFCC PROJECT
FAST TRACK

30 Day Implementation

Guiding Council decides if project should be "Fast Tracked" for rapid implementation

Administrative or Clinical Champion participates on the Project Team to facilitate urgent improvement/change

Action Steps:
- Dedicate a 4 hour block of meeting time rather than meet weekly

- At that meeting:
  *Follow Steps 3-6
  *Determine Pilot Group/Setting
  *Report Decisions and Launch Pilot at next Working Group Meeting
  *Implementation within Department/Unit by Day 30

Six Steps to form PFCC Project Improvement Teams

Step 1. Select a Project based on the perspectives of patients and their families

Step 2. Assign Project Team Co-Leaders

Step 3. Evaluate the Current State by Using Care Experience Flow Mapping, Patient and Family Shadowing, Patient Storytelling, and Patient and Family Surveys—Viewing All Care as an Experience through the Eyes of the Patient and Family

Step 4. Recruit Members for the Project Team Based on Care Giver Touchpoints Identified Through Care Experience Flow Mapping

Step 5. Create a Shared Vision by Writing the Story of the Ideal Patient and Family Care Experience for the Project as if you were the Patient and Family Member

Step 6. Get to Work....

Figure 6.1   PFCC Project fast-track card, front and back.

ideas, to contributing what we can, and to hearing weekly reports on your progress."

***

The next morning, each Project Team met to begin Step 6 of the PFCC "cycle within a cycle." They reread their Shadowing reports and Care Experience Flow Maps and compared the current state to their ideal stories. Then Project Team co-leaders asked Project Team members to identify the gaps between the current state and the ideal. The gaps were obvious. Some lively discussions ensued as each Project Team brainstormed ways to close the gaps.

An Emergency Department nurse on the Project Team to improve the collection and storage of patient belongings said, "Emergency Medical Services needs to know where to put the patients' belongings, like motorcycle helmets, when patients are wheeled into the Emergency Department.

And once their clothes are removed—along with their wallets, purses, jewelry, glasses, shoes, and other items—where can *we* put them so they stay together and don't get lost? It sounds so simple, why isn't this being done already? What do we need to do to make this happen routinely, for every single patient?"

In the meeting of the Project Team to restructure the Trauma Team, the intensive care unit Medical Director said, "We need to streamline the delivery of medical care so patients and families know who is responsible for their care, and so there is regular and seamless communication among doctors, nurses, patients, and families. What would doing this involve?"

The patient advocate on the Project Team to involve patients and families in the nursing change of shift report told team members, "We need to move the nursing change of shift report from the nurses' station to the bedside, despite the potential for the kind of resistance we've seen in the past. We can expect to encounter valid objections, including the amount of time such reports could take, privacy issues, discomfort speaking frankly in front of the patient and family, and so on. How do we overcome these objections so that nurses accept, and actually embrace, change?"

Alice, the former patient and member of the patient and family reunion Project Team, said, "We need to 'part the waters' for the family when they get here, just like our ideal story said. Instead of what feels like indifference, the family should be greeted immediately, given continual updates about the patient's condition, and treated with the utmost care and respect. How can we do that?"

A pharmacist and member of the Project Team to transform discharge prescriptions and medication education said, "Patients have made it clear they want to go home with their actual medications in hand—not just prescriptions they have to fill themselves—and they want to be sure they understand the instructions about how and when to take them. What can we do to make this happen?"

***

Immediately, the Project Teams got to work to close the gaps they identified between the current and the ideal state. To improve collecting and storing patient belongings, the Project Team decided to Shadow the current state to see why patients' belongings were being lost.

Here are the details Shadowing showed them: the bags meant for storing patient belongings weren't large enough to hold items such as motorcycle helmets, so helmets were being left on the floor next to, but not inside, the bags—and when caregivers retrieved and labeled the bags, they weren't always sure whether a helmet actually belonged to the patient whose items they'd just retrieved; the labels caregivers were using to identify a patient's belongings weren't sticky enough to adhere well to the bags, and often peeled off as the patient was being wheeled from the Emergency Department to another location in the hospital; and there was no system in place to alert those who were storing patient belongings that the patient was ready to be discharged and needed their bags to be returned.

"If express delivery services, airports, and hotels can manage customers' bags so they rarely get lost, we should be able to do this for our patients," Arthur White told the Project Team. And in one week, this is exactly what the Project Team did. They bought extra-large patient belongings bags that would hold big, bulky items like motorcycle helmets. They worked with the Patient Access Department to develop computer-generated, HIPAA (Health Insurance Portability and Accountability Act)-compliant patient labels with tracking numbers to affix to the bags. An hour before patients were ready to be discharged, a nurse sent a message requesting the bags, identified by tracking number, to be delivered to their rooms. And if patients requested their bags before discharge, nurses followed the same procedure for a speedy delivery.

As a result of the project Arthur White had called "low-hanging fruit," the number of lost patient belongings went from 15 to 25 per week to zero within the first week. With a small investment in new bags for patient belongings and an effective labeling and tracking system, Exemplar Memorial was able to save thousands of dollars annually by eliminating the need to reimburse patients for lost belongings.

"Can you imagine how much money we'd save if this process was spread hospital-wide or system-wide?" Michael Glass asked the PFCC Working Group at their meeting the following week.

"Not only that," Arthur White added, "but because patients now leave the hospital with all their belongings, their level of trust in our care and satisfaction with their discharge experience is higher than ever. Isn't that what it's all about?"

While Arthur White, Michael Glass, and the rest of their Project Team were working to transform the current state of the collection and storage of patient belongings, Team Trauma—the Project Team to restructure the Trauma Team—began their project to reorganize the delivery of medical care with the goal of transforming communication, safety, and peace of mind for patients and families. Meeting weekly as a Project Team and again as part of the Trauma Care Experience Working Group, Team Trauma brainstormed and tested ways to introduce a continuity of care that had not existed at Exemplar Memorial for 20 years.

Shadowing showed Team Trauma all of the details of the current state: doctors were assigned to patients based on the patient's location in the hospital, which changed often. Rotating teams of medical residents and fellows, as well as a revolving door of medical specialists, introduced yet another layer of doctors and confusion. As a result, patients and families didn't know who their doctors were and didn't have a consistent plan of care, making them feel continually anxious, uncertain, and unsafe.

Using the Care Experience Flow Map that resulted from Shadowing to target touchpoints, Team Trauma divided Exemplar Memorial's attending physicians, residents, and mid-level providers into three teams. They color-coded these teams Blue, Black, and Gold. Patients were assigned to the team that admitted them. That team would follow the patient throughout their stay, wherever they went in the hospital. A "float" team was assigned to cover the care of patients of the team on night rotation so there would be continuity of care at night as well as during the day.

Second, Team Trauma instituted a multidisciplinary, daily early morning report that included the night and the day teams for both trauma and critical care medicine. After presenting details about their patients, these teams would begin patient rounds. If patient rounds could begin earlier, Team Trauma reasoned, discharge decisions could be made earlier in the day.

Sounds simple? Well, although the solution *is* elegantly simple, the process of achieving it was anything but. As Paul Goode told the Working Group when their project was complete, "This was a complex project with many moving parts, and we needed to overcome many challenges to implementation. For example, since trauma patients and their families are in contact with so many different disciplines throughout their experience, we had to involve caregivers from each touchpoint to make this work. We had to consider communication with the entire hospital, from hospital operators and nursing units to other medical disciplines. And we needed to educate caregivers in all departments on the new process and schedule. Finally, we had to work with the e-record team to make each patient's team designation part of their e-record documentation. Nevertheless, despite these challenges, we met our deadline for implementation.

"PFCC has made me a believer," he added. "Because of this project, patients now know who their physicians are; they are able to establish a relationship with one person who is both in charge of their care and who knows them and their histories well, which makes them feel safer and more secure; they receive a consistent plan of care during their stay; and they are actually being discharged earlier in the day than they had been before. Of course, earlier discharges mean reduced lengths of stay, reduced costs, and more efficient patient flow since beds now open up earlier for patients waiting in the post-anesthesia care unit or the Emergency Department.

"As one patient told me when she left the hospital," Paul Goode continued, "'I've never been treated as well in any hospital, had so much peace of mind, or felt as confident about my treatment and recovery as I do now. Every step of the way, I understood the doctors' plans for my care and I knew who to talk to when I had questions. It seemed like everyone was working as a team and were not only communicating with me but with each other. A thousand thanks to you and your colleagues.' What more can a doctor or patient ask for?"

When the Project Team to include patients and families in the nursing change of shift report Shadowed the current state, they found change of shift reports that were either conducted at nurses' stations or tape recorded by nurses going off duty. The reports were often incomplete, incorrect, too long, difficult to understand, and beset by interruptions.

To close the gap between the current state and the ideal, the Project Team developed a six-week strategy and tool kit to move from centralized and taped reports to bedside nursing change of shift reports. The Project Team sent nurses an e-mail to introduce the bedside change of shift report, conveying that this change was meant to improve patient safety, patient satisfaction, and staff accountability. They shared results of literature reviews demonstrating the positive effects of conducting change of shift reports at the bedside and provided videos to demonstrate effective techniques for doing so. Nurses were given the opportunity to ask questions and express concerns. The Project Team also created educational materials to give to patients and families about the bedside reporting process and their roles.

In addition, the Project Team created a bedside nursing report checklist, which included the following prompts:

■ Introduce the oncoming nurse to patients and family members (if patients want family members present).
■ Conduct an S-BAR (Situation, Background, Assessment, Recommendations) review.
■ Conduct a patient safety check (identification band, incision site, IV site, patient-controlled anesthesia settings, drain/Foley catheter, fall risk).
■ Check the environment for safety (call bell, walker within reach, bed alarm).
■ Update whiteboard with name/phone number of nurses and aides or patient care technicians on duty.
■ Ask patient and family if they have anything to add or correct, or if they have questions.

As Jeanne Marshall told the Working Group, "When patients and their families began to tell us they felt included, respected, and safe during nursing shift changes, we knew we'd achieved something vitally important. And when nurses on different shifts told us they felt like a cohesive team, well, that was the icing on the cake."

The Project Team to redesign the patient and family reunion got to work to close the gaps between the current state and the ideal for families whose loved ones, as trauma patients, were transferred to Exemplar Memorial Hospital from elsewhere in the widespread Exemplar Health System. Project Team members shared their ideas with one another in their weekly meetings. And every Tuesday morning they asked the other members of the Trauma Care Experience Working Group for suggestions about how to smooth the way for and reduce the anxiety of affected families.

The result was the Trauma Gold Pass, which each Trauma Concierge in the Exemplar Health System now gives to families of trauma patients who have been helicoptered to the

Exemplar Memorial Hospital Emergency Department. Along with the Trauma Gold Pass, the Trauma Concierge gives each family a booklet that includes driving directions and maps to help them find Exemplar Memorial Hospital easily; instructions on what to do when they arrive in the Emergency Department; a list of information they may need to provide when checking in with the Trauma Concierge; and important telephone numbers.

Families place the Trauma Gold Pass on the driver's side windshield of their car and show it to the parking attendant. They then carry the Trauma Gold Pass into the Emergency Department, which signals everyone with whom they come into contact—whether the security guard, the Trauma Concierge, nurses, physician assistants, technicians, those responsible for patient transport, or doctors—that this is the family of a trauma patient. Any caregiver who sees someone carrying a Trauma Gold Pass knows their first priority is to reunite that person with the patient as quickly as possible.

The Trauma Gold Pass is shown in Figure 6.2.

"We knew we'd have to involve every hospital in the system if we wanted this to be implemented correctly and consistently," Joan Gardner recalled, "so we expanded our Project Team to include representatives of valet parking, security, reception, and nurses and attending physicians in the Emergency Departments of every hospital in the Exemplar Health System. They called into our Project Team meeting every Wednesday morning. And because we sought their input from the beginning, they were just as committed to making this work as we were."

Launching the Trauma Gold Pass was only the beginning of transforming the current state into the ideal for patients and families. Through re-Shadowing every few months, Project Team members re-evaluated this project to see whether it was working from patients' and families' point of view and whether any changes were needed. Re-Shadowing over time

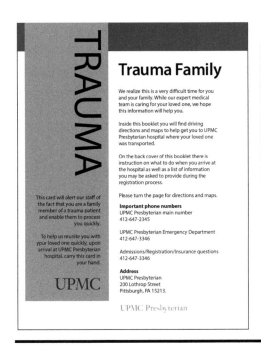

Figure 6.2 Trauma GOLD Pass.

showed Project Team members that the Trauma Gold Pass continued to promote speedy reunions between trauma patients and their families, and to facilitate brief meetings between the patient, family, and doctor.

In fact, re-Shadowing showed the Trauma Gold Pass was working so well the Project Team decided to expand it to the families of patients who arrived in the Emergency Department of any hospital in the Exemplar Health System. In response to comments and suggestions made by families during re-Shadowing, the Project Team developed a Web-based Trauma Gold Pass that family members could print out at home and bring with them to the hospital. The Project Team also developed a smartphone Trauma Gold Pass app that families can present to caregivers at each touchpoint from the time they arrive to park their cars to the time they arrive at the Trauma Concierge's desk.

When periodic re-Shadowing showed the Project Team that the Trauma Gold Pass continued to achieve its goals, they decided to close, or complete, their project. Ron Knightley sent

Jackie Jordan details about their project to enter into a shared database. This database now enables caregivers in other hospitals in the Exemplar Health System to learn from the Project Team's work. Jackie also entered "the Patient and Family Reunion" as the first of the PFCC Working Group's <u>Completed Projects</u>.

At the next Working Group meeting, Project Team members decided to take one of the projects on Jackie Jordan's <u>Future Projects</u> list and move it to the list of <u>Current Projects</u>. When Kate Starr reminded them that any new project should be one that patients and families have expressed a need for, they selected "the Day of Surgery Care Experience."

"We've reached our first milestone," Ben smiled and said. "We now have a list of <u>Completed Projects</u>, starting with "Redesigning the Patient and Family Reunion." We will add more completed projects to this list quickly. As our list grows, we'll be able to look back and see how many care experiences we've transformed for patients and families. This will give us a real sense of accomplishment and fuel our enthusiasm for doing more."

What do patients and families have to say about the Trauma Gold Pass? During re-Shadowing, the wife of one patient said, "For the first time, I feel supported in the hospital. Yes, I was anxious and frightened when I got the call to come to the Emergency Department. But from the moment I arrived here I felt that every person I saw was trying to help reunite me with my husband, which they did, and quickly. I will always be grateful. I tell my friends and family how great Exemplar Memorial is every chance I get. And if I ever need trauma care, this is the place I want to be."

Caregivers, too, have expressed the satisfaction the Trauma Gold Pass has given them. "I know as soon as the family member of a patient approaches me," said one Trauma Concierge, "I can reunite them with their loved one quickly and get them together with the doctor so they'll know exactly what's going on. I've always wanted to help people, and the Trauma Gold Pass helps me do that."

Like the other Project Teams, the Project Team to revise discharge prescriptions and medication education got to work to make the patient's and family's ideal state the current state—that is, to send them home with medications in hand and to help them understand how and when to take them. As Shadowing revealed, patients were receiving only prescriptions when they were discharged and often had trouble filling them in a timely way. As a result, despite their best intentions, many patients were not taking their medications as directed and would end up right back in the Emergency Department.

At a Working Group meeting one Tuesday morning, a pharmacist on the Project Team said, "Our pharmacists can see the patient and family right before discharge, hand them their medications if they're discharged on a weekday, and explain how and when to take them. But how can we hand patients their medications if they're discharged at night, after the hospital pharmacy has closed, or on weekends when it isn't open at all?"

The intensive care unit Medical Director and member of the Working Group and Team Trauma replied, "Have you ever thought about partnering with a local pharmacy to fill prescriptions when the Exemplar Memorial pharmacy is closed? I wouldn't be surprised if they'd agree to fill prescriptions and deliver their medications right to the patient's bedside."

"What a great idea! We hadn't thought of that. We talked about contacting the hospital pharmacy to see if it's feasible to keep someone on at night and to keep the pharmacy open on weekends. But if not, this sounds like a good alternative."

Alice asked, "Since you're going to be educating patients and families about how and when to take their medications, do you want to try putting a week's worth of medications in one of those Sunday–Saturday plastic pill holders? That way, patients will have their medications set up correctly for the first week and they can use this set-up as a model for doing it themselves at home. That really would have helped me when I was discharged."

Then she asked another question. "What if every doctor and nurse were to use the 'teach-back' technique to be sure patients and families really understand how and when to take their medications when they get home? You know that phrase 'never assume?' Well, you can't assume patients and families really understand just because they smile and nod.

"Don't forget," she went on, "when we're discharged from the hospital, patients and families usually feel a certain level of stress. Plus, the medications we're given in the hospital can make us feel a little 'fuzzy.' So even the sharpest among us often finds it difficult to understand instructions. My advice is to ask patients and families to repeat your instructions in their own words—and if they still don't understand, try explaining more simply and writing the instructions down clearly so they can read them later when they're feeling better."

At their Project Team meeting the next morning, Project Team members decided to put all of these ideas into practice. When Maria Gonzalez, Project Team co-leader, contacted the hospital pharmacy the next day and learned it wasn't feasible to have someone staffing the pharmacy at night or on weekends, she worked out a partnership with the local pharmacy to deliver prescription medications to patients' bedsides when the hospital pharmacy was closed.

Both the hospital pharmacy and the local pharmacy provided Sunday–Saturday pill holders with each medication, which a pharmacist organized at the patient's bedside with the involvement of patients and families right before discharge.

Before a patient was discharged, a nurse and a pharmacist also asked patients and families to explain, in their own words, how and when to take their medications; allowed time to answer any questions; and gave them a telephone number to call if they had any questions about their medications, day or night, when they got home.

As the pharmacist told the Working Group after their project was implemented, "One patient, an elderly man, grabbed my hand before he left the hospital and said, gratefully, 'I know I can take care of myself now. Thank you for giving me what I need to do that.'"

Then Phil Hart, Project Team co-leader, said, "Maria and I have noticed a decline in Emergency Department readmissions over the past few months. I'm not saying this project is solely responsible for that decline," he added, "but giving patients the ability to take their medications as prescribed makes it less likely they'll end up right back here."

When the last of the Project Team co-leaders had presented their projects' accomplishments to the Working Group, Ben beamed as he said, "Outstanding work, everyone. Our annual meeting is coming up. As promised, PFCC is now a reality at Exemplar Memorial Hospital. I can't wait to tell everyone what our work has meant to patients and families, how PFCC has affected each of us as caregivers, and how the Patient Centered Value System is helping to improve clinical outcomes, reduce waste, and lower costs."

***

The auditorium was packed for Exemplar Memorial Hospital's annual meeting. Standing at the podium, Ben Highland recalled sharing the story of his wife, Jane's, experience as a trauma patient at last year's annual meeting and his experience as her very worried husband.

"As I said last year," Ben began, "I felt panicked about my wife's condition and dissatisfied with the quality of trauma care as it applied both to Jane and to me. Like the family members of most patients, I felt powerless to understand, let alone navigate, a confusing and seemingly impenetrable hospital system where patient safety was sometimes jeopardized and communication was often fragmented. I realized then that this is how all family members must feel when they are thrust into the world of trauma care. I felt then, and continue to feel, a strong connection with ordinary patients and families; a deep empathy for their often frustrating and lonely hospital experiences; and a profound sense of urgency to transform the current state into the ideal as patients and families define it.

"I am delighted to tell you that one year later, we have transformed the trauma care experience for patients and families using Shadowing and the six-step PFCC Methodology, two of the three prongs of the Patient Centered Value System. Our care transformation projects have focused on collecting and storing patient belongings, restructuring the Trauma Team, involving patients and families in the nursing change of shift report, redesigning the patient and family reunion, and revising the discharge prescription and medication education process.

"While we were transforming the experiences of patients and families in trauma care," Ben continued, "we were also transforming the experience of caregivers and the culture of this organization. How? Well, caregivers now see the care experience through the eyes of patients and families and feel empowered to make needed changes as a result. This perspective, which will spread as more and more caregivers participate in PFCC Working Groups and Project Teams, is what will change the culture.

"What makes the PFCC Methodology sustainable is that these efforts to transform the experience of patients and families in trauma care will continue. We never rest on our laurels, knowing we can always do better to improve the current state. The Trauma Care Experience Working Group will re-Shadow to identify the ever-changing current state and will form new Project Teams to close the gaps between the current state and the ideal. After repeated re-Shadowing over time with sustained positive results, Project Teams may choose to close projects and reform to tackle new ones. Project Teams begin and end, but Working Groups are forever.

"We are now on the cusp of launching other care transformation projects at Exemplar Memorial. All we need are caregivers who are committed to seeing all care through the eyes of patients and families, and caregivers who are determined to Shadow and follow the six steps of the PFCC Methodology to transform care from the current state to the ideal as patients and families define it.

"If we start tomorrow, by this time next year we will have transformed the Day of Surgery Care Experience, the Total Hip and Knee Joint Care Experience, the Bariatric Surgery Care Experience, the Women's Cancer Care Experience, and others.

"So, don't be surprised to find me standing in your office doorway. I'll be stopping by to ask you to serve on a Guiding Council; to Shadow a patient's and family's care experience; to form a Working Group; to write the ideal story of a care experience through the eyes of patients and families; and to form Project Teams to transform the current state into the ideal. And when you're tapped by Guiding Council Co-Chairs to serve on Project Teams, I hope you'll feel inspired by what you've seen and heard today—that care transformation is possible and it has arrived!" Ben exclaimed, smiling and feeling humbled by the standing ovation and applause.

Chapter 7

The Patient Centered Value System: Fact, Not Fiction

> Know how to distill complexity into a [simple] message to reach the hearts as well as the minds of the larger world ...
>
> **Thomas Jefferson**

These are the facts: The Patient Centered Care Value System—comprising Shadowing, the Patient and Family Centered Care (PFCC) Methodology, and Time-Driven Activity-Based Costing—is an elegantly simple approach to transforming healthcare that improves the patient and family experience of care, improves clinical and operational outcomes, decreases waste, and lowers costs. The Patient Centered Value System is being implemented at the University of Pittsburgh Medical Center, and in hospitals nationally and internationally with positive results, as the second half of this book explains. Why, then, have we chosen to present the first half of this book in the form of a story?

The answer is that stories are at the heart of the Patient and Family Centered Care Methodology. In the PFCC Methodology, we listen to the stories patients and families tell about their experience of care when we Shadow. When we listen and observe, we see the care experience through their eyes, often for the first time: we learn what the current state looks and feels like to patients and families, and how the ideal state would look and feel to them. Their stories drive our sense of urgency to make needed changes in the delivery of care. Making changes to close the gaps between the current state and the ideal as patients and families define it is where care transformation begins.

Storytelling is also what Step 5 of the PFCC Methodology is all about. In Step 5, caregivers come together to write the ideal story of the care experience as if we were patients and family members. The ideal stories we write enable us to empathize with patients and families ("What would we want this care experience to look and feel like if *we* were the patient and family member?"), to brainstorm in new and creative ways, and then to work together in high-performance care teams to make the ideal, real.

Stories spark our imaginations, fire our sense of what is possible, and fuel our efforts to achieve our goals. Stories, integral to the PFCC Methodology and to this book, help us to see—and then go beyond—any limitations, real or imagined.

Like our fictional hero Dr. Benjamin Highland and the caregivers at Exemplar Memorial Hospital, all you need to do is follow the processes presented in Chapters 1 through 6 of our story—the "how-to" portion of this book—to implement the PFCC Methodology *right now* for results you will see in a matter of weeks.

Although Chapters 1 through 6 are told as a story, there is nothing fictional about the Patient Centered Value System, which is based on principles common in business but rarely, if ever, applied to healthcare. With the end of our story show-ing how to introduce and implement the PFCC Methodology in any size organization, the second section of this book turns to the third component of the Patient Centered Value System—Time-Driven Activity-Based Costing—and to the research underpinnings and practice of the Patient Centered Value System as a whole.

In Part II, Chapter 8 describes how Shadowing is used in Time-Driven Activity-Based Costing and explains how its application will help you to determine and drive down the *true* cost of healthcare delivery for any medical or surgical condition; identify the true cost drivers in any segment of care delivery and over the full cycle of care; and achieve the Triple Aim by driving down costs in a way that protects or improves outcomes and experiences.

In Part III, Chapter 9 presents the theoretical underpinnings of the Patient Centered Value System and how it is built on the shoulders of giants in the fields of organizational change (including disruptive change), design sciences and experience-based design, process improvement, psychology, business, marketing, and leadership. The Patient Centered Value System integrates these approaches into a *single tool* designed specifically for healthcare.

Chapter 10 explains how you can add the Patient Centered Value System to other process improvement approaches you may already be using (such as Lean) to accelerate the pace of improvement.

Finally, Chapter 11 describes how organizations nationally and internationally are using the Patient Centered Value System to improve patient engagement and clinical outcomes, improve the health of populations, reduce waste and inefficiency, and lower costs.

Following the Patient Centered Value System as shown in Chapters 1 through 6 and explained in Chapters 8 through 11 will enable your organization to achieve the Triple Aim: improving the patient experience of care, including quality and satisfaction; improving the health of populations; and reducing the per capita costs of healthcare.

DETERMINE AND DRIVE DOWN THE TRUE COST OF CARE DELIVERY AND ACHIEVE THE TRIPLE AIM

II

Chapter 8

Determine the True Cost of Care Using Shadowing and Time-Driven Activity-Based Costing

We have been living with the economic impact of the high cost of care for so long that it has become part of our expectations and is accepted as just the way things are... The sun is setting on that day in America.

Gene Lindsey, M.D.
President and CEO Emeritus, Atrius Health and Harvard Vanguard Medical Associates

What is the cost of delivering healthcare today? For that matter, what do we mean by cost? If, like most healthcare professionals, you think of charges and reimbursement, you are missing the granularity that would enable you to accurately answer this question. Actual, or true, costs include *all* of the expenses incurred by a provider, hospital, or other healthcare organization to provide patient care. Charges are simply the prices set by providers, hospitals, and other healthcare organizations for healthcare services. And reimbursement is the dollar amount a provider or hospital receives from insurance companies or the government (e.g., Medicare or Medicaid). These broad categories do not provide the granular data needed to determine the true costs of healthcare delivery for any medical or surgical condition and over the full cycle of care: that is, from the first office visit for knee pain to non-surgical treatment, to total joint replacement surgery, to rehabilitation and home care, to the 90-day follow-up visit, or for a much longer full cycle of care for a condition such as cleft palate, for which a patient may be followed for up to 20 years.

Without such data, providers do not know, for example, what it costs them to provide total joint replacement, heart bypass surgery, or diabetes care. They don't know their costs for any individual segment of care (such as a doctor's office visit or pre-surgical testing) and they don't know their costs over the full cycle of care.

Likewise, providers and organizations do not know the actual cost *drivers* within a clinical condition—which means they do not have a way to assure that driving down costs in one segment of care delivery won't increase costs in another. Nor do they know the impact of cost reductions on patient outcomes or experiences.

The uncertainty about what healthcare delivery actually costs is the result of the decades-long fee-for-service payment system in the United States, in which charges to patients (and insurers) have not been based directly on costs but, rather, have been based on volume: that is, on providing more services to more people. In addition, the fragmentation of healthcare delivery also practiced in the fee-for-service model has led to patients receiving healthcare services from a variety of providers and organizations across functional silos and over time, making a determination of costs over a complete cycle of care for any given patient virtually impossible.

Consider this example: a patient experiencing knee pain may visit a primary care physician, an orthopedic specialist, a sports medicine physician, a chiropractor, an acupuncturist, a physical therapist, a physiatrist, or all of the above. The patient may get x-rays or an MRI (magnetic resonance imaging) at a free-standing imaging center, an ambulatory care center, a physiatrist's or chiropractor's office, an orthopedic surgeon's office, or a hospital. The x-rays may be done in one such facility and the MRI in another. And they may be done multiple times and longitudinally over time, depending on the patient's motivation to address the problem, the progression/regression of the pain, insurer allowances or restrictions, and varying (sometimes conflicting) treatment plans from different care providers. A patient may try therapeutic injections or fluid drainage administered by a sports medicine physician, a rheumatologist, or an orthopedic surgeon, or may instead (or in addition) try a course of physical therapy or pursue weight loss to fend off surgery. If joint replacement surgery becomes necessary, the patient may receive additional diagnostic testing and have one or more appointments at an orthopedic surgical office, either affiliated or unaffiliated with the hospital or free-standing surgical center where surgery is later performed. Post-surgically, the patient may experience an inpatient hospital stay followed by inpatient and/or outpatient rehabilitation, physical therapy, home care, and return doctors' office visits. Each step of this scenario generates charges that are not only disconnected from actual costs but, necessarily, given the fragmentation, charges that may have no relation to outcomes and experiences.

The Institute for Healthcare Improvement's Triple Aim, a term coined in 2008 (Berwick et al., 2008), equalizes the goals of achieving better care, better health, and reduced costs. We must not pursue one without the others. Yet, it is a tremendous challenge to be accountable for all three goals when we do not have efficient, real-time, accurate knowledge of the true cost of delivering healthcare; and when we have a fragmented healthcare system in which patients receive and are billed for services across multiple providers. Until now, individual health-care providers and organizations simply have not had a way to assure that improvements in costs are pursued in concert with improvements in outcomes and experiences—and that no one prong of the Triple Aim is left behind.

This chapter explains how to use Shadowing and Time-Driven Activity-Based Costing in the context of the Patient Centered Value System to: (1) determine the true (actual) cost of delivering care for any specific medical or surgical condition; (2) identify true cost drivers in any segment of care delivery and over the full cycle of care; and (3) achieve the Triple Aim by driving down costs in a way that protects or improves outcomes and experiences.

Origins of the Patient Centered Value System

In 2006, Dr. Anthony M. DiGioia, III, and colleagues in the Bone and Joint Center at Magee-Womens Hospital of UPMC developed the Patient and Family Centered Care (PFCC) Methodology. Its purpose, as demonstrated in the first half of this book, is to see the care experience from the perspective of patients and families and to create a simple approach to transforming each step of the care experience from the current state to the ideal.

Five years after the PFCC Methodology was first developed, Robert S. Kaplan and Michael Porter, at the Harvard Business School, applied Time-Driven Activity-Based Costing (Kaplan and Anderson 2007) as a method for determining the true cost and value (i.e., outcomes achieved per dollar spent) of deliver-ing healthcare over the full cycle of patient care (Kaplan and Porter 2011).

While developed independently and for different pur-poses, the PFCC Methodology and Time-Driven Activity-Based Costing share certain fundamental similarities. Most important, each focuses on the care experience from the point of view of the patient and family. Each defines the beginning and end points of the patient's care, thereby setting the parameters for measurement. Each maps the patient's journey to identify all of the touchpoints along the way, and each measures the amount of time every caregiver (and patient) spends at each step of the care process.

Along with the similarities, there are also differences between the PFCC Methodology and Time-Driven Activity-Based Costing. While Time-Driven Activity-Based Costing relies on clinicians and managers to describe and estimate basic information such as care pathways, care processes, personnel, minutes spent per process or activity, and space and equipment used, the PFCC Methodology uses Shadowing rather than discussion-based estimates—in other words, real-time observation—that enables Shadowers to record every touchpoint and resource used as they occur. It has been found time and again that estimates of care pathways and processes miss a lot; the only accurate and efficient way to identify pathways, processes, and resources is by Shadowing (DiGioia et al. 2016). Once these are identified, the PFCC Methodology provides the structure for building high-performance implementation teams to verify the data and develop plans to drive and sustain change.

What Is Time-Driven Activity-Based Costing in the Context of the Patient Centered Value System?

In the Patient Centered Value System, Time-Driven Activity-Based Costing uses Shadowing to accurately and efficiently identify the care pathway and the four buckets of resources that must be examined in order to calculate the true cost of care delivery for any medical or surgical condition: personnel, space, equipment, and consumables. By applying Shadowing,

Time-Driven Activity-Based Costing efficiently identifies the actual cost and cost drivers of delivering care (as opposed to charges or reimbursements) in each segment of care and over the full cycle of care.

Integrating Shadowing, Time-Driven Activity-Based Costing, and the PFCC Methodology—the three equally important parts of the Patient Centered Value System—allows for the development of high-performance implementation teams that can put process improvements into place to drive down costs while protecting and/or improving patient and family experiences and clinical outcomes. Such integration is at the heart of the Patient Centered Value System.

Benefits of Time-Driven Activity-Based Costing

Shadowing plus Time-Driven Activity-Based Costing yields information on the types, utilization, and cost of each resource and the duration of activities for each step of care delivery. This methodology also accounts for "back office" processes such as billing and central sterilization activities that are often missed by other costing tools. Accurate cost knowledge allows providers to enter into alternative payment and care delivery models with minimal financial risk.

Shadowing plus Time-Driven Activity-Based Costing guides high-performance care teams as they conduct the following activities:

- Identify accurate care pathways for a specific medical or surgical condition.
- Identify the resources (personnel, consumables, equipment, and space) used throughout the care pathway (e.g., 30 days pre- to 90 days post-hip replacement surgery).
- Identify the amount of time each resource is used per activity, per segment of care, and in total.
- Calculate the actual cost of each of these resources.

- By activity (e.g., physical assessment in an exam room or chest x-ray process).
- By segment of care (such as a doctor's office visit, pre-surgical testing, surgery in the operating room, etc.).
- Over the full cycle of care (i.e., 30 days pre- to 90 days post-surgery).

Shadowing combined with Time-Driven Activity-Based Costing thereby provides organizations with the unique ability to reduce costs thoughtfully rather than making across-the-board cuts, as is more typical, and to do so while enhancing or protecting outcomes and patient experiences, thus creating true value for patients, families, providers, and organizations.

In addition to explaining how to use Shadowing with Time-Driven Activity-Based Costing, this manual pinpoints cost drivers, variations in processes, and potential gaps in care within each segment of care (pre-hospital, hospital, and post-hospital); provides the foundation for internal and external benchmarking between similar service lines to drive the adoption of best practices; and will enable you to operationalize process improvement by tightly coupling clinical and financial performance.

Time-Driven Activity-Based Costing Plus Shadowing: A User's Manual

Time-Driven Activity-Based Costing in the context of the Patient Centered Value System consists of three steps:

Step 1: Shadow the care segment(s)
Step 2: Develop Time-Driven Activity-Based Costing process maps
Step 3: Calculate costs in four buckets of resources—personnel, space, equipment, and consumables—to determine cost drivers and start process improvement efforts

Step 1: Shadow the Care Segment(s)

It is essential to begin using Time-Driven Activity-Based Costing by Shadowing the care segments that make up a care experience and then creating process maps (see the figures throughout this chapter for guidance) in much the same way as a Care Experience Flow Map is created in Step 3 of the PFCC Methodology (described in Chapter 3). The first step is to divide complex care experiences into smaller segments, then Shadow *each segment* to build a full experience process map. Templates for Shadowing are available at GoShadow.org.

Figure 8.1 illustrates the full cycle of care for a patient requiring hip or knee replacement surgery or, for that matter, any type of surgery. This figure, which can be adapted easily for any clinical care experience, shows each segment involved in the care process. Once the segments that make up a care experience have been identified, Shadowing each segment individually and then combining segments will enable you to determine the true costs over the full cycle of care. One recommendation is to Shadow first to construct a general process

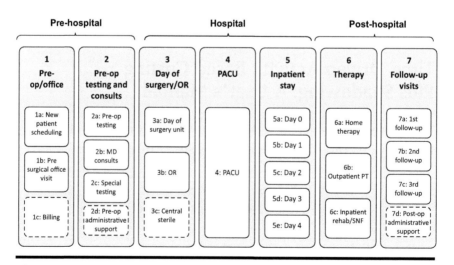

Figure 8.1 (See color insert.) Segments and sub-segments for the full cycle of care for a patient requiring surgery.

map, then re-Shadow to collect details pertaining to time, resources, and consumables.

Applying Shadowing to Time-Driven Activity-Based Costing requires a slight shift of focus from Shadowing in the PFCC Methodology. Instead of focusing on the experience of care, as in the PFCC Methodology, Shadowing in the context of Time-Driven Activity-Based Costing focuses on capturing specific details of personnel, space, and activities, and the amount of time they are used; equipment used (or available for use); and the compilation of a list of consumables used. (In Time-Driven Activity-Based Costing, consumables are defined as any disposable medical items, medications, operating room instruments, and implants.)

Time Detail for Personnel, Space, and Activities

Shadowing requires recording the starting and ending times of caregivers' activities and changes in location (touchpoints), such as when a nurse enters and leaves an examination room, what time a procedure starts and ends, or when a patient leaves the x-ray room and returns to the waiting room.

Photo Option for Consumables and Equipment

While you are Shadowing, taking a picture can be an effective way to capture consumables and equipment used or available during a segment of care. These photos can be used to verify, with the appropriate clinicians and leaders, the type and number of consumables and equipment used in any segment of a care experience.

Step 2: Develop Time-Driven Activity-Based Costing Process Maps

After Shadowing, you can now develop Time-Driven Activity-Based Costing process maps for each segment of care. These process maps show the actual steps in the care pathway as they occur, the caregivers (personnel) with whom the patient and family come into contact, and the touchpoints (where patients and families go) during the care experience. In addition, these process maps summarize the activities that take place at each step and the amount of time it takes to complete each activity. Let the Care Experience Flow Map developed during Shadowing in Step 3 of the PFCC Methodology (shown in Chapter 3, Figure 3.1) serve as the model for Time-Driven Activity-Based Costing process mapping.

In the "pre-operative testing" segment of the Time-Driven Activity-Based Costing process map (Figure 8.2), each caregiver is represented by a different type of shaded box that shows the activity performed and the average length of time (for all of the patients and families Shadowed) the activity took to complete.

Time-Driven Activity-Based Costing process maps reveal resources and activity time used to determine actual costs (for personnel, consumables, equipment, and space); where patient and families go—that is, all locations during a care experience—and for how long; resources with substantial unused capacity; care providers not working at the "top of their licenses" in order to best match personnel by cost for each task; and unnecessary redundancies, waste, and inefficiencies.

Time-Driven Activity-Based Costing process maps also show variations among patients who have the same medical or surgical condition, such as total joint replacement. These variations can be illustrated by adding decision nodes to these process maps; each node represents a point of variation in which a non-standard activity takes place for individual patients. For example, it is standard practice for patients who will have total joint replacement surgery to receive an electrocardiogram (EKG) during pre-operative testing. However, as the pre-operative testing process map (Figure 8.2) shows, if a patient has had an EKG in the past 30 days, he or she can skip Step 4 (represented as a decision node) and move directly to Step 5 in the pre-operative testing process. Process maps

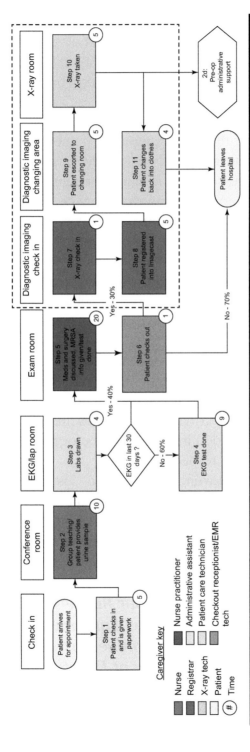

Figure 8.2   (See color insert.) Time-Driven Activity-Based Costing process map for the pre-operative testing segment of care.

enable you to account for the percentage of time such changes in activity take place. For instance, about 40 percent of this patient population has received their EKG in the past 30 days.

Time-Driven Activity-Based Costing process maps must also include "back office" processes. These processes are defined as activities that occur to support the care of the patient throughout the care experience, some of which may not be captured during actual Shadowing of patient experiences. These processes include staff scheduling appointments, entering data into and studying electronic health records, obtaining authorizations from insurance companies, billing (Figure 8.3), and central sterilization and preparation of surgical instruments and trays for the operating room (Figure 8.4). To determine back office processes, one-on-one interviews are conducted with the appropriate personnel and leaders who are familiar with the processes. Once this information is gathered, these activities can become their own segments within the care experience or be integrated into other segments. For example, processes such as patient scheduling and billing are often considered to be their own segments of care, while activities such as preparing charting notes and surgical trays could easily be included in the segments for the office visit and operating room, respectively.

When the Time-Driven Activity-Based Costing process maps are complete, you will know the total number of minutes each resource is utilized. You can then use this information to calculate the actual cost for the clinical condition over a full cycle of care.

Step 3: Calculate Costs in Four Buckets of Resources—Personnel, Space, Equipment, and Consumables—to Determine Cost Drivers and Start Process Improvement Efforts

When you have Shadowed the actual care pathway and created your process map, you can begin to evaluate the

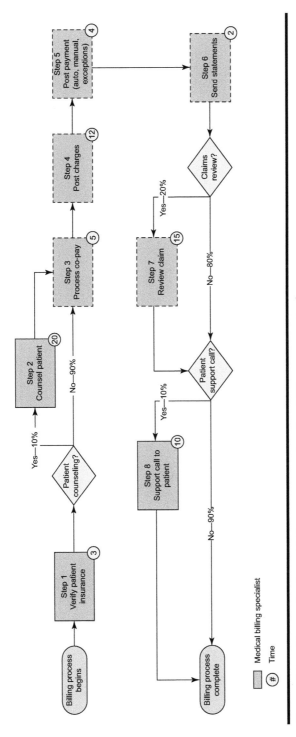

Figure 8.3 (See color insert.) Process mapping the billing segment of care.

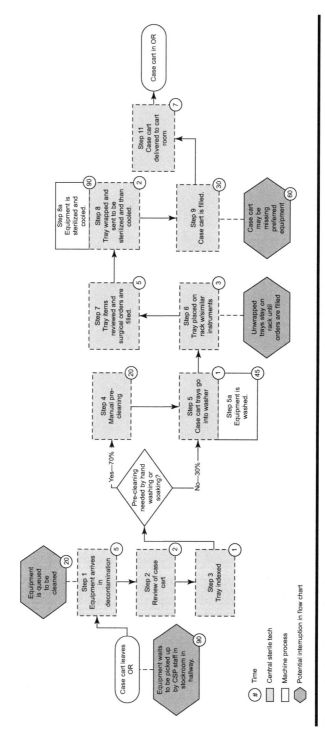

Figure 8.4 (See color insert.) Process mapping for the central sterilization of the operating room.

Figure 8.5   (See color insert.) Combining the time used with the cost per minute to calculate the actual cost to deliver care.

resources used in each segment of care and calculate the actual costs of delivering that care for the full cycle. You can collect information on the resources used from a variety of sources, such as frontline staff, hospital leadership, the Finance Department, and the Facilities Management Department.

The actual cost of care is calculated by multiplying the number of minutes a resource is used by the cost per minute of each resource, first over a segment of care and then over the full cycle of care, as illustrated in Figure 8.5.

Personnel

To determine the cost per minute of the personnel involved in delivering care, you'll need to collect the total annual cost incurred for each personnel type, as well as the total time each personnel type is available for treating or caring for patients. The total annual personnel costs include annual salary, benefits, supervision, training/travel, information technology support, and so on; these can be collected during one-on-one meetings with leaders and/or frontline staff.

For example, to determine the cost per minute for an x-ray technician in the pre-operative testing segment, you'll first need to determine the total annual cost for the x-ray technician by adding the cost types as shown in Figure 8.6a. After calculating the total annual cost of an x-ray technician, you'll then need to calculate the capacity rate as 365 days minus the total time (in minutes) the x-ray technician is not available for

Title	Department	Cost type	Amount ($)	Total ($)
X-ray technician	Imaging	Annual salary	32,000	46,996.00
		Benefits	8,320	
		Supervision	4,676	
		Assistant/admin support	0	
		Training and travel	1,000	
		IT (hardware and support)	1,000	
		Office expenses	0	
		Malpractice insurance	0	
		Miscellaneous	0	

(a)

Title	Department	Capacity calculation	Allocated time (per day)	Total time (min/year)	Cost rate ($/min)
X-ray technician	Imaging	Hours/day (hrs)	8.5	94,080.00	0.50
Annual salary: $46,996.00		Breaks (lunches, etc.) (hrs)	1.0		
		Meetings/non-patient time (hrs)	0.5		
		Training and conference days/year	5.0		
		Weekends and public holidays/year	110.0		
		Vacation and PTO/year	26.0		

Net 7 hrs/day x 60 min/hr = 420 min/day
420 min/day x net 224 working days/yr = 94080 min/year

(b)

Figure 8.6 (See color insert.) (a) Determining costs for an x-ray technician, (b) calculating personnel capacity for an x-ray technician.

work, as shown in Figure 8.6b. The cost per minute for an x-ray technician in this example is calculated as follows:

$$\frac{\text{Total Cost}}{\text{Total Time}} = \text{X-ray Technician Cost per Minute}$$

$$\frac{\$46,996}{94,080 \text{ Minutes}} = \frac{\$0.50}{\text{Minute}}$$

Consumables

As already mentioned, consumables are defined here as any disposable medical item (e.g., dressing supplies, needles, and blood tubes), medications, operating room instruments, and implants. The most efficient way to collect information on the consumables used, as well as their associated cost, is to obtain

Operating room consumable name	Consumable cost ($)	Quantity	Total cost
Hip implant	4,500.00	1	4,500.00
Custom hip pack	350.00	1	350.00
Saw blade	55.00	2	110.00
Suture material	18.00	4	72.00

Figure 8.7   (See color insert.) Calculating the cost of consumables in the operating room.

a supplies list from unit directors and/or department managers. The calculation to determine the cost of each consumable is the most straightforward of any resource and is the only cost not based on time; simply multiply the cost per item by the quantity used, as shown in Figure 8.7.

Space

To determine the cost per minute for space, you'll need to know the relevant square footage and real estate value per square foot, as well as annual depreciation, operating, maintenance, and housekeeping costs. The square footage and costs associated with space can typically be collected from a contact in Facilities Management. The amount of time each space is available is based on the normal availability of that space for patient-focused work; the analyst determines whether the space is open for use only during normal business hours (e.g., Mon–Fri. 8:30 a.m.–5:30 p.m.), or for extended hours up to 24 hours per day. Figure 8.8 shows the costs associated with the radiology suite, which in this example is calculated as follows:

$$\frac{\text{Total Annual Space Cost}}{\text{Availability Time Frame}}$$

$$\frac{\$7,840}{115,785\ \text{Minutes}} = \frac{\$0.07}{\text{Minute}}$$

Space name	Area (sq ft)	New construction costs per sq ft ($/sq ft)	Useful life (yrs)	Annual construction depreciation per sq ft ($/sq ft)
X-ray room	150	250	15	16.67

Annual maintenance costs per sq ft ($/sq ft)	Annual operating costs (incl. utilities) per sq ft ($/sq ft)	Yearly housekeeping costs per sq ft ($/sq ft)	Real estate value per sq ft ($/sq ft)	Real estate life (yrs)	Yearly real estate cost per sq ft ($/sq ft)	Total annual space cost per square ft ($/sq ft)	Total annual space cost ($)	Availability timeframe	Availability (minutes)	Total annual space cost per minute ($/min)
15	12	7	40	25	1.6	52.27	7840	Normal hours	115,785	0.07

Figure 8.8 (See color insert.) **Calculating the space costs associated with the radiology suite.**

Equipment

In most care experiences, equipment is one of the lower-cost resources because equipment is used by a large number of patients over a long period of time (i.e., years); yet, capturing equipment costs is still important. Knowing the cost of equipment and the amount of time it is used may help departments considering annual capital requests, calculating the return on investment for new equipment, or determining the unused capacity of the equipment already purchased.

To determine the cost per minute for each piece of equipment used over the full cycle of care for the clinical condition, you will need to know the replacement cost, yearly depreciation, and maintenance costs. Similar to space, you will need to know the amount of time the equipment is available for use. Figure 8.9 is an example of the costs associated with the x-ray machine. In this example, the cost per minute for the x-ray machine is calculated as follows:

Equipment	Replacement cost	Useful life (years)	Yearly depreciation	Yearly maint. costs (%)	Yearly maint. costs ($)	Equipment cost per year ($/yr)	Availability timeframe	Availability (minutes)	Capacity cost rate ($/min)
X-ray machine	90,000	10	9,000	10%	9,000	18,000	Normal hours	115,785	0.16

Figure 8.9 (See color insert.) **Costs associated with the x-ray machine.**

$$\frac{\text{Annual Equipment Cost}}{\text{Total Minutes Available}}$$

$$\frac{\$18,000}{115,785 \text{ Minutes}} = \frac{\$0.16}{\text{Minute}}$$

Calculate the Actual Cost of Each Care Segment and the Full Cycle of Care

Now that you have calculated your cost per minute for each resource used, you can determine the cost of each step in the care pathway and the full cycle of care (Figure 8.10).

Figure 8.11 shows how we calculated the cost of taking an x-ray (Step 10 in Figure 8.10) in the pre-operative testing segment of the Time-Driven Activity-Based Costing process map. The cost per minute for each resource is simply multiplied by the average number of minutes it took to complete the task based on Shadowing results. In this case, the total cost for an x-ray technician to complete a five-minute x-ray was $3.65.

The Patient Centered Value System: Identify Cost Drivers to Begin Improvements

Improving value in healthcare depends on knowing the major contributors to high costs, or cost drivers, over a full cycle of care and having the tools to drive down costs while protecting outcomes and experiences. This is what the Patient Centered Value System is all about. For the first time, process improvement efforts are tightly coupled with financial and clinical performance.

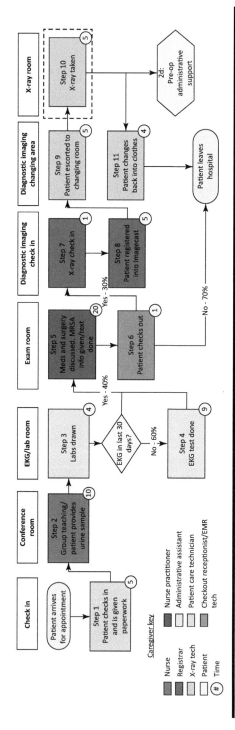

Figure 8.10 (See color insert.) Example of Time-Driven Activity-Based Costing process map for a new patient office visit.

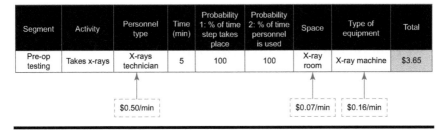

Segment	Activity	Personnel type	Time (min)	Probability 1: % of time step takes place	Probability 2: % of time personnel is used	Space	Type of equipment	Total
Pre-op testing	Takes x-rays	X-rays technician	5	100	100	X-ray room	X-ray machine	$3.65

$0.50/min $0.07/min $0.16/min

Figure 8.11   (See color insert.) Calculating the cost of an x-ray taken in the pre-operative testing segment of the Time-Driven Activity-Based Costing process map.

Cost Drivers

Now that you've calculated the actual cost of care delivery for your defined care experience (i.e., clinical condition), the next step is to delineate the resources and activities of the care experience that *drive* costs. Care providers, leaders, and managers now have greater insight into the financial side and actual costs associated with the care delivery process and can begin to identify the root causes of high costs. The comprehensive Time-Driven Activity-Based Costing report gives you a complete picture of the processes (for each segment and in total), time, and resources involved.

We have found that the cost drivers—that is, costs that have the greatest effect on an organization's bottom line—fall into the following categories:

■ **Personnel:** Personnel costs make up the largest portion of the overall cost of care delivery, typically about 65 percent of total costs. In reviewing personnel costs and capacity, note which personnel aren't working to the top of their license. For example, perhaps a physician is performing work that can be transferred to a mid-level provider or a nurse practitioner is doing work that can be taken over by a non-advanced practice nurse or a case manager. Also, the more inefficient the process, the more time spent on non-value added steps and practices, which increases costs. Focus on providing the right care at the right time with the right personnel.

■ **Consumables:** Implants and devices often make up the largest portion of the consumable costs, especially if the care experience under review includes surgery. One way to reduce these costs is to collaborate with supply chain leaders (if you don't already) and revisit your buying power to negotiate with suppliers.

Depending on the type of care experience, additional cost drivers can include medication therapy, anesthesia protocols, number of office visits, non-evidence-based variations in procedures, inpatient length of stay, discharge disposition (i.e., home vs. skilled nursing facilities or rehabilitation centers), and the number and types of outpatient therapies.

Implement the Patient Centered Value System

With this information, including actual costs, you can use the entire Patient Centered Value System to move toward creating value for patients and families and your healthcare organization by eliminating non-value added practices and processes while maintaining or improving outcomes at lower costs. PFCC Working Groups and Project Teams can use the cost information, along with the experiential information already collected through Shadowing, to implement changes that lower costs but protect, and even improve, experiences and outcomes.

By collecting information on costs and the care pathway and by identifying cost drivers within every segment of care while seeing the current state of the care experience through Shadowing, your PFCC Working Group will be able to tightly couple clinical and financial performance. Using the information collected will help you to improve care processes and deliver value to patients and families as well as to your healthcare organization.

The case study on pre-operative testing, shown next, shows how one care delivery team was able to reduce costs while improving patient outcomes and experiences.

CASE STUDY: PRE-OPERATIVE TESTING PROCESS IMPROVEMENT

During the pre-operative testing portion of the total joint replacement care experience, Shadowing plus Time-Driven Activity-Based Costing showed that all patients were receiving a chest x-ray prior to surgery. By implementing updated protocols as to when it is medically necessary to obtain a chest x-ray, the team was able to reduce pre-surgical chest x-rays by 70 percent, resulting in total annual cost savings of $7500 for one surgeon. The savings will grow accordingly when the protocol is extended to additional surgeons. In addition to cost savings, this initiative improved the patient experience by lessening testing time and radiation exposure.

Figure 8.12 shows the total cost calculation for a patient receiving a chest x-ray.

Segment	Activity	Personnel type	Time (min)	Probability 1: % of time step takes place	Probability 2: % of time personnel is used	Space	Type of equipment	Total
Pre-op testing	X-ray check in	Registrar	1	100	100	Imaging check in		$0.45
Pre-op testing	Patient registered into Imagecast	Registrar	5	100	100	Imaging check in		$2.25
Pre-op testing	Patient escorted to changing room	X-ray technician	5	100	100	Changing area		$2.60
Pre-op testing	Takes x-rays	X-ray technician	5	100	100	X-ray room	X-ray machine	$3.65
Pre-op testing	Patient changes back into clothes	X-ray technician	4	100	100	Changing area		$2.08
	Total cost of receiving chest x-ray							$11.03

Figure 8.12 (See color insert.) Total cost calculation for patient receiving a chest x-ray.

After you've applied Shadowing to Time-Driven Activity-Based Costing and implemented improvements, be sure to re-Shadow the care experience periodically to see how your improvement efforts are working, and to identify additional improvement opportunities. Shadowing is built on a philosophy of continuous improvement, reinvigorating team members to move beyond their initial goals and providing an opportunity to re-assess the metrics of implemented projects.

The Need for the Patient Centered Value System in Today's Healthcare Environment

In order to achieve the IHI's Triple Aim and compete in value-based care delivery systems, healthcare organizations and providers must know the true cost of delivering care over the full cycle; understand that costs, charges, and reimbursement are not the same and are not directly related under fee-for-service payment systems; and learn how to drive down costs without compromising outcomes or patient experiences.

Such an understanding would lead to positive results for patients, families, providers, and organizations: first, patients and families would be able to learn, in advance, the price of medical services, be able to compare costs across providers, and then budget to pay for them; and second, healthcare providers and organizations would be better equipped to enter into bundling or shared risk programs with insurers in a way that minimizes their financial risk. Knowing their true costs to deliver care over the full cycle of care would give healthcare organizations and providers all of the information they need to succeed under alternative payment and service models (see sidebar).

In the end, patients and families are the best sources to help us to understand and deliver value. Only by following patients and families through their healthcare journeys can we collect all of the information needed to record, evaluate, and then optimize their experiences, outcomes, and costs. By providing value for patients and families, we also deliver value for caregivers and organizations.

Accountable Care Organizations comprise multiple "medical homes"—that is, many primary care providers and/or practices that work together. The difference between Accountable Care Organizations and the Patient Centered Medical Home (defined in the next section) is that the former are accountable for the cost and quality of care, both within and outside of the primary care relationship. Therefore, Accountable Care Organizations must include specialists and hospitals to control costs and improve health outcomes across the entire care continuum. Accountable Care Organizations have led to the development of new payment models, which are in turn leading to new delivery systems requiring greater communication, care coordination, and quality measurement reporting. (Council of Accountable Physician Practices)

Bundled Payment Programs refer to a type of risk contracting that assigns a fixed, negotiated fee to cover a set of treatment services, encouraging providers to manage costs while meeting high-quality care standards. If the cost of the service is less than the bundled payment, participating providers retain the difference. But if the cost exceeds the bundled payment, providers are not compensated for the difference.

Comprehensive Care Joint Replacement Model is a program being proposed by the Centers for Medicare and Medicaid Services to support better and more efficient care for beneficiaries undergoing hip and knee replacements, the most common type of inpatient surgery for Medicare beneficiaries. This model would test bundled payment and quality measurement for an episode of care associated with hip and knee replacements to encourage hospitals, physicians, and post-acute care providers to work together to improve the quality and coordination of care from the initial hospitalization through recovery.

Patient Centered Medical Home is an enhanced primary care delivery model that strives to achieve better access, coordination of care, preventive care, quality, and safety within the primary care practice while creating a strong partnership between the patient and primary care physician. In this model, payers often reward providers with a per-month "bonus" for improving primary care services for each patient in the medical home (National Committee for Quality Assurance).

Reference-Based Pricing allows plans to negotiate prices with high-quality providers and encourages plan participants and beneficiaries to use those providers. A health plan offers to pay a fixed amount, which certain providers will accept as payment for a particular procedure. Plan participants and beneficiaries using a provider who does not accept the reference price must pay the difference between the provider's charge and the reference price out of pocket. These out-of-pocket payments do not count toward the statutory maximum out-of-pocket limits.

Shared Savings Programs are generating a great deal of interest as an approach to healthcare payment reform. "The basic concept is: if a healthcare system or provider reduces total healthcare spending for its patients below the level that the payer (e.g., Medicare or a private health insurance plan) would have otherwise expected, the provider is rewarded with a portion of the savings. The result is that the payer still spends less than it would have otherwise, and the provider gets more revenue than it would have otherwise expected" (Center for Healthcare Quality & Payment Reform). Medicare has established a Shared

Savings Program that facilitates coordination and cooperation among providers to improve the quality of care
for Medicare fee-for-service beneficiaries and to reduce
unnecessary costs. Participation in Medicare's Shared
Savings Program is open to all providers, hospitals, and
suppliers that create or participate in an Accountable Care
Organization. The Shared Savings Program will reward
Accountable Care Organizations that lower their growth in
healthcare costs while meeting performance standards in
quality of care and putting patients first.

References

Berwick, DM, Nolan, TW, Whittington, J. 2008 May/June. The triple
    aim: Care, health, and cost. Health Aff 27(3):759–769.
Council of Accountable Physician Practices. Accountable Care Facts.
    http://www.accountablecarefacts.org.
DiGioia, AM, Greenhouse, PK, Giarrusso, ML, Kress, JM. 2016
    January. Determining true cost to deliver total hip and knee
    arthroplasty over the full cycle of care: Preparing for bundling
    and reference-based pricing. *J Arthroplasty* 31(1):1–6.
Kaplan, RS, Anderson, SR. 2007. *Time-Driven Activity-Based Costing:
    A Simpler and More Powerful Path to Higher Profits.* Boston,
    MA: Harvard Business School Publishing Corp.
Kaplan, RS, Porter, ME. 2011 September. The big idea: How to
    solve the cost crisis in healthcare. *Har Bus Rev* https://hbr.
    org/2011/09/how-to-solve-the-cost-crisis-in-health-care.
National Committee for Quality Assurance. http://
    www.ncqa.org/Programs/Recognition/Practices/
    PatientCenteredMedicalHomePCMH.aspx.

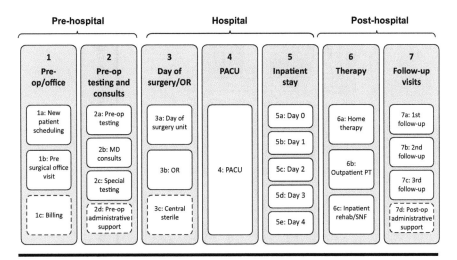

Figure 8.1   Segments and sub-segments for the full cycle of care for a patient requiring surgery.

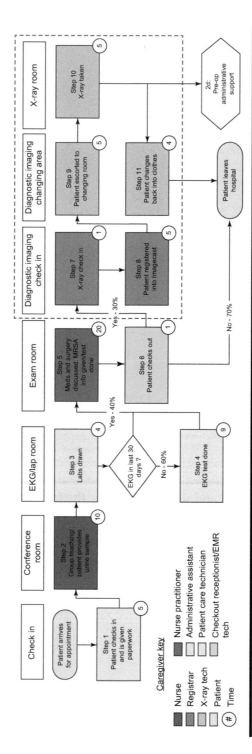

Figure 8.2   Time-Driven Activity-Based Costing process map for the pre-operative testing segment of care.

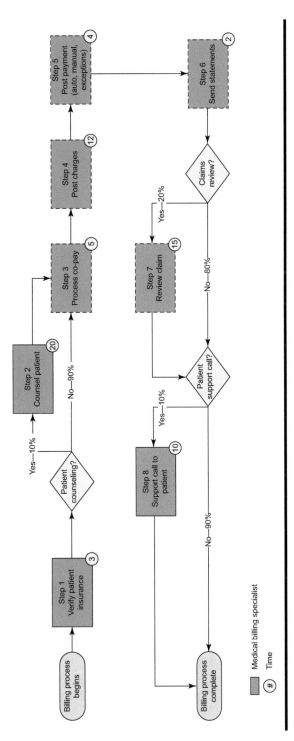

Figure 8.3 Process mapping the billing segment of care.

Legend:
- Medical billing specialist
- (#) Time

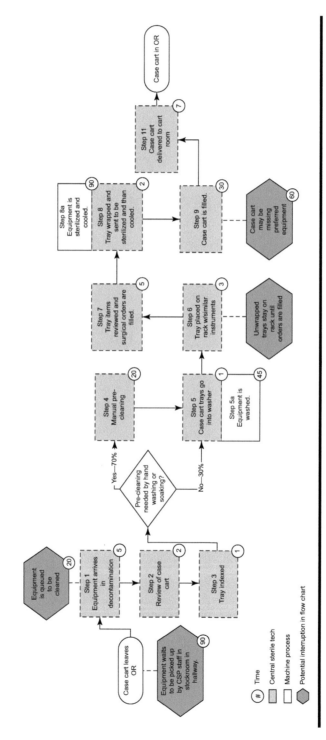

Figure 8.4 Process mapping for the central sterilization of the operating room.

Clinical side

Financial side

Minutes used ✕ Cost per minute

= $/Resource

Figure 8.5 Combining the time used with the cost per minute to calcu-late the actual cost to deliver care.

Title	Department	Cost type	Amount ($)	Total ($)
X-ray technician	Imaging	Annual salary	32,000	46,996.00
		Benefits	8,320	
		Supervision	4,676	
		Assistant/admin support	0	
		Training and travel	1,000	
		IT (hardware and support)	1,000	
		Office expenses	0	
		Malpractice insurance	0	
		Miscellaneous	0	

(a)

Title	Department	Capacity calculation	Allocated time (per day)	Total time (min/year)	Cost rate ($/min)
X-ray technician	Imaging	Hours/day (hrs)	8.5	94,080.00	0.50
Annual salary: $46,996.00		Breaks (lunches, etc.) (hrs)	1.0		
		Meetings/non-patient time (hrs)	0.5		
		Training and conference days/year	5.0		
		Weekends and public holidays/year	110.0		
		Vacation and PTO/year	26.0		

Net 7 hrs/day x 60 min/hr = 420 min/day
420 min/day x net 224 working days/yr = 94080 min/year

(b)

Figure 8.6 (a) Determining costs for an x-ray technician, (b) calculat-ing personnel capacity for an x-ray technician.

Operating room consumable name	Consumable cost ($)	Quantity	Total cost
Hip implant	4,500.00	1	4,500.00
Custom hip pack	350.00	1	350.00
Saw blade	55.00	2	110.00
Suture material	18.00	4	72.00

Figure 8.7   Calculating the cost of consumables in the operating room.

Space name	Area (sq ft)	New construction costs per sq ft ($/sq ft)	Useful life (yrs)	Annual construction depreciation per sq ft ($/sq ft)
X-ray room	150	250	15	16.67

Annual maintenance costs per sq ft ($/sq ft)	Annual operating costs (incl. utilities) per sq ft ($/sq ft)	Yearly housekeeping costs per sq ft ($/sq ft)	Real estate value per sq ft ($/sq ft)	Real estate life (yrs)	Yearly real estate cost per sq ft ($/sq ft)	Total annual space cost per square ft ($/sq ft)	Total annual space cost ($)	Availability timeframe	Availability (minutes)	Total annual space cost per minute ($/min)
15	12	7	40	25	1.6	52.27	7840	Normal hours	115,785	0.07

Figure 8.8   Calculating the space costs associated with the radiology suite.

Equipment	Replacement cost	Useful life (years)	Yearly depreciation	Yearly maint. costs (%)	Yearly maint. costs ($)	Equipment cost per year ($/yr)	Availability timeframe	Availability (minutes)	Capacity cost rate ($/min)
X-ray machine	90,000	10	9,000	10%	9,000	18,000	Normal hours	115,785	0.16

Figure 8.9   Costs associated with the x-ray machine.

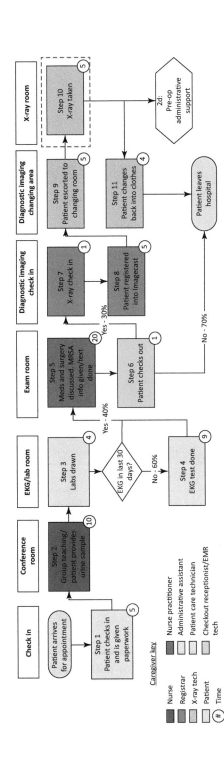

Figure 8.10 Example of Time-Driven Activity-Based Costing process map for a new patient office visit.

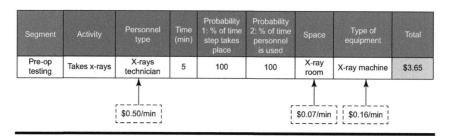

Segment	Activity	Personnel type	Time (min)	Probability 1: % of time step takes place	Probability 2: % of time personnel is used	Space	Type of equipment	Total
Pre-op testing	Takes x-rays	X-rays technician	5	100	100	X-ray room	X-ray machine	$3.65

$0.50/min

$0.07/min $0.16/min

Figure 8.11   Calculating the cost of an x-ray taken in the pre-operative testing segment of the Time-Driven Activity-Based Costing process map.

Segment	Activity	Personnel type	Time (min)	Probability 1: % of time step takes place	Probability 2: % of time personnel is used	Space	Type of equipment	Total
Pre-op testing	X-ray check in	Registrar	1	100	100	Imaging check in		$0.45
Pre-op testing	Patient registered into Imagecast	Registrar	5	100	100	Imaging check in		$2.25
Pre-op testing	Patient escorted to changing room	X-ray technician	5	100	100	Changing area		$2.60
Pre-op testing	Takes x-rays	X-ray technician	5	100	100	X-ray room	X-ray machine	$3.65
Pre-op testing	Patient changes back into clothes	X-ray technician	4	100	100	Changing area		$2.08
Total cost of receiving chest x-ray								$11.03

Figure 8.12   Total cost calculation for patient receiving a chest x-ray.

THE PATIENT CENTERED VALUE SYSTEM: THEORY AND PRACTICE

Chapter 9

The Science behind the Patient Centered Value System: Built on the Shoulders of Giants

> … One new idea leads to another … and so on throughout the course of time, until someone, to whom no one of these ideas was original, combines all together and produces what is justly called a new invention.

Thomas Jefferson

Previous chapters have explained that implementing the Patient Centered Value System will take your organization or practice from its current state of care delivery to the seemingly elusive ideal state as patients and families define it; improve clinical and operational outcomes; help you understand the true cost of delivering healthcare through the full cycle of care; and decrease waste and lower costs while increasing value for patients, families, and organizations. Earlier chapters have also shown that implementing the Patient Centered

Value System generates communities of continuous learning and improvement and involves minimal costs. This chapter explains the scientific and theoretical underpinnings of the Patient Centered Value System, which are significant, have been well researched, are used by many of the most successful organizations today, and have now been intentionally designed for healthcare.

The Patient Centered Value System was built on the work of leaders in the fields of organizational change (including disruptive innovation and change), design sciences and experience-based design, process improvement, psychology, business, marketing, leadership, and economics. They include John Kotter, Tim Brown, Paul Bate and Glenn Robert, Nobel Prize winner Herbert Simon, B. Joseph Pine II and James Gilmore, Clayton Christensen, Jon R. Katzenbach and Douglas K. Smith, Stephen Denning, Ty Montague, Robert S. Kaplan, and Michael Porter.

The Patient Centered Value System integrates all of their approaches—some complementary, some disparate—into a *single tool*. For example, John Kotter's (1996, 2008) groundbreaking work in the field of organizational behavior and change management has made major contributions to the structure of the Patient Centered Value System, particularly his eight steps for leading organizational transformation and culture change. These steps are: (1) establish a sense of urgency; (2) create a guiding coalition; (3) develop a change vision; (4) communicate the vision for buy-in; (5) empower broad-based action; (6) generate short-term wins; (7) never let up; and (8) incorporate changes into the organization's culture.

The work of Kotter and others, which has so profoundly influenced the development of the Patient Centered Value System, is the subject of the first part of this chapter. The second part explains how the Patient Centered Value System has adapted their ideas—in essence, how we borrowed brilliance and built on the shoulders of giants.

***

Collectively, the work of visionaries has influenced the development and refinement of the Patient Centered Value System around four key concepts:

Key Concept 1. Seeing all care as an *experience* through the eyes of patients and families and creating a sense of urgency to drive change.

Key Concept 2. Involving patients, families, and caregivers in co-designing care delivery.

Key Concept 3. Creating a simple approach to determining your own current state and moving toward the ideal while breaking down silos and overcoming expected hurdles.

Key Concept 4. Determining the actual (true) cost to deliver care for any specific medical or surgical condition—and tightly coupling clinical with financial performance—to deliver true value.

Key Concept 1. *Seeing all care as an experience through the eyes of patients and families and creating a sense of urgency to drive change.*

The first key concept of the Patient Centered Value System is based on the work of B. Joseph Pine II and James Gilmore, John Kotter, and Tim Brown. In *The Experience Economy,* Pine and Gilmore (1999) write about **experience-based design**; that is, the overarching importance of a customer's experience while purchasing a good or service. They note that the experience may be even more important, and often more memorable, than the service being provided because it is the experience, rather than the good or service, that engages people's emotions.

Tim Brown's construct of **design thinking** also underpins the Patient Centered Value System. President and CEO of the design and innovation consulting firm, IDEO, Brown (2008, 2009) notes that although after-the-fact information and data such as letters, surveys, and focus groups are important tools for understanding patient and family perceptions of care delivery, they do not provide the *immediacy* required to ignite and sustain a sense of urgency to drive change. According to Brown, it is direct observation that creates an emotional connection that leads to insight—that "ah-ha!" moment. According to Brown (2009), the rationale for keeping the end user (in the case of healthcare, this means patients and families) at the forefront of innovation is that it is only end users who can tell us what they want and need. The strength of design thinking is evident in the implementation phase, which is explained in Key Concept 3.

Key Concept 2. *Involving patients, families, and caregivers in co-designing care delivery.*

The second key concept of the Patient Centered Value System is based in part on the work of Paul Bate and Glenn Robert (2006), who suggest that the patient and family *experience* is equally as important as clinical outcomes and process improvement efforts. They say the challenge is to find a way to understand the experience of care subjectively—at a deep level as patients and families do—which will open the door to effective care redesign, moving the care experience from its current state ever closer to the ideal. Bate and Robert suggest that the design sciences should be the third science of healthcare, after the clinical and process sciences.

Like Pine and Gilmore, Bate and Robert (2006, p. 308) describe experience-based design, defining it not only as an experience, but as "a design process with the goal of making user experience accessible to the designers, to allow them to conceive of designing experiences rather than designing services." They describe a process by which key moments and places that contribute to the user's subjective experience (i.e., touchpoints) should be captured and suggest that "working with the front-line people who bring alive those various touch points in the journey—it is possible to begin designing experiences rather than processes" (Bate and Robert 2006, p. 308).

Bate and Robert (2006) also propose involving patients directly in redesigning care delivery and advise moving past asking them what was good about their experience to seeking details that can be more effectively acted on. To discover the types of experiential details needed for action, the authors draw on the design sciences, "in which the traditional view of the user as a passive recipient of a product or service has begun to give way to the new view of users as integral to the improvement and innovation process" (Bate and Robert 2006, p. 308).

Finally, Bate and Robert (2006) describe a "continuum of patient influence" that starts with the least effective form of influence—that is, complaining—and progresses to increasingly more effective forms of influence, including giving information, listening and responding, consulting and advising, and, finally, experience-based co-design.

Key Concept 3. *Creating a simple approach to determining your own current state and moving toward the ideal while breaking down silos and overcoming expected hurdles.*

The third key concept of the Patient Centered Value System is based on the work of Nobel Prize winner Herbert Simon, Paul Bate and Glenn Robert, Clayton Christensen, John Kotter and Dan Cohen, Stephen Denning, Ty Montague, and Jon R. Katzenbach and Douglas K. Smith, whose work contributed to the implementation phase of disruptive innovation. These experts in their own fields write about the benefits of simplifying and streamlining organizations, and about the kinds of leadership and tools needed to get us there.

According to Simon's (1996) seminal work, *Sciences of the Artificial*, and later interpreted and applied by Bate and Robert (2006), a goal of the design sciences is to systematically and scientifically design approaches that make things better for the end user.

Bate and Robert (2006) suggest that making things better for the end user can best be done by focusing on their experience from the "inside out" as they move through the service and interact with its various parts.

Christensen (1997) writes about the need to break down organizational silos so prevalent in healthcare using what he calls **disruptive innovation theory**. He describes this theory as "the process by which complicated, expensive products and services are transformed into simple, affordable ones" (Christensen 1997, p. 3). Christensen describes the unique hurdles involved in introducing disruptive technologies and processes in organizations and explains the need to understand the current state, or environment, in which they are introduced so these hurdles can be anticipated and overcome.

Kotter and Cohen (2002) advance the idea that silos prevent organizations from acting quickly in a rapidly changing world by destroying trust, preventing communication, and fostering complacency. He notes that silos are best broken down through regular forums in which all viewpoints are represented, where the expectation is that the group's pronouncements will be taken seriously, and where skilled leaders help to drive the change process.

Denning (2005) believes that the role of a leader in breaking down silos—getting people to work together and communicate openly—is facilitated through **storytelling**. Denning champions storytelling as a powerful tool for sharing knowledge and for driving change in organizations. Montague (2013) takes this concept one step further. To Montague, storytelling leads to **"storydoing"** and is vital to organizational change. According to Montague, the benefits of storytelling and storydoing include having a more clearly defined purpose, creating intense customer and employee loyalty, and having "an authenticity and humanity that make a company magnetic," noting that "storydoing is a team sport. You cannot do this alone. You need to build a cross-disciplinary team to accomplish this" (Montague 2013, p. 208).

Katzenbach and Smith (2005) write about the importance of teams, especially **high-performance teams**, to break down silos and meet challenges needing immediate attention. In fact, they believe, high-performance teams both thrive on and are driven by urgent performance challenges. According to Katzenbach and Smith (2005), successful teams depend on having members with complementary skills, a common purpose, a set of common performance goals, a working approach on which all team members agree, and mutual accountability for performance. And while changing organizational culture can be daunting for individuals working alone, teams motivate and reward their members for working to achieve mutually agreed-upon goals.

Key Concept 4. *Determining the actual (true) cost to deliver care for any specific medical or surgical condition—and tightly coupling clinical with financial performance—in order to deliver true value.*

The fourth key concept of the Patient Centered Value System is based on the work of Kaplan and Porter (2011) at the Harvard Business School, who applied Time-Driven Activity-Based Costing (originally developed by Kaplan and Anderson, 2007) as a method for determining the true cost and value (i.e., outcomes achieved per dollar spent) of delivering healthcare over the full cycle of patient care. Time-Driven Activity-Based Costing in the context of the Patient Centered Value System focuses on the care experience from the point of view of the patient and family; defines the beginning and end points of the patient's care, thereby setting the parameters for measurement; maps the patient's journey to identify all of the touchpoints along the way; and measures the amount of time every caregiver (and the patient) spends at each step of the care process. How to use Shadowing plus Time-Driven Activity-Based Costing is described in detail in Chapter 8.

"Borrowing Brilliance"

As Murray (2009) advocates in his book *Borrowing Brilliance,* the Patient Centered Value System has borrowed brilliance from the thought leaders just mentioned. Their work has influenced the way caregivers Shadow patients and families through their care experiences; harness the power of storytelling and storydoing; form and sustain high-performance care teams; and overcome the expected hurdles to organizational change.

Shadowing Patients and Families

As Nancy Byrd, Chief Nursing Officer at fictional Exemplar Memorial Hospital says in Chapter 1, "Starbucks takes an impersonal experience and makes it personal; healthcare takes a personal experience and makes it impersonal…." Pine and Gilmore's (1996) concept of experience-based design informs the goals and terminology of the Patient Centered Value System as an approach to viewing all care as an *experience.* The Patient Centered Value System uses the essential, powerful tool of Shadowing to turn an impersonal healthcare encounter into a personal experience for patients and families. Building on the work of Bate and Robert (2006), Shadowing enables caregivers to see the care experience through the eyes of patients and families and to understand, perhaps for the first time, the care experience "from the inside out." Care Experience Flow Mapping, which is vital to recording caregivers' observations during Shadowing, is also based on the work of Pine and Gilmore (1996).

Influenced by the work of Bate and Robert (2006), Kotter (1996, 2008), and Brown (2008), Shadowing moves us away from the least effective form of patient engagement and moves us toward engaging patients and families most effectively, as full partners in co-designing care delivery. Fixing things after receiving a complaint can be difficult. The Patient Centered

Value System enables caregivers to see patients' and families' care experiences in real time; to see how patients and families react to their care experiences; and to hear and note their concerns, comments, and suggestions as they move through each stage of their care experience.

It is the real-time observation afforded by Shadowing that sparks an emotional connection between caregivers and patients and families, creating and sustaining a sense of urgency to drive the changes patients and families say they want and need. This emotional connection leads to insight and an understanding of, and commitment to, the need for immediate and sustained transformational change. According to Kotter (2008, p. 8), feelings of urgency "quite naturally lead to behavior in which people are alert and proactive, in which they constantly scan the environment around them, both inside and outside their organizations, looking for information relevant to success and survival….With a true sense of urgency, people want to come to work each day ready to cooperate energetically and responsively with intelligent initiatives from others. And they do."

Sustaining innovation and an ongoing sense of urgency to drive change are built into the Patient Centered Value System by requiring each Working Group and Project Team to conduct periodic re-Shadowing. New opportunities to move care ever closer to the ideal state are identified by re-Shadowing over time.

Shadowing to Determine Actual (True) Costs

Shadowing is the linchpin in the Patient Centered Value System, the single tool that enables caregivers to see the care experience from the perspective of patients and families, and enables providers and organizations to discern the actual, or true, costs of delivering healthcare for any medical or surgical condition over the full cycle of care. Based on the work of Kaplan and Porter (2011), Time-Driven Activity-Based

Costing in the Patient Centered Value System uses Shadowing to accurately identify the care pathway and the four buckets of resources that must be examined in order to calculate the true cost of care delivery: personnel, space, equipment, and consumables. As Chapter 8 explains, Time-Driven Activity-Based Costing can be used to efficiently identify the actual cost and cost drivers to deliver care (as opposed to charges or reimbursements).

By linking the Patient and Family Centered Care (PFCC) Methodology and Shadowing with Time-Driven Activity-Based Costing, Shadowing enables high-performance implementation teams to put process improvements into place to drive down costs while protecting and/or improving patient and family experiences and clinical outcomes. Such integration is at the heart of the Patient Centered Value System.

Storytelling and Storydoing

The Patient Centered Value System channels the work of Denning (2005) on storytelling and Montague (2013) on storydoing as critical business tools and as starting points for sparking thoughts and igniting change about the present (current state) and the future (the ideal). Storytelling is fundamental to the Patient Centered Value System, in which caregivers observe and then formulate patients' and families' stories through Shadowing; invite patients, families, and caregivers to tell their stories when they share their thoughts and feelings about their experience of care; and, of course, Working Groups use storytelling to write the story of ideal care as if they, themselves, were patients and family members. Through storytelling, caregivers put themselves in the shoes of patients and families, empathizing in a new way with their care experiences. Stories are both directive and aspirational. Storytelling, like Shadowing, helps us to understand both the current state and the ideal state as patients and families see it. In writing the ideal story, Working Groups are inspired to implement projects to close the gaps between the current state of care delivery and the ideal.

In the Patient Centered Value System, as Montague (2013) writes, storytelling leads seamlessly to storydoing. While the story is both the true current state and the idealized future state, the "doing" is what happens when high-performance care teams such as Working Groups, which include representatives from every touchpoint of the care experience, create a shared vision of the ideal and have the tools to bring the vision to life. In "doing," the gaps are closed between the current and the ideal state, making the ideal state a reality. As Montague asserts, storytelling and storydoing can be learned, replicated, and spread from one area to the rest of the organization.

High-Performance Care Teams

Guiding Councils, Working Groups, and Project Teams are high-performance care teams, a concept influenced by the work of Katzenbach and Smith (2005) and John Kotter (1996, 2008). Creating and sustaining high-performance teams is a function of shared vision and goals; a sense that change is needed here and now; shared leadership and accountability; continuous learning and development; a customer (i.e., patient and family) focus; and the ability to gather, use, and learn from feedback and data.

The shared vision of Guiding Councils, Working Groups, and Project Teams enables team members to work toward mutually agreed-upon goals. As recommended by Katzenbach and Smith (2005), team members work to achieve goals they themselves, rather than someone at the top of the organization, have set. In the Patient Centered Value System, leadership responsibilities are shared among Guiding Council co-leaders, Working Group co-leaders, and Project Team co-leaders. Working Group members, whose skills and areas of expertise are complementary, come from multiple areas of the organization.

Successful teams meet frequently to review current performance and develop improvement plans using clear performance measures. It is important and highly recommended that Working Groups meet weekly in order to maintain their focus, stay on track, and continually move projects forward. Developing clear baseline measures and goals for Patient Centered Value System projects help Project Teams to track progress and evaluate their effectiveness.

Overcoming Expected Hurdles

The Patient Centered Value System is also based on Clayton Christensen's (1997) disruptive innovation theory, which served as a guide to developing a new process of care delivery that would be more streamlined and less expensive than the old one. The key would be to introduce a process in which simplicity and low-tech solutions would replace complexity. Christensen's (1997) work was instrumental in helping to prepare for hurdles and to strategize the best ways to overcome them. Christensen (1997) taught the overarching importance of taking into account the environment in which an innovation is introduced, the significance of not being contrite in introducing the innovation, and the crucial need for support from the CEO and other leaders.

The Patient Centered Value System started small, with one care experience, and was then applied to one additional care experience, and then another, as the hurdles in each version were recognized and overcome. This method of identifying and overcoming hurdles along the way enabled the Patient Centered Value System to be disseminated widely, spreading through word of mouth and at an increasing pace over the years since its inception. There have been more than 65 active Working Groups at UPMC, some of which have been active for many years.

Conclusion

Foundational thought leaders such as Kotter and Cohen, Pine and Gilmore, Brown, Bate and Robert, Simon, Christensen, Denning, Montague, Kaplan and Porter, and Katzenbach and Smith cross disciplinary boundaries. Their multidisciplinary ideas have been intentionally adapted for healthcare and are reflected throughout the Patient Centered Value System, completely integrated and, in the background, always at work.

Dozens of healthcare organizations outside of UPMC have adopted the Patient Centered Value System, reflecting growing interest not only nationwide but internationally. Chapter 10 suggests ways that organizations can add the Patient Centered Value System to other improvement methods they may already be using, such as Lean, to accelerate the pace of improvement. Finally, Chapter 11 explains how organizations have used the Patient Centered Value System to improve patients' and families' experiences of care, clinical outcomes, and population health.

References

Bate, P, Robert, G. 2006 Oct. Experience-based design: From redesigning the system around the patient to co-designing services with the patient. *Qual Saf Health Care* 15(5):307–310.

Brown, T. 2009. *Change by Design: How Design Thinking Transforms Organizations and Inspires Innovation*. New York: HarperCollins.

Brown, T. 2008 June. Design thinking. *Har Bus Rev* 85–92. http://hbr.org/2008/06/design-thinking/.

Christensen, CM. 1997. *The Innovator's Dilemma: When New Technologies Cause Great Firms to Fail*. Boston, MA: Harvard Business Press.

Denning, S. 2005. *The Leader's Guide to Storytelling: Mastering the Art and Discipline of Business Narrative*. San Francisco, CA: Jossey-Bass.

Kaplan, RS, Anderson, SR. 2007. *Time-Driven Activity-Based Costing: A Simpler and More Powerful Path to Higher Profits*. Boston, MA: Harvard Business School Publishing Corp.

Kaplan, RS, Porter, ME. 2011 Sept. The big idea: How to solve the cost crisis in healthcare. *Harv Bus Rev* 47–64. https://hbr.org/2011/09/how-to-solve-the-cost-crisis-in-health-care.

Katzenbach, JR, Smith, D. 2005 July. The discipline of teams. *Harv Bus Rev*. 162–171 http://hbr.org/2005/07/the-discipline-of-teams/ar/pr.

Kotter, JP. 1996. *Leading Change*. Boston, MA: Harvard Business Press.

Kotter, JP. 2008. *A Sense of Urgency*. Boston, MA: Harvard Business Press.

Kotter, JP, Cohen, DS. 2002. *The Heart of Change: Real-Life Stories of How People Change their Organizations*. Boston, MA: John P. Kotter and Deloitte Consulting LLC.

Montague, T. 2013. *True Story: How to Combine Story and Action to Transform Your Business*. Boston, MA: Harvard Business Press.

Murray, DK. 2009. *Borrowing Brilliance: The Six Steps to Business Innovation by Building on the Ideas of Others*. New York: Gotham Books.

Pine, JB, Gilmore, JH. 1999. *The Experience Economy: Work is Theatre and Every Business a Stage*. Boston, MA: Harvard Business School Press.

Simon, HA. 1996. *The Sciences of the Artificial*. Boston, MA: Massachusetts Institute of Technology Press.

Chapter 10

Patient Centered Value System + Lean or Other Process Improvement Approaches = Rapid Improvement

> If you want others ... to be on this journey with you ... teach the path both by imparting knowledge and walking the path yourself, and by having all the leadership team walking the path.
>
> **Patricia Gabow, M.D.**

Process improvement approaches such as Lean (Deblois and Lpanto 2016), Six Sigma (Kaplan 2013), and the Toyota Production System (DiGioia et al. 2015) play an important role in transforming healthcare by shining a laser-like focus on waste and perfecting processes that can exhaust ever-scarcer resources. Many healthcare organizations that have invested time and money in these approaches are also becoming

increasingly interested in the Patient Centered Value System (Bisognano and Kenney 2012). We suggest that integrating the Patient Centered Value System with these other approaches, which are complementary, can quicken the pace of improvement. This chapter explains the similarities and differences between the Patient Centered Value System and other process improvement approaches such as Lean; the ways in which adding the Patient Centered Value System to Lean can speed the pace of improvement and healthcare delivery redesign; how integrating the Patient Centered Value System with other process improvement approaches will enhance your ability to address what's important to patients, families, caregivers, and your organization; and how your organization can adopt the Patient Centered Value System quickly, at a minimal cost.

Similarities between the Patient Centered Value System and Other Process Improvement Approaches

If you've been using Lean, Six Sigma, the Toyota Production System, or other process improvement approaches, you may be interested to learn that these share a number of overlapping principles and features with the Patient Centered Value System. Like other process improvement tools, the Patient Centered Value System seeks to fundamentally transform the way a product or service is provided and to embed a new way of thinking—and behaving—into the "DNA" of an organization. The Patient Centered Value System, like the process improvement tools you may already be using, is methodical and replicable, based on the science of improvement (DiGioia et al. 2010), and has built-in sustainability. Each of these approaches advocates going to where the work is done. They use time studies and flow maps to identify the true current state and toolkits for implementing process change. Each of these approaches crosses departments in order to tap into the power of cross-functionality to create high-performance teams. Combining the Patient Centered Value System with other process improvement tools can help you create a more comprehensive approach to improving care delivery (DiGioia et al. 2010).

Differences between the Patient Centered Value System and Lean or Similar Process Improvement Approaches

The differences between the Patient Centered Value System, Lean, and similar process improvement approaches can spark a powerful synergy, leading to rapid improvement when used within a single organization. Unlike other approaches, the Patient Centered Value System focuses on the patient and family in collaboration with providers to guide improvement efforts in *each segment* of the patient and family experience throughout their healthcare journey, seeking to identify every opportunity to move from the current state to the ideal. This broad focus necessarily expands the array of improvement opportunities being addressed simultaneously as well as the number of staff members who have a chance to be involved.

Unlike other process improvement approaches, the Patient Centered Value System includes the family as well as the patient as the equal focus of improvement efforts. The patient and family form a single unit in terms of health and wellness; thus, the Patient Centered Value System seeks to optimize the experience of patients *and* families.

Equally important in the Patient Centered Value System is Time-Driven Activity-Based Costing: its focus is on determining the actual (true) cost of healthcare, and helping to reduce costs and increase value while protecting and improving clinical outcomes and patient and family experiences (DiGioia et al. 2016; Millenson et al. 2013; DiGioia and Greenhouse 2011). (A manual for how to use this approach is presented in Chapter 8.)

While improving the care of patients is the primary goal of all process improvement, Lean and the Patient Centered Value System differ in their approach to meeting this goal. For example, Lean focuses on the real-time observation of processes to reduce waste and inefficiencies; the Patient Centered Value System focuses on the real-time observation of patients and families by Shadowing them through their care experiences. Like Lean, the Patient Centered Value System reveals opportunities to eliminate waste and inefficiencies. But, unlike Lean, the Patient Centered Value System guides organizations in eliminating waste step-by-step (see Chapter 8) while identifying opportunities to improve care delivery as articulated by patients and families (DiGioia et al. 2015).

Lean emphasizes managing processes and "things" (e.g., creating more efficient medication dispersal methods, reducing wasted footsteps for care providers, improving blood tube labeling efficiency and accuracy, and so on); the Patient Centered Value System emphasizes (1) the transformation of performance, with a primary focus on transforming the care experiences of patients and families; and (2) the tight coupling of clinical and financial performance to deliver true value. This dual focus of the Patient Centered Value System leads organically to the perfecting of processes and non-human components of care delivery while at the same time leading to performance improvement.

Shadowing

Shadowing is the single tool in the Patient Centered Value System that accomplishes multiple goals. First, Shadowing enables patients and families both to be engaged in their care and to co-design the care experience; creates a powerful emotional connection between caregivers and patients and families; and motivates caregivers to transform care experiences from the current state to the ideal. The powerful emotional investment that caregivers feel as a result of Shadowing the care experiences of patients and families distinguishes the Patient Centered Value System from other process improvement approaches (DiGioia and Greenhouse 2011).

Second, Shadowing as used in Time-Driven Activity-Based Costing of the Patient Centered Value System accurately identifies the care pathway and the four buckets of resources that must be examined in order to calculate the true cost of care delivery for any medical or surgical condition: personnel, space, equipment, and consumables. Time-Driven Activity-Based Costing can be used to efficiently identify the actual cost and cost drivers to deliver care (as opposed to charges or reimbursements) in each segment of care and over the full cycle of care (DiGioia et al. 2016). (See Chapter 8 for details.)

Performance Improvement

The Patient Centered Value System is both a pathway to process improvement and a pathway to *performance* improvement: high-performance implementation teams put process improvements into place to reduce costs and increase value while protecting and improving patient and family experiences and clinical outcomes.

Unlike other process improvement approaches, the Patient Centered Value System breaks down organizational silos so prevalent in healthcare by creating cross-functional high-performance care teams known as Working Groups. A representative from every touchpoint identified during Shadowing is included as an equal member of the Working Group. Covering the full cycle of care, the Working Group may include representatives from pre-hospital, outpatient, inpatient, procedural, and post-hospital segments of the healthcare continuum.

Caregivers who are part of a Working Group together address the entire care experience in a way that a single caregiver, or caregivers working in single departments, cannot. Weekly Working Group meetings provide a forum for caregivers from disparate parts of the organization to interact and problem-solve, usually for the first time, sharing a common purpose, clear performance goals, and an agreed-upon working approach. Working Group members hold each other mutually accountable for their performance and are driven by each other's sense of urgency to drive change. They set for themselves clear and compelling performance challenges, celebrate their wins, re-group to take on new challenges, and re-Shadow over time in an effort to continually see the current state of any care experience from the patient's and family's point of view.

In organizations using Lean or similar approaches, improvement projects are usually prioritized by hospital or practice leadership. In organizations using the Patient Centered Value System, improvement projects are prioritized by what patients and families say is important to them. Using Lean together with the Patient Centered Value System enables organizations to drive improvement from the "top down" *and* from the "bottom up," as multiple staff representing varying levels, roles, and responsibilities see the care experience from the patient's and family's point of view.

The Patient Centered Value System changes the culture by engaging the emotions of caregivers from every part of the organization. This emotional engagement leads caregivers to commit to align their goals for change with their performance, both individually and collectively. Our emotional connection to the need for change, not someday but *now*, is what changes the culture and inspires performance improvement, so that continuous improvement becomes woven into the fabric of the organization (Kotter 2007, 2012; Katzenbach and Smith 1993). In the Patient Centered Value System, caregivers feel an emotional commitment to "walk the talk," living and working this system of care delivery in every instance, every day.

As Kate Starr, Scott Long, Jackie Jordan, and other characters in our story found, caregivers' insights resulting from using the Patient Centered Value System motivate care transformation in a way that traditional observations and reviewing survey data and reports simply do not.

Integrating the Patient Centered Value System with Lean and Similar Process Improvement Approaches

While Lean and similar process improvement approaches can take time and training to master, the Patient Centered Value System can be implemented quickly and is easy to learn. For organizations interested in creating synergy by integrating the Patient Centered Value System with Lean or similar process improvement approaches, we recommend the following:

■ Add Shadowing to Value Stream Mapping (Lean's 2 P and 3 P events) and Rapid Improvement Events by adding team members to Lean improvement teams; this will provide a more complete picture of the patient and family care experience.
■ Elevate improving the patient's and family's experience of care as a goal that is equally important as eliminating waste. Seeing the "ideal state" from the patient's and family's perspective can lead to new, simpler processes that improve care, improve the experience, and lower costs.
■ Have staff who have had Lean training, as well as those who haven't, identify a process they care deeply about and Shadow that process, both from the patient's and family's point of view as well as from the perspective of Time-Driven Activity-Based Costing. Through Shadowing, staff members will see care through the eyes of patients

and families and will learn which costs can be saved as they work to improve clinical outcomes and experiences.

■ Include Patient Centered Value System stories and metrics on Managing for Daily Improvement boards. These bring data boards to life and engage staff around what they care about most—the improved well-being and experiences of patients and families.

■ Consider incorporating the Patient Centered Value System as the overarching approach to transforming care delivery, thereby taking advantage of the language and the emotional hook of direct observation that engages caregivers in driving change. This can be done by forming a Guiding Council, Working Groups, and Project Teams, and championing their efforts (as described in Chapters 1 through 6). Through this process, you may see that the Patient Centered Value System aligns well with the mission of your organization.

Conclusion

The Patient Centered Value System complements Lean and similar process improvement approaches by engaging patients and families in redesigning care delivery, broadening the identification of opportunities to transform care and create value, and deepening the engagement and emotional investment of the entire care team in addressing these opportunities. Integrating the Patient Centered Value System with other approaches will enable you to bridge the "top down" with the "bottom up." For organizations already committed to Lean process improvement, adding the Patient Centered Value System will quicken the pace of improvement by focusing the efforts of all caregivers on the goal of creating ideal care delivery, broadly defined.

References

Bisognano, M, Kenney, C. 2012. *Pursuing the Triple Aim: Seven Innovators Show the Way to Better Care, Better Health, and Lower Costs*. San Francisco: John Wiley & Sons.

Deblois, S, Lpanto, L. 2016 March. Lean and six sigma in acute care: A systematic review of reviews. *Int J Health Care Qual Assur* 29(2):192–208.

DiGioia, AM, Greenhouse, PK. 2011. Patient and family shadowing: Creating urgency for change. *J Nurs Adm* 41(1):23–28.

DiGioia, AM, Greenhouse, PK, Giarrusso, ML, Kress, JM. 2016 January. Determining the true cost to deliver total hip and knee replacement over the full cycle of care: Preparing for bundling and reference-based pricing. *J Arthroplasty* 31:1–6.

DiGioia, AM, Lorenz, H, Greenhouse, PK. 2010. A patient-centered model to improve metrics without cost increase. *J Nurs Adm* 40(12):540–546.

Kaplan, GS. 2013 Spring. Pursuing the perfect patient experience. *Front Health Serv Manag* 29(3):16–27.

Katzenbach, JR, Smith, DK. 1993. *The Wisdom of Teams: Creating the High Performance Organization*. Cambridge, MA: Harvard Business School Press.

Kotter, JP. 2007. Leading change: Why transformation efforts fail. *Har Bus Rev* 96–103. https://hbr.org/2007/01/leading-change-why-transformation-efforts-fail.

Kotter, JP. 2012. Accelerate! *Har Bus Rev* 44–58. https://hbr.org/2012/11/accelerate.

Millenson, ML, DiGioia, AM, Greenhouse, PK, Swieskowski, D. 2013. Turning patient centeredness from ideal to real: Lessons from 2 success stories. *J Ambul Care Manage* 36(4):319–334.

Chapter 11

The Patient Centered Value System in Practice

Change is inevitable. Change is constant.

Benjamin Disraeli

Adopting the Patient Centered Value System, an approach to improving the patient and family experience of care while improving financial performance, is the right thing to do for patients, families, caregivers, and organizations. But sometimes, doing the right thing is insufficient incentive to get everyone on board. How, then, can you introduce the Patient Centered Value System and sustain this new healthcare operating system in your organization? One way is by seeing how other organizations are using the Patient Centered Value System and the results they have achieved.

This chapter describes how a number of hospitals have implemented the Shadowing and Patient and Family Centered Care (PFCC) Methodology components of the Patient Centered Value System. This chapter also explains how some are using Shadowing and Time-Driven Activity-Based Costing (the third component of the Patient Centered Value System, described in detail in Chapter 8) to determine the actual (true) costs of healthcare through the full cycle of care for any medical or surgical condition.

Patient Partnerships = Engagement = Better Outcomes

The Problem

There is a growing body of evidence that patients who are engaged in their care have better clinical outcomes, better care experiences, lower healthcare costs (Cosgrove et al. 2013; Langel 2013; Roseman et al. 2013; Carman et al. 2013), and improved healthcare quality and patient safety (Langel 2013) compared with patients who are not actively involved in their care. Patients who are engaged in their care tend to ask questions, participate in shared decision making, serve on patient and family advisory councils, and participate in the design and execution of quality improvement projects (Carman et al. 2013). Hospital policies that enable families to be present 24 hours a day, nursing change of shift reports that take place at the patient's bedside, and patient centered discharge planning are examples of practices that foster patient and family engagement and improved outcomes (Carman et al. 2013).

Yet, although research demonstrates that engaging patients in their care leads to a range of improved outcomes for patients, families, and organizations, engaging patients and families in their care productively and organization-wide is still the exception rather than the rule. Healthcare organizations can move to a culture that promotes patient and family engagement and a practice that fosters it by implementing the Patient Centered Value System.

The Real-World Solution

Patients and families need to know who their caregivers are and be able to interact with them effectively in order to be engaged in their care, but patients and families arriving at **UPMC Presbyterian Hospital** for trauma care didn't always know who their doctors were, when their doctors (and which ones) would conduct rounds, or what their plan of care was (which seemed to change depending on which doctor they spoke to). Far from feeling engaged in their care, patients and families felt anxious and confused. And patients and families weren't the only ones who were confused. Nurses, residents, therapists, and other caregivers were often confused by the wide array of doctors (e.g., hospitalists, surgeons, and specialists) and their sometimes contradictory or confusing plans of care. As shown in Chapter 6 of our story, caregivers at UPMC Presbyterian listened to what patients and families (and caregivers) had to say about the current state and used the PFCC Methodology to transform the trauma care experience from the current state to the ideal as patients and families define it.

Caregivers at UPMC Presbyterian formed a Trauma Working Group. They Shadowed the trauma care experience to see the current state from the patient's and family's point of view, and then wrote the ideal story of the trauma care experience as patients and families defined it. The ideal story served as their touchstone and road map, expressing the need for patients and families to see the same doctors throughout their hospital stay, regardless of their location in the hospital. The ideal story also made it clear that patients and families wanted their nurses, doctors, and other caregivers to communicate closely with each other, wanted to participate in information sharing and decision making, wanted to better understand and contribute to their plan of care, and wanted their caregivers to communicate with them regularly by conducting rounds at predictable times.

The Working Group formed a Trauma Restructuring Team to close the gaps between the current state and the ideal. Closing the gaps involved assigning providers to one of three care teams—Black, Gold, or Blue. Each trauma patient who enters the Emergency Department is now assigned to one of these teams, and team members see this patient and family wherever they go in the hospital throughout their stay until the time of discharge. Each team comprises an attending physician, a senior resident/fellow, a junior resident, and an intern or mid-level practitioner.

In addition, the Trauma Restructuring Team made changes to daily patient rounds, making them team based rather than location based; restructured the morning report; assigned specific roles and responsibilities to members of each team; established predictable lines of communication between team members and with patients and families; established call schedules; worked within the constraints of resident schedules; and explained the new procedures to all hospital nursing units.

By being responsive to the expressed needs of patients and families, this project has improved the continuity of care, improved communication with patients and families, improved caregiver satisfaction, and has been associated with improved discharge times.

University Hospital, North Staffordshire, England, is one of the largest hospitals in the United Kingdom, is a designated trauma center, and serves a local population of 500,000. University Hospital has one of the highest admission rates for asthma among children in England, with 100–120 children arriving in the Emergency Department with asthma each month. Despite the existence of local and national clinical guidelines for asthma treatment, caregivers and administrators at University Hospital knew that variations existed in asthma management and discharge planning, and many caregivers did not feel confident about their ability to treat asthma.

In an effort to improve and standardize asthma care for children and their families, University Hospital began to implement the PFCC Methodology. Administrators, caregivers, and patients and families formed a Guiding Council, Working Group, and Project Teams to help them understand the current state of asthma care, envision the ideal state, and implement projects to close the gaps between them.

They used Shadowing and Care Experience Flow Mapping, wrote their shared vision of the ideal care experience, and selected improvement projects in response to what patients and families said was most important to them. As a result, Project Teams chose to focus on ensuring that caregivers were motivated and competent; that clinical care processes, communication, and information sharing was excellent; that the hospital environment meets patient and family needs; and that patients and families are consistently treated with dignity and respect.

To address families' need for motivated and competent staff, a Project Team developed a questionnaire for caregivers about their self-confidence in treating asthma, and then held one-on-one asthma care training sessions to improve their confidence, knowledge, and skills. The Project Team then surveyed caregivers about their confidence in treating asthma after the training.

In response to patients' and families' expressed needs for excellent clinical care processes, communication, and information sharing, Project Teams created an asthma algorithm, which set out the treatment pathway for patients presenting with asthma. They also created an "asthma clock," a visual tool that enables children and parents to note the timing of the care they receive alongside the ideal treatment scenario. Families are encouraged to use this asthma clock to make enquiries of staff if the care isn't following the ideal pathway. Project Teams also developed a respiratory admission packet containing a personal asthma action plan, an asthma clock questionnaire (which asks children and parents when caregivers provided specific types of care), and a discharge summary sheet to help families better manage their children's asthma at home. Project Teams also developed an information sheet to tell families what to expect while they're in the hospital and a poster-like "tree" for bulletin board posting on which patients and families can write comments about their asthma care experience.

Responding to the need for an environment that better serves patients, families, and caregivers, Project Teams collected patient and family stories; developed a Shadowing packet for caregivers; established links with university medical and nursing students; improved signage; and launched an Asthma Active website.

To address the need to treat patients and families with dignity and respect, Project Teams developed patient and family surveys; convened patient and family focus groups; created surveys for caregivers; and reported the findings of all surveys and the comments tree to the Working Group, enabling Project Teams to continue to close the gaps between the current state and the ideal.

Project Teams have undertaken additional caregiver training in asthma management and caregivers' confidence in managing asthma has grown. Patients have reported caregivers' increasing interest in and enthusiasm for managing asthma. Ongoing projects include developing an asthma library, an exercise program aimed at patients with asthma, and new patient information resources. There are also plans for the development of an online support group for parents and an interactive Internet application for the management of asthma (PFCC Team, University Hospital of North Staffordshire).

The city of Walsall, England, has a population of 67,000 children, 6,000 of whom have asthma and another 600 of whom are diagnosed with asthma each year. Short-term stays for children who arrived at **Walsall Manor Hospital** with asthma attacks had increased every year for 10 years. Caregivers believed that many children admitted to the hospital could have been managed in primary care, and that 90 percent could have been treated effectively at home if families had known what to do. Yet, hospital audits of pediatric asthma management showed that only 50 percent of patients and families received interventions to promote asthma management at home, including information booklets, instructions on inhaler use, and an asthma plan at discharge. And fewer than

30 percent of patients and families were advised to visit their pediatricians following discharge.

After the death of a child following an asthma attack, caregivers recognized that their management of asthma needed improvement. For example, they needed to pay particular attention to the anxieties of patients and families and improve communication among caregivers. Later the same year, Walsall Manor Hospital implemented the PFCC Methodology to engage caregivers, patients, and families in co-designing a new asthma care pathway; transform the admissions and discharge process; reduce unplanned admissions and readmissions; and improve the patient and family journey and care experience.

Shadowing, Care Experience Flow Mapping, and patient and family questionnaires, focus groups, and interviews showed the Guiding Council, Working Group, and Project Teams the current state of pediatric asthma care from the patient's and family's point of view: signage was poor and patient resources were not easily accessible; the environment was sterile and unwelcoming; patients and families were not always listened to and their anxieties were not always adequately addressed; treatments often differed from one area and provider to another; the patient's and family's journey through the pediatric assessment unit could be disjointed and slow; patients and families were not given a clear indication of what would happen and when, which often left them feeling frustrated and confused; and patients and families were given limited discharge information, which resulted in an inability to adequately manage their child's asthma at home, increasing the risk for readmission.

To transform the admissions and discharge process for patients and families and to address their concerns about not knowing what to expect during the asthma care process, the Working Group—with significant input from patients and families—created an evidence-based management tool called an Asthma Plan, tailored for each child. The Asthma Plan is an integrated care pathway for caregivers designed to ensure that patients and families receive consistent, high-quality care throughout the hospital.

To ensure that the discharge process begins at the time of admission, Project Teams created a four-part evidence-based discharge package that promotes asthma management by the patient and family and ensures continuity of care with the child's primary care doctor. The discharge package, co-designed with patients and families, ensures that patients are clinically ready for discharge; that families feel able to take care of their child at home; that the patient is competent in using the asthma inhaler; that the patient is given an asthma self-management plan, printed advice about how to take their medication and use their inhaler, a peak expiratory flow rate meter, diary, and medication; and that before discharge the patient is given a follow-up appointment with a doctor or nurse either in the community or in the hospital.

To address additional concerns expressed by patients and families, Project Teams created an illustrated, child-friendly Journey Map to help orient patients and families to the asthma care experience and chart their progress every step of the way; introduced clear signage; decorated the pediatric unit to be more welcoming and child friendly; created a welcome package for families to inform them of all the resources available in the hospital; and instituted mandatory training for nurses and doctors, along with a clinical competencies checklist for all caregivers, to ensure their confidence in managing a child's asthma symptoms.

To improve the pediatric experience, the Working Group reduced waiting times and introduced a Rapid Access Clinic and specialty multidisciplinary clinics for allergy and asthma.

As a result of these projects, patients now receive standardized, evidence-based asthma care; caregivers' confidence in their ability to deliver appropriate asthma care has increased; and more than 80 percent of patients and families now receive evidence-based treatment and discharge information, compared to 4 percent when the project began (Abdalla et al. 2013).

Alder Hey Children's Hospital, Liverpool, England, has one of the busiest children's departments in Europe, with 68,000 admissions per year. One of the most common reasons children come to Alder Hey is for treatment of acute abdominal pain. A number of parents lodged serious complaints about their children's care, the root causes of which hospital administration wanted to understand and address.

Working with parents, caregivers at Alder Hey launched the PFCC Methodology to better understand the current state, generate a shared vision of the ideal, and close the gaps between the two. Shadowing and Care Experience Flow Mapping, along with patient and family stories, revealed the current state: Alder Hey did not have an existing pathway in place to treat children with severe abdominal pain; the time between admission and a decision about the need for surgery could take more than six hours; the delivery of care for abdominal pain among caregivers was inconsistent; and communication with patients and families was often inadequate.

When the Working Group wrote their story of ideal care, their shared vision of the ideal state emerged: this included timely diagnosis and treatment, effective pain management, rapid decisions about the need for surgery, the communication of adequate and appropriate information to patients and families, and a positive care experience for children, families, and caregivers.

To go from the current state to the ideal, Project Teams developed a multi-professional acute abdominal pain pathway setting out clearly the ideal treatment scenario for people presenting with acute abdominal pain. They created a surgical decision unit to ensure that opinions about the need for surgery can be made quickly.

As a result of implementing the PFCC Methodology, the average time for a child to be seen by the surgical team was reduced to less than two hours. The average length of stay for acute surgical patients was reduced from five to two days. The percentage of patients who said their pain was well managed improved from 48 percent to 100 percent. Ninety-five percent of families said their overall waiting time was what they expected or less, compared to 45 percent before the PFCC Methodology was introduced. Eighty-six percent of families, compared with 28 percent at baseline, said they felt well informed (Minford et al. 2013).

The Dubowitz Children's Neuromuscular Centre at Great Ormond Street Hospital for Children, London, is a national outpatient service providing clinical assessment, diagnostic services, and advice on treatment and rehabilitation for boys with muscular dystrophy. The Great Ormond Street Hospital houses a clinic for children with Duchenne muscular dystrophy—a severe, life-limiting disease that affects boys and results in progressive muscle weakness. Treatment depends on coordination among members of a multidisciplinary team including physiotherapists, dieticians, nursing specialists, family care advisors, consultants, and lung physiologists, as well as caregivers conducting bone density testing and heart scanning.

Great Ormond Street Hospital launched the PFCC Methodology to improve the care experience of boys with Duchenne muscular dystrophy and their families. A Guiding Council and Working Group—in collaboration with families—used Shadowing, Care Experience Flow Mapping, and parent questionnaires to determine the current state, which they found to be as follows: each time patients and families come to Great Ormond Street Hospital they have several hours of multiple appointments. The fact that they often travel from areas outside of London makes these visits particularly stressful. Therefore, avoiding delays—the ideal state—is essential to help reduce stress levels that are already high due to the nature of the disease and the complexity of the clinical pathway.

To transform the current state to the ideal, Project Teams created a new appointments schedule; developed clinic preparation packages for appointments to ensure the medical team has a full clinical history for each patient; engaged volunteers to help patients and families navigate the clinic to get to their appointments on time and to provide play activities for children; telephoned families before their appointments to confirm their attendance; created a text alert system to remind them of their appointments and reduce non-attendance; developed a more realistic appointment schedule for patients and families; created a single-page appointment letter to consolidate all appointments into one document; and developed an updated hard copy plan to give patients and families when they arrive at the clinic, which provides current team contact details and information about appointments. In addition, the Working Group, in collaboration with patients and families, designed a family information and communication package that is given to all new patients, and developed a new web page providing resources for all patients with Duchenne muscular dystrophy and their families.

As a result of these efforts, 91 percent of families attending the clinic now report receiving a care plan on arrival compared to 25 percent when the project began; 90 percent of families report waiting less than 30 minutes compared to 58 percent at baseline; more than 80 percent report that clinic appointment coordination is good or very good; and more than 90 percent of families report that their children's concerns are listened to and their management plan is explained in a way they understand (Manzur et al. 2013).

The Royal United Hospital, Bath, England, provides acute treatment and care for approximately 500,000 people in Bath and surrounding areas. Because Shadowing and the PFCC Methodology can be used to benefit any "end user"—including patients, families, and caregivers—caregivers at Royal United Hospital decided to implement this methodology to help them improve their delivery of care at the end of life. Caregivers at Royal United Hospital recognized the need to improve their end of life care and communication, both with each other and with patients and families during this difficult time.

Specifically, caregivers wanted to understand the experience of patients and families, as well as their own experiences and reactions, at the end of life. Caregivers wanted to be able to identify when a patient is approaching the end of life at an earlier stage, help them manage the uncertainties they and their families face, and provide appropriate support. Caregivers wanted to have earlier conversations with patients and families about the uncertainty of the illness and future care; improve their communications skills with patients and families at the end of life; document clear medical plans and conversations they have with patients and families in the notes so this information can be shared; see that a patient's end of life care wishes are met; and improve the coordination of care.

Caregivers at Royal United Hospital implemented the PFCC Methodology to achieve these goals through a global Institute for Healthcare Improvement (IHI) initiative called The Conversation Project. As a result of Shadowing, Care Experience Flow Mapping, focus groups, and one-on-one conversations with caregivers, the Working Group saw the current state of end of life care: they were not confident in their ability to have conversations with dying patients and their families unless death was imminent; nurses often felt uncomfortable voicing their opinions to doctors about when to withdraw treatment; junior doctors felt unsupported in their decisions regarding when to treat and when to maintain comfort; caregivers commented on a lack of clear decisions or documentation in the medical notes, which was especially problematic when they were on call at night and on weekends; there was a lack of teamwork in decision making at the end of life, particularly between doctors and nurses; and caregivers were not emotionally prepared to cope with death and dying.

While caregivers were aware of the inadequacies in their end of life care, families said they weren't being given the information they needed. They said they needed to feel more confident in their caregivers and to experience greater consistency in the caregivers they saw and the information they received.

After Shadowing and using the other tools in the PFCC Methodology, the Working Group defined the ideal state as one in which there is evidence of a clear plan in the medical notes, a discussion with the patient and family, and advance care planning being shared with the patient's primary care physician.

To close the gap between the current state and the ideal, the Working Group held more open discussions about patients who were identified as approaching the end of life; used a communication sheet in the notes to document the important decisions and discussions they had with the patient and family; and fostered a greater understanding that the end of life is not just about care in the last days of life but about planning in advance, which may be weeks or months before death.

The benefits of this project for patients and families are difficult to measure, given that identifying an opportunity to ask patients near the end of life and their families about their feelings is challenging. The benefits for caregivers, however, are quantifiable. In only six months, the percentage of caregivers reporting a clear plan documented in the medical notes increased from 25 percent to 100 percent in the wards implementing The Conversation Project; the percentage of caregivers who documented discussions with the patient went from 0 percent to 100 percent; the percentage of caregivers reporting discussions with the family increased from 50 percent to 100 percent; and evidence of advance care planning being communicated to the primary healthcare team went from 0 percent to 100 percent.

Meeting the goals of The Conversation Project requires a change in mind-set and culture, which cannot be achieved overnight. Although junior doctors now receive mentorship and support by end of life and palliative care specialists, Royal United Hospital recognizes a continuing need to train staff around advance care planning and communication skills, and will continue to use the PFCC Methodology to reach their goals (The Kings Fund, 2013).

Other hospitals in the United Kingdom are using Shadowing and other tools in the PFCC Methodology to improve end of life care through co-design with patients and families. These include the Dorset HealthCare University (Purbeck), Great Western Hospitals, Kent Community Health, Oxford University Hospitals, Portsmouth Hospitals, University Hospital Southampton, and Western Sussex Hospitals (Point of Care Foundation 2016/17).

Eliminating Waste and Creating Efficiencies While Improving Clinical Outcomes

The Problem

Waste in healthcare has been estimated to account for more than 20 percent of total healthcare costs and could well be higher (Berwick and Hackbarth 2012). Waste includes over-utilization; spending on services or processes that lack evidence of effectiveness over less expensive alternatives; inefficiencies in the provision of healthcare goods and services; redundant activities that increase the potential for over-processing, unnecessary wait times and unnecessary motion; and costs incurred while treating preventable medical injuries such as patient falls or hospital-acquired infections. Waste can also include staff not working at the top of their license and fluctuating or excess capacity of personnel, space, and equipment.

After studying regional variations in Medicare spending, researchers at the Dartmouth Institute for Health Policy and Clinical Practice estimated that 30 percent of all Medicare spending on clinical care could be eliminated without negatively affecting health outcomes (Skinner and Fisher 2010). The key to economic success for healthcare organizations in the current climate is to identify which aspects of care delivery constitute waste and can therefore be eliminated without harming patients or reducing their quality of care.

The Real-World Solution

Magee-Womens Hospital of UPMC established a Hand Hygiene Working Group to address the need to prevent infections and reduce the costs that result. After Shadowing and following the PFCC Methodology of the Patient Centered Value System, this Working Group realized the need to conduct a hand hygiene education awareness campaign for patients, families, and caregivers. The Working Group had hand sanitizer stations placed at key locations identified by Shadowing and at entrances to buildings, units, and rooms; made hand hygiene education for caregivers and visitors more frequent and more visible; and provided all caregivers with personal hand hygiene devices. As a result, there has been an 85-percent improvement in hand hygiene among caregivers, and feedback from patients and families has been positive.

The Bone and Joint Center at Magee-Womens Hospital of UPMC has reduced waste by using the Patient Centered Value System to develop a blood conservation program that has reduced transfusion rates; eliminated routine type and cross and then screens in all primary total joint replacement patients; initiated the use of non-invasive bloodless hemoglobin monitoring to eliminate finger sticks for blood samples; and discontinued the use of autotransfusion devices following surgery. This blood conservation program has reduced transfusion rates for patients having primary total knee replacement from 14 percent to 1 percent, and has reduced transfusion rates for those having primary total hip replacement from 9 percent to 1 percent. These reductions translated into savings of $148,000.

With fewer patients requiring blood transfusions, length of stay has decreased by 0.9 days. For the Bone and Joint

Center at UPMC in 2014, eliminating routine type and cross saved $208 per patient, or $242,112, a significant amount for a high volume practice; eliminating routine type and screen for all patients having primary total joint replacement reaped an annual saving of $240,657; and the discontinuation of auto-transfusion devices resulted in savings of more than $75,951.

By adopting the Patient Centered Value System, the Bone and Joint Center has achieved the lowest cost per case in the UPMC system, and has achieved better-than-national-average indicators in length of stay; percentage of patients discharged directly to home; mortality rates; and compliance with the Surgical Care Improvement Project initiative (DiGioia et al. 2012; Millenson et al. 2013), resulting in bonus payments to the hospital, lower readmission rates, and improved functional outcomes, which have led to a greater number of patients returning to work more quickly.

Wake Orthopaedics, in Raleigh, North Carolina, collaborated with the Bone and Joint Center in using Shadowing and the PFCC Methodology to improve the value, quality, and cost of orthopedic services. Focusing on improving total knee replacement procedures and the total joint replacement pathway, Wake Orthopaedics formed a Working Group and Project Teams to overhaul pre-operative testing and education, improve screening methods for methicillin-resistant staphylo-coccus aureus (MRSA) and methicillin-sensitive staphylococcus aureus (MSSA), provide greater antibiotic choices and improve delivery times, prioritize communication among caregivers, and redesign the pain management pathway.

One year after the Wake Orthopaedics initiative began, 100 percent of patients, compared to 98.28 percent before the initiative started, received antibiotics one hour before incision; the surgical infection rate declined from 2.99 percent to 0 percent; patients' length of stay for knee and hip surgery was reduced from 3.90 days and 3.5 days to 3.4 days and 2.2 days, respectively; unplanned readmissions 30 days after elective primary knee and hip surgery declined from

6.2 percent to 3.61 percent; patient satisfaction rose from 79.7 percent to 92.9 percent; and the average total direct cost per patient declined by 7.8 percent, falling from $13,014 to $12,072.

Reducing Readmissions

The Problem

In 2012, the Center for Medicare & Medicaid Services began reducing payments to hospitals for Medicare beneficiaries who were readmitted within 30 days for heart failure, acute myocardial infarction, and pneumonia. In the last quarter of 2012, the Center for Medicare & Medicaid Services reported that the readmission rate fell to 17.8 percent—down from a rate of between 18.5 percent and 19.5 percent—prompting government officials to conclude that the hospital readmissions reduction program is making a difference. During the 2013 fiscal year, more than 2200 hospitals paid a penalty of up to 1 percent of their Medicare base payments—a total of $280 million in penalties. The Center for Medicare & Medicaid Services projected that during the 2014 fiscal year, 2225 hospitals would incur penalties amounting to $227 million (Pagan 2014).

In addition to financial incentives to reduce readmission rates, decreasing readmissions also reduces the risk for infections and other potentially negative clinical outcomes that increase the cost of care.

The Real-World Solution

The components of the Patient Centered Value System provide the tools to identify and rectify many of the factors that contribute to unnecessary readmissions, as illustrated by the following examples.

The **Bariatrics Working Group** at Magee-Womens Hospital of UPMC analyzed reasons for readmissions and saw that the lack of sufficient hydration was a common thread. Shadowing identified appropriate time points for and methods of improving hydration education, which led to the following PFCC projects:

- Development of a quiz to assess patient understanding of dehydration
- Development of a Hydration Fact Sheet
- Staff education on the "teach back" technique
- Development of a Bariatric Surgery Discharge Journal for patients to log fluid intake at home (and to log wound assessment, pain score, nausea assessment, signs and symptoms of dehydration, and fluid/ml ounce conversation tables)
- Pilot testing of the distribution of "calibrated" water bottles
- Post-operative telephone calls to patients by nurses and assessment of journal use

After the Bariatrics Working Group implemented these projects, the readmission of 22 patients who had bariatric surgery during the first 30 days declined from an average of 9.5 to 1. These results have been maintained.

The Bariatrics Working Group is also focusing on reducing other common complications of bariatric surgery that result in readmission within 30 days, including wound infection, pain, vitamin deficiency, weight gain, and deep vein thrombosis/pulmonary embolism. The improved paradigm resulted in increased collaboration between inpatient and outpatient teams, increased collaboration among care disciplines, increased communication with patients and families about how to prevent the symptoms associated with unnecessary readmission, and increased collaboration among the various bariatrics programs in the health system.

The **Gynecological Oncology Working Group** at Magee-Womens Hospital of UPMC focused one of their projects on reducing unnecessary readmissions as a result of what patients described as inadequacies in the discharge process and follow-up components of care. To address these concerns, the Working Group revised patient education materials and processes; identified patients at high risk for early readmission; had a multidisciplinary team review each readmission monthly; telephoned patients after discharge to go over their discharge instructions; implemented educational activities targeting the top three reasons for readmission; and established patient advisory groups.

Working Group projects further resulted in revising workflows; reviewing surgery-specific educational materials with patients and families before surgery; creating new dietary "refrigerator reference guides" to give to patients before discharge; and developing a new model of care on the inpatient unit by which a bedside nurse became a discharge educator.

Readmission rates in the Gynecologic Oncology Program decreased from 8.7 percent to 4.9 percent in one year.

Members of the **Discharge Prescriptions and Medication Education Working Group** at Magee-Womens Hospital of UPMC realized that patients' inability to fill prescriptions after discharge or to take their medications as prescribed accounted for a significant percentage of avoidable readmissions. As described in Chapter 6, the Working Group listened to what patients and families said they wanted and needed on hospital discharge and made the current state the ideal as patients and families define it.

As a result of Shadowing and following the PFCC Methodology, a pharmacist now comes to the patient's bedside just before discharge and gives the patient and family the necessary medications. And if a patient is due to be discharged on a day or time when the hospital pharmacy is closed, a local pharmacy delivers the medications directly to the patient's room. Since this project was implemented, readmission rates associated with medication noncompliance have decreased.

This project has also been adopted by the Children's Hospital of Pittsburgh of UPMC.

At the **Baptist Memorial Hospital** in Collierville, Tennessee, a Working Group created medication cards to teach patients and families about new medications prescribed in the hospital. These cards have improved communication between nurses and patients and families; improved patient and family understanding of their new medications and how to take them; improved collaboration between nurses and the hospital pharmacy; improved patient safety and satisfaction; and have been associated with reduced readmissions and decreased costs.

Reducing Staff Turnover

The Problem

Despite the recent easing of the nursing shortage, a shortage is projected in 16 states by 2025 (HRSA 2014) and nursing turnover continues to be a problem (Kovner et al. 2014). Nurses reportedly leave their jobs for a variety of reasons, including feeling overextended and emotionally and physically depleted as a result of chronic job stressors (McHugh et al. 2011).

Staff satisfaction and retention are an issue at UPMC, just as they are at most healthcare organizations. The average cost of replacing a registered nurse (RN) is estimated to be anywhere from $22,000 to more than $64,000 (RWJF 2009). Contributing to these costs are lost productivity before departure; separation costs due to factors such as exit interviews and paperwork; coverage costs, including hiring temporary workers and overtime pay; recruiting costs, which include advertising and interviewing; hiring costs, which include hiring bonuses, search firm fees, and relocation reimbursement; the lost productivity of vacancy periods; and lost productivity for new nurses.

There are, of course, additional costs associated with staff turnover. Temporary employees are often in short supply, they have higher hourly rates to make up for the lack of benefits, and the permanent staff must provide a great deal of oversight and support to ensure that temporary staff members meet quality of care expectations. This creates more work for the existing staff, which can lead to a vicious cycle of lower job satisfaction and increased staff turnover. Many hospitals resort to paying current staff overtime rates, which is clearly a poor financial solution and a trend that is at odds with increasing regulatory changes preventing mandatory overtime.

The Real-World Solution

There is abundant anecdotal evidence that the Patient Centered Value System improves caregiver satisfaction and reduces staff turnover, and that those involved report feeling empowered to identify the gaps between the current and ideal states of care delivery and then to close those gaps. Enabling caregivers to identify problems in care delivery and then to fix them engenders a sense of professional satisfaction, empowerment, and joy in work, which translates into loyalty to the organization.

Furthermore, there is evidence of a quantitative correlation between the implementation of the Patient Centered Value System and a reduction in staff turnover at UPMC. Within the first 18 months of adopting the Patient Centered Value System, the **Day of Surgery Working Group** at UPMC Presbyterian reported a 75-percent decrease in nursing turnover (from 60 to 15) in the operating room, a 100-percent decrease in the pre- and post-anesthesia care unit (from 1 to 0), and a 73-percent decrease (from 11 to 3) in same day surgery. And within the first two years of adopting the Patient Centered Value System in the Trauma Care continuum at UPMC Presbyterian—which includes the Emergency Department and several inpatient units—staff turnover decreased by 66 percent (from

35.1 percent to 25.1 percent and then to 11.9 percent) (DiGioia
and Greenhouse 2012). Imagine the cost savings associated
with these two examples alone, let alone the cost savings that
could result from a hospital-wide or system-wide implementation of the Patient Centered Value System.

Reducing the Cost of Care

The Problem

How can the cost of healthcare be reduced if we don't know
what the true cost of care—over the full cycle of care, not just
our particular segment—really is? As Chapter 8 explains, the
actual cost of delivering healthcare over the full cycle of care
for any medical or surgical condition is unknown because
until now there has been no systematic approach to measuring these costs. While Chapter 8 provides details about this
approach, which combines Shadowing with Time-Driven
Activity-Based Costing, this section explains how it is being
used in the Patient Centered Value System and the cost savings
that have resulted.

The Real-World Solution

The **Bone and Joint Center at Magee-Womens Hospital of
UPMC** used Shadowing combined with Time-Driven Activity-
Based Costing to identify the true cost of primary total hip
and knee replacement surgery by resource type (personnel,
space, equipment, and consumables) over the full cycle of
care (30 days pre- to 90 days post-surgery) and by segment
of care (pre-hospital, hospital, and post-hospital). The operating room accounted for the largest portion of the overall cost:
58 percent and 51 percent for total hip replacement and total
knee replacement, respectively (DiGioia et al. 2016). Implants
and personnel accounted for the second largest portion of

the overall cost: 53 percent and 44 percent for total hip and total knee implants, respectively; and personnel accounted for 44 percent and 50 percent of the overall cost for total hip replacement and total knee replacement, respectively (DiGioia et al. 2016). The cost of space and equipment accounted for only 3 percent and 6 percent of the overall cost of total hip replacement and total knee replacement, respectively (DiGioia et al. 2016).

In addition, as highlighted in a case study in Chapter 8, applying Shadowing to Time-Driven Activity-Based Costing emphasized the fact that all patients were receiving a chest x-ray prior to surgery and that protocols needed to be updated and revised. Once protocols were revised, only patients at risk—not all patients routinely—received chest x-rays. The number of pre-surgical chest x-rays declined by 70 percent for a total annual cost saving of $7500 for one surgeon. Less testing time and lower radiation exposure also led to increased patient satisfaction (DiGioia et al. 2016).

Shadowing plus Time-Driven Activity-Based Costing was also used to compare the total joint replacement service lines of four surgeons at two urban and two community hospital systems in 2015. The analysis showed large variations in care pathways, resource costs, and total costs. In addition, Shadowing combined with Time-Driven Activity-Based Costing showed that pre-operative testing protocols, time in the operating room, types of personnel used, protocols for follow-up visits, discharge disposition (home vs. nursing facilities or rehabilitation centers), and the number of outpatient therapy sessions were also highly variable.

Conclusion

A Buddhist quote states, "When the student is ready, the teacher will appear." The Triple Aim (IHI) and the ever-changing healthcare environment have made students of us all as we seek new ways to improve the healthcare experience, improve clinical outcomes, and reduce healthcare costs. The need for the Patient Centered Value System becomes clearer all the time.

We hope you will consider this book the proverbial teacher. Our story (Chapters 1 through 6) has shown you how to introduce and implement the Patient Centered Value System in any organization, whatever its size. The remaining Chapters 7 through 11 explain why you should. As Lao Tsu said, "A journey of a thousand miles begins with one step." It's time to get started.

References

Abdalla, H, Whyte, C, Hughes, E, Killops, A. 2013. Paediatric asthma: Improving patient and staff experience. http://www.kingsfund.org.uk/sites/files/kf/walsall-poster-poster-asthma-nov13.pdf.

Berwick, D., Hackbarth, A.D. 2012. Eliminating waste in U.S. health care. *JAMA* 307(14):1513–1516.

Carman, KL, Dardess, P, Maurer, M, et al. 2013. Patient and family engagement: A framework for understanding the elements and developing interventions and policies. *Health Aff* 32(2):223–231.

Cosgrove, DM, Fisher, M, Gabow, P, et al. 2013. Ten strategies to lower costs, improve quality, and engage patients: The view from leading health system CEOs. *Health Aff* 32(2):321–327.

DiGioia, AM, Greenhouse, PK. 2012. Care experience-based methodologies: Performance improvement roadmap to value-driven health care. *Clin Orthop Relat Res* 470:1038–1045.

DiGioia, AM, Greenhouse, PK, DiGioia, CS. 2012. Digital video recording in the inpatient setting: A tool for improving care experiences and efficiency while decreasing waste and cost. *Qual Manag Health Care* 21(4):269–277.

HRSA. 2014. Future of the nursing workforce: National- and state-level projections, 2012–2025. http://bhpr.hrsa.gov/healthworkforce/supplydemand/nursing/workforceprojections/index.html.

Institute for Healthcare Improvement. The Conversation Project. http://www.ihi.org/Engage/Initiatives/ConversationProject/ Pages/default.aspx.

The Kings Fund. Case study 3: The conversation project. http:// www.kingsfund.org.uk/projects/pfcc/conversation-project

Kovner, CT, Brewer, CS, Fatehi, F, Jun, J. 2014 Aug–Nov. What does nurse turnover rate mean and what is the rate? *Policy Polit Nurs Pract* 15(3–4):64–71.

Langel, S. 2013. Pioneering new ways to engage the disabled. *Health Aff* 32(2):216–222.

Manzur, A, Barratt, R, Byrne, L. 2013. Multidisciplinary outpatient review clinic for boys with Duchenne Muscular Dystrophy (DM). http://www.kingsfund.org.uk/sites/files/kf/gosh-poster-neuro-nov13.pdf.

McHugh, MD, Kutney-Lee, A, Cimiotti, JP, Sloane, DM, Aiken, LH. 2011 Feb. Nurses' widespread job dissatisfaction, burnout, and frustration with benefits signal problems for patient care. *Health Aff* 30(2):202–210.

Millenson, ML, DiGioia, AM, Greenhouse, PK, Swieskowski, D. 2013 Oct–Dec. Turning patient-centeredness from ideal to real: Lessons from 2 success stories. *J Ambul Care Manage* 36(4):319–334.

Minford, J, Grice, J, Williams, K, Hibberd, S. 2013. Acute abdominal pain pathway. Alder Hey Children's Hospital. http://www. kingsfund.org.uk/sites/files/kf/alder-hey-poster-acute-abdominal-pain-pathway-nov13_0.pdf.

Pagan, J. 2014 July. Examining medicare's hospital readmissions reduction program. *Health Aff* http://www.healthaffairs.org / blog/2014/07/24/examining-medicares-hospital-readmissions-reduction-program/.

PFCC Team, University Hospital of North Staffordshire. 2013. Patient and carer empowerment: A children's asthma improvement project. http://www.kingsfund.org.uk/sites/files/kf/north-staffordshire-poster-asthma-nov13.pdf.

The Point of Care Foundation. 2016. Living well to the very end: Patient and Family Centred Care programme. England: The Health Foundation, National Health Service. https://www.pointofcarefoundation.org.uk/news/ living-well-end-pfcc-project-update/.

Robert Wood Johnson Foundation. 2009. Evaluation of the Robert Wood Johnson wisdom at work: Retaining experienced nurses research initiative—Final report. Princeton, NJ: Robert Wood Johnson Foundation.

Roseman, D, Osborne-Stafsnes, J, Amy, CH, Boslaugh, S, Slate-Miller, K. 2013. Early lessons from four 'Aligning Forces for Quality' communities bolster the case for patient-centered care. *Health Aff* 32(2):232–241.

Skinner, J, Fisher, ES. 2010 May. *Reflections on Geographic Variations in U.S. Health Care.* Lebanon, NH: The Dartmouth Institute for Health Policy & Clinical Practice.

Glossary

Accountable Care Organizations: Accountable Care Organizations are groups of doctors, hospitals, and other healthcare providers who come together voluntarily to deliver coordinated, high-quality care to their Medicare patients. The goal of coordinated care is to ensure that patients, especially the chronically ill, get the right care at the right time while avoiding unnecessary duplication of services and preventing medical errors. When an Accountable Care Organization succeeds in both delivering high-quality care and spending healthcare dollars more wisely, it will share in the savings it achieves for the Medicare program (Center for Medicare & Medicaid Services).

Bundled Payment Programs: in a Bundled Payment Program, a single, "bundled" payment covers services delivered by two or more providers during a single episode of care or over a specific period of time. This is a type of risk contracting that assigns a fixed, negotiated fee to cover a set of treatment services, encouraging providers to manage costs while meeting high-quality care standards. If the cost of the service is less than the bundled payment, participating providers retain the difference. But if the cost exceeds the bundled payment, providers are not compensated for the difference (Center for Medicare & Medicaid Services).

Care Experience: a care experience refers to the way patients and families experience, or perceive, any and all aspects of their healthcare, including clinical outcomes; interactions (including written and verbal communication) with and among care providers and anyone else with whom they come into contact (such as parking attendants, receptionists, and technicians); the environment; transitions in care; safety; costs; and efficiency. A care experience can be as broad as an entire hospital stay, or as narrow as an office visit or, simply, patient registration.

Care Experience Flow Map: a Care Experience Flow Map is always completed during Step 3 of the Patient and Family Centered Care (PFCC) Methodology. The Care Experience Flow Map highlights the caregivers and touchpoints the patient and family encounter during their healthcare journey (or the segment of care being focused on for improvement) identified through Shadowing (defined below). The Care Experience Flow Map can be as simple as a bulleted list of each step in the care experience or a diagram or chart showing each step. The idea is to "map" the actual journey of patients and families through the care experience.

Data captured in the Care Experience Flow Map includes the following details:

- The actual flow of care (sometimes referred to as the care pathway) for the patient and family; the patient and family may have either the same, or different, Care Experience Flow Maps
- Caregivers and touchpoints
- Organizational silos that present barriers to optimal care experiences.
- Time (how long the patient and family spend at each touchpoint) and efficiency notes
- Specific actions taken by caregivers

- Subjective information such as impressions, interpretations of body language, and the feelings identified through both observation and conversation

Caregiver: a caregiver is anyone in the healthcare setting who influences the experiences of patients and families, whether directly or behind the scenes. This includes doctors, nurses, aides, technicians, therapists, dietitians, schedulers, housekeepers, parking attendants, administrators, and others.

Current State: the current state is the existing condition. In the Patient Centered Value System, it is critical to understand the current state (i.e., what the patient and family currently experience in a primary care doctor's office, on a hospital trauma unit, or in any other healthcare setting) before setting out to improve it.

Design Thinking: design thinking is an approach to developing innovative solutions—whether products, services, processes, or experiences—that meet the needs and desires of end users. Design thinking transforms the existing condition to a preferred condition (Simon 2002).

Disruptive Innovation Theory: disruptive innovation, a term coined by Clayton Christensen, describes a process by which a product or service takes root initially in simple applications at the bottom of a market and then relentlessly moves up the market, eventually displacing established competitors. Disruptive innovation describes how industries transform to provide increasingly affordable and conveniently accessible products and services to consumers (Christensen et al. 2009).

Experience-Based Design: experience-based design refers to involving end users in the design or redesign of a process or service (Bate and Robert 2006). In healthcare, the end users are patients and families. Experience-based design offers an alternative to the traditional view of patients and families as passive recipients of care and provides a way to see patients and families as integral to the improvement and innovation process.

Healthcare Experience Co-Design: co-design of the healthcare experience means that healthcare providers design the ideal state of healthcare delivery *in collaboration* with patients and families after listening to their wants and needs. Providers then test and implement projects to close the gaps between the current state and the ideal as patients and families define it.

High-Performance Care Teams: a high-performance care team is a group of people who share a common vision, goals, and metrics, and who collaborate, challenge, and hold each other accountable to achieve outstanding results (Society for Human Resource Management).

Ideal State: the ideal state of a care experience is an experience that meets and exceeds all the needs and desires of end users—in this case, patients and families.

Patient and Family Centered Care Methodology: the Patient and Family Centered Care (PFCC) Methodology is a process *and* performance improvement tool that focuses on the patient and family to guide improvement efforts. The second prong of the Patient Centered Value System, the PFCC Methodology, is a simple, replicable, and sustainable six-step approach for viewing all care through the eyes of patients and families, and creating Working Groups and Project Teams to transform care from the current state to the ideal as patients and families define it (Figure G.1).

Patient Centered Medical Home: the Patient Centered Medical Home is an enhanced primary care delivery model designed to achieve better access to and coordination of care while delivering preventive services and assuring quality and safety within the primary care practice. The Patient Centered Medical Home seeks to create a strong partnership between the patient and

Six Steps to Transform Care from the Current State to the Ideal

| Step 1: Select a care experience | Step 2: Establish the care experience guiding council | Step 3: Evaluate the current state | Step 4: Expand the guiding council into the working group | Step 5: Write the ideal story | Step 6: Identify projects and form project teams |

Figure G.1   The six steps of the Patient and Family Centered Care Methodology to transform care from the current state to the ideal.

primary care physician. Payers often reward providers with a per-month bonus for improving primary care services for each patient in the medical home (National Committee for Quality Assurance).

Patient Centered Value System: the Patient Centered Value System is a relationship-based approach to transforming care delivery that focuses on the needs of patients and families, improves care experiences and clinical outcomes, and reduces costs. The Patient Centered Value System is a comprehensive approach to healthcare delivery comprising Shadowing, the Patient and Family Centered Care Methodology (defined previously), and Time-Driven Activity-Based Costing (both defined hereafter). The Patient Centered Value System provides the structure and mechanism to reduce costs while protecting and/or improving patient and family experiences and clinical outcomes.

Guiding Council: The Guiding Council serves as the foundation and leadership of a Working Group. The Guiding Council is a small, strategic group of "Champions," who serve as catalysts to initiate and set the stage for care transformation using the PFCC Methodology. At a minimum, a Guiding Council is made up of an Administrative Champion (or Co-Champions), a Clinical Champion (or Co-Champions), and a Coordinator. Members of the Guiding Council are the first Shadowers of the care experience selected for improvement. They expand into a Working Group by inviting representatives from every touchpoint of the patient and family care experience identified during Shadowing. Guiding Council members should be well respected by their peers, familiar with the care experience being improved, and passionate about improving the experience of care for patients and families.

Project Teams: Project Teams implement projects that the Working Group has identified to close the gaps between the current and ideal states of a care experience. Project Teams begin when an improvement project is chosen by the Working Group and ends when the project is completed.

Reference-Based Pricing: reference-based pricing allows health plans to negotiate prices with providers and encourages plan participants and beneficiaries to use those providers. A health plan offers to pay a fixed amount, which certain providers will accept as payment for a particular procedure. Plan participants and beneficiaries using a provider who does not accept the reference price must pay the difference between the provider's charge and the reference price out of pocket (SHRM 2014).

Shadowing: Shadowing is the first prong and cornerstone tool of the Patient Centered Value System. As used in the PFCC Methodology, Shadowing is the direct, real-time observation of patients and families as they move through each step of a care experience to identify the current state. As used with Time-Driven Activity-Based Costing, Shadowing is the direct, real-time observation of the four buckets of resources used to deliver care (i.e., personnel, space, equipment, and consumables). Shadowing can be accomplished using the goShadow® application for mobile devices coupled with a cloud-based collaborative platform that permits automatic report generation (available at GoShadow.org).

Shadowing Reports: Shadowing reports are narrative descriptions of everything that was seen and heard during Shadowing. Shadowing reports convey the current state of any care experience from the perspective of patients and families to the full Working Group after Shadowing and Care Experience Flow Mapping. The Shadowing report, delivered in person in the form of a (true) story by those who Shadowed the care experience, presents the data captured in the Care Experience Flow Map (defined previously) along with observations, impressions, and recommendations of patients, families, caregivers, and Shadowers. You can create Shadowing reports automatically by synchronizing your Shadowing notes with the reporting function using the goShadow® platform (GoShadow.org).

Shared Savings Programs: Shared Savings Programs facilitate coordination and cooperation among providers to improve the quality of care for Medicare fee-for-service beneficiaries and to reduce unnecessary costs. Participation in Medicare's Shared Savings Program is open to all providers, hospitals, and suppliers that create or participate in an Accountable Care Organization. The Shared Savings Program will reward Accountable Care Organizations that lower their growth in healthcare costs while meeting performance standards in quality of care and putting patients first (Center for Healthcare Quality & Payment Reform).

Storydoing©: a term coined by Ty Montague, author and Chief Executive Officer of Co: Collective, storydoing means using the tool of storytelling to drive action in a business environment (Montague 2013).

Storytelling: storytelling is the expression of events, thoughts, and feelings in words, sounds, images, or all of these. In the context of the PFCC Methodology, storytelling is used during Shadowing and when presenting the Shadowing report to capture each aspect of the care experience from the patient's and family's perspective. Storytelling is also used when caregivers envision the ideal care experience (including information patients and families provide during Shadowing) and write this as a collective story, also from the patient's and family's point of view.

Touchpoints: touchpoints refer to key moments and places in which patient and family care experiences are directly or indirectly affected by any caregiver. Touchpoints include places where patients and families go at each step of their care experience and those with whom they come into contact.

Time-Driven Activity-Based Costing: Time-Driven Activity-Based Costing, developed by Robert Kaplan and Steven Anderson of the Harvard Business School (Kaplan and Anderson 2007), is the third component of the Patient Centered Value System. Used with Shadowing, Time-Driven Activity-Based Costing identifies the actual (true) cost of providing care for any medical or surgical condition.

Time-Driven Activity-Based Costing Process Maps: Time-Driven Activity-Based Costing process maps show the actual steps in the care pathway as they occur, the caregivers (personnel) with whom the patient and family come into contact, and the touchpoints (where patients and families go) during the care experience. In addition, these process maps summarize the activities that take place at each step and the amount of time it takes to complete each activity. Time-Driven Activity-Based Costing process maps reveal the resources and activity time used to determine actual costs (for personnel, consumables, equipment, and space); where patient and families go—that is, all locations during a care experience—and for how long; resources with substantial unused capacity; care providers not working at the "top of their licenses" in order to best match personnel by cost for each task; and unnecessary redundancies, waste, and inefficiencies.

Working Group: the Working Group is a cross-functional and cross-hierarchical team representing every touch-point of a care experience identified by members of the Guiding Council during Shadowing. The close collaboration of Working Group members breaks down the silos ubiquitous in healthcare. Working Groups are responsible for identifying gaps between the current state of the care experience and the ideal from the patient's and family's point of view, and then launching Project Teams to close the gaps. Working Groups are permanent, re-Shadow periodically over time, and continually identify new current states and new opportunities for improvement.

References

Bate, P, Robert, G. 2006. Experienced-based design: From redesigning the system around the patient to co-designing services with patients. *Qual Saf Health Care* 15:307–310.

Center for Healthcare Quality & Payment Reform. Paths to Healthcare Payment Reform: Is "Shared Savings" the Way to Reform Payment? http://www.chqpr.org/downloads/sharedsavings.pdf

Center for Medicare & Medicaid Services. Accountable Care Organizations (ACOs). https://www.cms.gov/Medicare/Medicare-Fee-for-Service-Payment/ACO/index.html?redirect=/Aco.

Center for Medicare & Medicaid Services. Bundled payments for care improvement (BPCI) initiative: General information. https://innovation.cms.gov/initiatives/bundled-payments/.

Christensen, CM, Grossman, JH, Hwang, J. 2009. *The Innovator's Prescription: A Disruptive Solution for Health Care.* New York: McGraw-Hill.

Kaplan, RS, Anderson, SR. 2007. *Time-Driven Activity-Based Costing: A Simpler and More Powerful Path to Higher Profits.* Boston, MA: Harvard Business School Publishing Corp.

Montague, T. 2013. *True Story: How to Combine Story and Action to Transform your Business.* Boston, MA: Harvard Business Review Press. http://www.storydoing.com

National Committee for Quality Assurance (NCQA). Patient-centered medical home recognition. http://www.ncqa.org/Programs/Recognition/Practices/PatientCenteredMedicalHomePCMH.aspx

Simon, H. 2002. *The Sciences of the Artificial.* Boston, MA: Massachusetts Institute of Technology Press Books.

Society for Human Resource Management (SHRM). Developing and Sustaining High Performance Work Teams. http://www.shrm.org/templatestools/toolkits/pages/developingandsustaininghigh-performanceworkteams.aspx

Society for Human Resource Management. 2014. Employers turn to reference-based health pricing. https://www.shrm.org/resourcesandtools/hr-topics/benefits/pages/reference-based-pricing.aspx.

Appendix

UPMC, an internationally known integrated health system, provides more care to the regions' most vulnerable citizens than any other healthcare institution and integrates 65,000 employees, more than 25 hospitals, more than 600 doctors' offices and outpatient sites, and a more than 3 million- member Insurance Services Division. To date, Working Groups have been launched for more than 65 different care experiences in 9 UPMC hospitals and counting, as well as by healthcare organizations around the country and around the world. Interest in the Patient Centered Value System as a means to improve clinical outcomes and lower costs continues to spread.

Although this book focuses on the successes organizations have achieved using the Patient Centered Value System, such success is not inevitable and is not guaranteed. In fact, success sometimes requires trial, error, and learning from failure. For example, approximately one-quarter of Working Groups that have been launched at UPMC are not currently active—that is, they have failed to be maintained. The question is, why? There are several possible reasons.

- There may be turnover in Champions (that is, Guiding Council members), which can lead to stalled momentum and, ultimately, cessation of Working Group efforts.
- Champions may not be right for their roles—unlike Kate Starr and Scott Long in Chapter 2, they may not have

the skills or personality required to serve as Champions, which can negatively affect Working Group functioning.

■ Re-Shadowing of a defined care experience may not be conducted routinely to identify gaps between the ever-changing current state and the ideal; the result is stagnation and maintenance of the status quo for patients and families.

The failure of a Working Group has a lot to teach us, and it is important to use failure as an opportunity to learn. Keep track of Working Groups and notice signs of flagging. If a Working Group seems to have stalled, find out why. Then, if appropriate, take steps to re-invigorate or re-launch the Patient and Family Centered Care (PFCC) Working Group as needed.

Current Care Experience Working Groups at UPMC

Children's Hospital of Pittsburgh of UPMC
Champion Working Group
Ambulatory Super Group (Ear, Nose, and Throat, Pediatric Outpatient Surgery Care Experience, Dental Care Experience)
Surgical Care Experience
Pediatric ICU Care Experience
ER Registration Care Experience
Radiology Care Experience

Magee-Womens Hospital of UPMC
Network and Shadowing Exchange
HCAHPS—Cleanliness and Noiselessness
Antepartum Care Experience
Bariatric Care Experience
Emergency Room Care Experience
End of Life Care Experience
Hand Washing Care Experience
Hysterectomy Care Experience
ICU Care Experience
Life after Weight Loss Care Experience

Medical Inpatient Care Experience
Mother and Baby Care Experience
Total Hip and Knee Joint Replacement Care Experience
Urology Care Experience

UPMC McKeesport
Emergency Department Care Experience
Surgical Care Experience

UPMC Mercy
Comprehensive Stroke Care Experience
Emergency Department Experience
Rehabilitation Care Experience
Surgical Care Experience

Mon Yough Community Services
Adult Outpatient Care Experience

UPMC Health Plan
Employee Injured at Work Care Experience

UPMC Northwest
Orthopedic Surgery Care Experience

UPMC Passavant
Orthopedic Specialists Care Experience

UPMC Presbyterian
PFCC Super Working Group
Ambulatory-Outpatient Communications Care Experience
Cardiothoracic Surgical Care Experience
Endocrine Care Experience
Imaging Patient Access Care Experience
Dining Experience
Environment of Healing Experience
Surgical Care Experience
Pre-Transplant (Evaluation) Care Experience
Transplant Care Experience
Trauma Care Experience

UPMC St. Margaret's
Employee Inclusion Experience
First Contact Care Experience
Surgical Care Experience

UPMC System-Wide
Patient and Family First
Surgical Care Network
UPMC Lactation Care Experience

Index

T - #0212 - 160425 - C312 - 234/156/14 - PB - 9780367735838 - Gloss Lamination